RENAISSANCE DRAMA
New Series V 1972

Renaissance Drama

New Series V

*Essays Principally
on Comedy*

Edited by
S. Schoenbaum and Alan C. Dessen

Northwestern University Press

EVANSTON 1972

THE ILLUSTRATION on the front cover is the earliest known likeness of Ben Jonson, an engraving by Robert Vaughan made around 1627. Courtesy of the Ashmolean Museum, Oxford.

THE BACK COVER is an illustration of Act II, scene V, of Terence's *Andria* from the 1493 edition of his comedies. By permission of the Folger Shakespeare Library, Washington, D.C.

TO THE MEMORY OF
BERNARD WEINBERG
1909–1973

Editorial Note

RENAISSANCE DRAMA, an annual publication, provides a forum for scholars in various parts of the globe: wherever the drama of the
Renaissance is studied. Coverage, so far as subject matter is concerned,
is not restricted to any single national theater. The chronological limits of
the Renaissance are interpreted liberally, and space is available for essays
on precursors, as well as on the utilization of Renaissance themes by
later writers. Editorial policy favors articles of some scope. Essays that are
exploratory in nature, that are concerned with critical or scholarly
methodology, that raise new questions or embody fresh approaches to
perennial problems are particularly appropriate for a publication which
originated from the proceedings of the Modern Language Association
Conference on Research Opportunities in Renaissance Drama.

For Volume VI of this series our topic will be Renaissance plays and
their dramatic antecedents. Manuscripts, for which the deadline is 1
March 1974, should be addressed to the guest editor for this volume,
Professor Alan C. Dessen, Department of English, University of North
Carolina, Chapel Hill, North Carolina 27514. The guest editor for
Volume VII will be Professor Joel Kaplan, University of British Colum-
bia; the tentative topic is Renaissance drama and the other arts. Prospec-
tive contributors are requested to follow the recommendations of the
MLA Style Sheet (second edition) in preparing manuscripts. For quota-
tions from Shakespeare the Alexander edition is used.

Contents

ix

RENAISSANCE DRAMA

New Series V ❧ *1972*

Feasting and Judging in Jonsonian Comedy

JONAS A. BARISH

NEAR THE BEGINNING of *Every Man in his Humor*, Young Lorenzo receives a letter from his friend Prospero inviting him to Florence for a spree. As inducement, Prospero proposes to display *"two of the most perfect, rare, & absolute true Gulls, that ever thou saw'st"* (I.i.154–155). Lorenzo looks up from his reading of the letter to see his foolish cousin Stephano approaching, upon which he comments, "Nay then, Ile furnish our feast with one Gull more toward a messe; hee writes to mee of two, and here's one, that's three, Ifayth" (I.ii.66–69). Prospero's promise of a pair of gulls, that is, is taken as the promise of a meal, with the gulls as dishes or courses. Comic diversion, traditionally associated with feasting, has here become the feast itself.

In revising the play for the Folio of 1616, Jonson clarified and amplified this analogy. Prospero, now Wellbred,[1] invites his friend much more explicitly to a meal:

1. The following list gives the Quarto and Folio names of characters mentioned in the present discussion:

Q	F
Lorenzo Junior	Edward Knowell
Prospero	Wellbred
Stephano	Stephen

3

. . . pr'y thee, come over to me, quickly, this morning: I have such a present for thee. . . . One is a Rimer sir, o' your owne batch, your owne levin. . . . The other—I will not venter his description with you, till you come, because I would ha' you make hether with an appetite.

(F, I.ii.80–87)

Of the two gulls, then, one is a loaf of bread, baked in the same oven, from the same yeast, as Young Knowell himself, being a poet; the virtues of the other are not to be divulged beforehand, so that Knowell will hasten to the encounter with a keener appetite. As before, his answer follows upon the arrival of his kinsman: "What! my wise cossen! Nay, then, Ile furnish our feast with one gull more, to'ard the messe. He writes to me of a brace, and here's one, that's three: O, for a fourth" (F, I.iii.70–73). Knowell undertakes, that is, to augment the fare, to add game of his own catching to Wellbred's "brace" of gulls.

It would seem that between the initial writing of the play in 1598 and its revision in (probably) 1612, Jonson's imagination seized more firmly on the connection between eating and laughing; this is confirmed by other appearances of the same trope. Volpone, licking his chops at the prospect of duping his greedy heirs once more by feigning dead, exclaims, "O, 'twill afford me a rare meale of laughter" (V.ii.87). When the meal has been savored, and he and Mosca are alone again, he cries, exultantly, "Who would have lost this feast?" (V.iii.107–108). Laughter, then, is nutrition; it replenishes and fortifies.[2] As Old Merrythought, in *The*

Bobadilla	Bobadil
Matheo	Matthew
Musco	Brainworm
Giuliano	Downright
Clement	Clement

I have differentiated as needed, for clarity, but have also not hesitated to mingle Quarto and Folio nomenclature for ease of reference (for example, by using the form "Bobadil" throughout, never "Bobadilla"). Citations from Jonson are to Ben Jonson, *Works,* ed. C. H. Herford and Percy and Evelyn Simpson, 11 vols. (Oxford, 1925–1952), with "u," "v," "i," and "j" altered to conform to modern practice.

2. It is also evacuation—of the lungs, of the spleen, of pent-up currents and vapors. Cf. Brainworm, "O that my belly were hoopt now, for I am ready to burst with laughing! never was bottle, or bag-pipe fuller" (F II.v.133–135); and Mosca, "Contayne / Your fluxe of laughter, sir" (*Volpone,* I.iv.133–134). Psychoanalytically,

Knight of the Burning Pestle, a connoisseur of laughter, puts it: " 'Tis mirth that fils the veines with bloud, / More then wine, or sleepe, or food" (II.444-445).[3] And one way to arouse mirth, in the Jonsonian world, is to provide matter for ridicule. Doll Common makes this clear when she congratulates her accomplices on settling their quarrel, so that no "sober, scirvy, precise neighbours" will reap "a feast of laughter, at our follies" (*Alchemist,* I.i.163-166). The pleasure of the feast of fools, however, lies in its rarity. The partakers think of themselves as gourmets, not gluttons, and those who undertake to please them stress that they are offering something choice and special, not mere belly satisfaction. The comic poet, presenting his wares, is in an analogous position. Jonson often imagines himself as a host welcoming spectators to a banquet. When in an expansive mood, as in the Prologue to *Epicoene,* he can make cheerful acknowledgment of the playgoers' right to like or dislike. He can stress the variety as well as the deliciousness of his cates. In more saturnine moments, or when stung by rejection, he can resentfully underscore the fact that while he offers his audiences full trenchers, solid nourishment, other playwrights insult them with broken meats, moldy dishes, bits, scraps, and leavings from the table.

A feast traditionally includes music, and Jonson occasionally suggests that a choice assortment of follies constitutes a concert as well as a meal. When Lorenzo joins Prospero in Florence, the latter questions him concerning Stephano, "what strange peece of silence is this? the signe of the dumbe man?" "Oh sir," answers Lorenzo, "a kinsman of mine, one that may make our Musique the fuller and he please, he hath his humor sir" (II.iii.55-58). Again the Folio version seizes the trope and explores it energetically. Instead of simply urging his friend to "be acquainted with my two *Zanies* heere, thou wilt take exceeding pleasure in them if thou hearst them once" (II.iii.52-54), Prospero's Folio counterpart makes the introduction in pointedly musical terms: "I pray thee be acquainted with my two hang-by's, here; thou wilt take exceeding pleasure in 'hem if thou

---

the relation between alimentation and excretion is close. Jonson thinks of laughter as something to be ingested and expelled, in either case heartily and wholesomely. Nicole, in *Le Bourgeois Gentilhomme,* III.ii, wishes to get drunk on laughter: "Tenez, Monsieur, battez-moi . . . et me laissez rire tout mon soûl."

3. Dramatic Works of F. Beaumont and T. Fletcher, ed. Fredson Bowers (Cambridge, 1966), I, 42.

hear'st 'hem once goe: my wind-instruments. Ile wind 'hem up—" (*F*, III.i.59–62). "Wind-instruments" has Swiftian implications; it conjures up visions of inert bladders waiting to be inflated with hot air, a notion pursued in Wellbred's declared intention to "wind 'hem up"—to puff them full of wind so that they will produce their characteristic gasps and wheezes. A moment later, in answer to Lorenzo's request for his verdict on Stephano, Prospero says, "I can compare him to nothing more happely, then a Barbers virginals; for every one may play upon him" (II.iii.183–185). Devastating enough, one would think, yet the Folio manages to be much more crushing: "I can compare him to nothing more happily, then a drumme; for every one may play upon him"—to which Young Knowell now replies, "No, no, a childes whistle were farre the fitter" (*F*, III.ii.23–25). The original analogy allowed Stephen too much range: a virginal, even a barber's virginal, requires skill; it is potentially capable of complex effects. But Stephen's reactions are crude and limited. Anyone can provoke them, as anyone can thump a drum. A drum, however, has martial and ceremonial associations; it suggests soldiership, discipline, and masculinity. The final, fittest term, then, in this search for an apt simile, proves to be the child's whistle, which pipes and squeaks, and which any child can play.

As with the image of the feast, that of the concert appears in the colloquy between Mosca and Volpone on the pleasure to be had from fools. Congratulating themselves on escaping the perils of the court, hoodwinking the magistrates and fastening the guilt onto the innocent, all with the unwitting aid of their dupes, they boast of making "So rare a musique out of discordes" (V.ii.18). Once again, like the meal of laughter—or like the dolphin's milk butter in which Sir Epicure Mammon's shrimps will swim—the symphony of folly is "rare," something to be cherished by collectors. Individual elements are synthesized to produce an unusual new compound, appealing in one case to the discerning ear, in the other to the discriminating palate.

"Palate," indeed, forms a key term in Jonson's culinary metaphor, and emphasizes the factor of judgment involved. The receiving organism is not a mere granary; it is a sensibility, capable of making fine distinctions. Jonsonian cuisine aims at subtleties that will appeal to the sophisticated taste. As he casts himself as host or master chef, so Jonson imagines his audience as composed of "Judging Spectators," who will scrupulously assay the quality of the food. "Before you judge," he admonishes us in the Prologue to *The New Inn*, "vouchsafe to understand, / Concoct, digest." The feast of folly, then, leads to judgment, within the play as well as without. The impulse to judge—to sift, to grade, weigh, and evaluate—culminates characteristically in Jonsonian comedy in a judgment scene in which scores are settled, penalties prescribed, and rewards bestowed.[4] Along with our judicial sense, such scenes satisfy our aesthetic sense; they bring all the strands of the plot into a close weave; they pass its elements in review and formulate a conclusive attitude toward them— one with which we may not always agree.

"Poetic justice," whether in life or art, implies that a person receives his "just deserts," often by some stroke of luck, some unexpected or even magical turn of events. According to Miss Prism in *The Importance of Being Earnest,* the good end happily and the bad end unhappily, and "that is what fiction means." That is also, in essence, what poetic justice means. It brings about a truer justice than the more prosaic sort. It fits punishment more perfectly to crime; it satisfies our desire to see order prevail, and our wish to allow appropriate mitigations and exceptions. It may, on occasion, confirm the world's coarser judgments, but usually it also refines on them. The fact that Jonson's plays frequently end with court scenes affords clear evidence of his concern for justice, but equally notable is the fact that these scenes trade so heavily in fantasy: they imaginatively allude to, rather than literally reproduce, the processes of actual courts. Their verdicts preserve a mysteriously self-validating quality not to be found outside such archetypes as the judgment of Solomon or the decrees of Daniel. They feed our craving for equity with small reference to mere law, for which Jonson shows increasingly scant respect.

Jonson, as critics have noticed, was haunted throughout his career by the problem of authority: who has the right to administer justice, and

---

4. See the paragraphs on this subject by Harry Levin, "An Introduction to Ben Jonson," in *Ben Jonson: A Collection of Critical Essays,* ed. Jonas A. Barish (Englewood Cliffs, N.J., 1963), pp. 48–49 (originally published as Introduction to *Selected Works of Ben Jonson* [New York, 1938]).

how does he acquire that right?[5] Each play grapples anew with the question and propounds its own experimental answers. Glancing over Jonson's output as a whole, we can perceive a gradual abandonment of the attempt to embody justice in figures of authority or public institutions, and an increasing reliance on the happy conjunctions of wit and chance. We discover also a rough inverse correlation between severity of judgment and feasting. Where judicial stringency prevails, the festive element tends to remain tentative and muted. Where the festive note is strongly struck, judgment tends toward leniency. The following pages will try to particularize.

Setting aside *A Tale of a Tub* as of uncertain date, we find in Jonson's earliest surviving play, *The Case is Altered* (1597), a quasi-romantic Plautine intrigue plot brought to an unusually full close by Jonson's judicial concerns. A series of lucky accidents reunites two sundered families, at the same time uncovering two crimes that must be dealt with. Jonson vests corrective power in the oldest and highest-ranking character on the stage, the Count Ferneze, who in turn invites the younger Count Chamount to deal with the transgressions of his father's former steward, the miser Jaques de Prie. Before wielding corrective authority, Ferneze has himself gone through a series of purifications, renouncing his unjust courtship of the miser's daughter, apologizing to Chamount for his irascible outbursts, and begging forgiveness from his own son for having threatened him with torture. These penances rid him of his choleric humors, and fit him, as it would seem, to assume his rightful role as governor of his household. It is to him that the distracted miser directs his plea for justice against the thieves who have fled with his gold. When the thieves prove to be Ferneze's own servants Juniper and Onion, and when these two swagger drunkenly onto the stage, vociferously offering to buy up lordships, it is only the work of a moment to dispatch them to the stocks and refer the disposal of their stolen treasure to Chamount. Chamount, surprisingly, not only pardons Jaques but bids him keep for his own the treasure he has in his turn stolen long ago.

5. The fullest treatment of this theme to date appears in John J. Enck, *Jonson and the Comic Truth* (Madison, Wis., 1957), especially in the passages indexed under "Justice."

One's first impulse might be to find an irritating imbalance here. Jaques has violated a post of high trust, that of steward. He has stolen not only his master's gold but also his child, and he breaks silence after so many years only to accuse that child, now his stepdaughter, of conspiring to rob him. Juniper and Onion, by comparison, oafs with no developed sense of right and wrong, have merely yielded to a moment of temptation, and then lacked the guile to protect their loot by deceit. Jaques is plainly the serious offender. But even in a writer with Jonson's vivid sense of retribution the laws of comedy must take precedence over the *lex talionis,* and those laws decree that what redresses the balance is not necessarily a strict allotment of grains of punishment to grams of crime, but an imaginative reordering that takes account of all complexities—such as Jonson's own axiom, to be spelled out in *Cynthia's Revels,* that "vice / Is like a furie to the vicious minde, / And turnes delight it selfe to punishment" (V.xi.131–133). By allowing for such deeper elements, it allows for a correspondingly profounder satisfaction. In the present case Onion and Juniper have enjoyed a hectic fling with their stolen coin; they have played the lords to the point of disciplining their own pages for pilfering from their purses, which they in turn have pilfered from Jaques. Novices in crime, innocents in the world, they form ideal candidates for exemplary correction. Nothing could more aptly conclude their escapade than a brief cooling-off period in the stocks. Jaques, on the other hand, has long ago passed beyond correction. He has also suffered years of punishment in his enslavement to his own fright. Rather like Spenser's Malbecco, he has become a living emblem of his crime, a tormented, wraithlike creature with scarcely anything human left about him, obsessed by the conviction that other men are plotting to rob him as he once robbed his master. With the kidnapped child returned, the lost gold ceases to matter; one may even suppose that the public bestowal of it on Jaques will break the nightmare that has haunted him for so long. Jonson of course spells out none of this. He merely arranges matters in such a way as to satisfy, despite superficial inequities, our sense that on the deeper levels justice has been done. Moving in the realm of comic law, he can devise vindications that have little to do with the criminal code.

In *Every Man in his Humor* (1598), Jonson begins to experiment with a more explicitly judicial finale, in which a spokesman for law presides over the disentangling of the plot and the distribution of deserts. Justice Clement is at once a properly constituted magistrate, "a Justice here, an excellent good Lawyer, and a great scholler," in Wellbred's reassuring credentials, but also "the onely mad, merrie, old fellow in *Europe!*" (*F*, III.v. 53–55), whose whimsical humors insure that his justice will be anything but cut and dried. And so it proves. Clement holds court with a nice sense of theater. He illustrates his fitness to judge an announced soldier (Bobadil) and a supposed poet (Matthew) by donning armor to receive the one, and reciting a sample of his own muse before hearing the verse of the other. Discovering Brainworm to be at the root of the day's confusions, he is prompted by Brainworm's happy skill in disguise to renounce all rigor; twice he exuberantly toasts the offender. Then comes the unorthodox sentence: "Pledge me. Thou hast done, or assisted in nothing, in my judgment, but deserves to bee pardon'd for the wit o' the offence" (*F*, V.iii.112–114). Brainworm's virtuosity in jest and his theatrical talent thus call forth the judge's own vein of mirth; judicial correction gives way to festive invitation. Keeping the promise of his name, Clement proceeds to play the peacemaker with the rest as well, urging them to drop their mutual grievances. Only two claimants seem to warrant some stringency: Matthew, whose verses are burned in a fiery sacrifice to the muses, and Bobadil, whose suit against Downright is stingingly spurned. The sentence on these two is unorthodox in a new way:

Well now my two Signior Out-sides, stand foorth, and lend me your large eares, to a sentence, to a sentence: first you signior shall this night to the cage, and so shall you sir, from thence to morrow morning, you signior shall be carried to the market crosse, and be there bound: and so shall you sir, in a large motlie coate, with a rodde at your girdle; and you in an olde suite of sackcloth, and the ashes of your papers (save the ashes sirha) shall mourne all day, and at night both together sing some ballad of repentance very pitteously, which you shall make to the tune of *Who list to leade and a souldiers life.*

(*Q*, V.iii.355–365)

The most striking feature of this penance is that for all its intricacy it possesses only poetic validity. Clement, a fantast of a justice, imposes a justice that is itself a fantasy. For neither Matthew nor Bobadil has broken the law. Doubtless it is immoral to be a coward, as it is shameful to pillage other men's verses, but to these as to multitudes of other delinquencies the law does not extend. Clement ignores, at the same time, offenses genuinely subject to statute and for which warrants have been issued, such as Stephen's theft of the cloak or Bobadil's beating of Cob. The punishments contemplated for Bobadil and Matthew—the one to dress in motley with a rod at his girdle, the other in sackcloth and in the ashes of his burnt poems, both to stand first in a cage, then in the marketplace, bound, mourning all day prior to singing a ballad of repentance at night, with the tune carefully specified—these recall hallucinations by Bosch or Brueghel more than they do the proceedings of courts of law. The whole device aims to turn the culprits into emblems of themselves, transfixing them with shame, and us with recognition, at this revelation of their natures.

In the Folio, Clement explains why his corrective hand falls so heavily on Bobadil and Matthew after brushing the rest so lightly: "Only these two, have so little of man in 'hem, they are no part of my care" (*F,* V.v.2–3). This confirms our sense that the two are being punished not for what they have done but for what they are. What they are is unmanly: imposture, especially the forging of false credentials of valor or letters, constitutes a dereliction of manhood. Clement is chastising most stingingly the faults Jonson finds hardest to forgive, momentarily excluding these characters from the ranks of men, while letting the rest pass unreprimanded. But even the scorned pair receive gentler shrift in the Folio:

. . . to dispatch away these, you signe o' the Souldier, and picture o' the *Poet* (but, both so false, I will not ha' you hang'd out at my dore till midnight) while we are at supper, you two shall penitently fast it out in my court, without; and, if you will, you may pray there, that we may be so merrie within, as to forgive, or forget you, when we come out.

(F, V.v.48–54)

The twain will not, this time, have to drink the cup of humiliation to the dregs; they will not have to parade in public as allegories of themselves; they will simply be barred from the general mirth. Stephen, Cob, and Tib are to be segregated in the buttery and provided with napkins and trenchers—Jonson leaves it uncertain whether he means this as a social or a moral segregation. The rest march off to a feast, at which the guest of honor, for his inventiveness in sport, will be Brainworm, invested (in the Quarto version) in the very robes of justice. Somewhat like a boy bishop or a king of fools, he will preside for the duration of the feast in the magisterial chair itself.

We may pause to reflect that Jonson would have found small precedent for his judicial finales in classical comedy, but much in native English drama. The debate among the Four Daughters of God in *The Castle of Perseverance* (as well as in the Ludus Coventriae *Salutation and Conception*) revolves precisely around the question of justice: can the protagonist, Humanum Genus, having died a slave to avarice, be allowed to proceed to heaven, or must he pay the price of his sins? The merciful verdict hinges on the fact that he has invoked Mercy with his dying breath, and in so doing won the remission promised by Christ. This is in the highest sense a case of "poetic" justice, which could never be duplicated in an earthly court. When the judge is human, as in *Fulgens and Lucrece,* the sentence can at best approximate ideal justice, never fully embody it. Despite Lucrece's wish for "some indifferent man" to arbitrate between her suitors, they insist on making her their judge. She, in turn, protects herself from the subversive implications of her choice by renouncing any general application of it: it will refer to this case and no other. Medwall thus anticipates and disarms disapproval of his heroine's preference for the churl over the nobleman, but thereby robs her decision of some of its resonance. Similarly, in Heywood's *The Four P's,* the Pedlar disclaims competence to referee the dispute among his companions: "it is no whit my sleight / To be a judge in matters of weight. / It behoveth no pedlars nor proctors / To take on them judgment as doctors" (ll. 384–387).[6] He does, however, agree to judge a matter he knows something about—lying—but having done so he retreats hastily to the posture of ignorance, urging his comrades and listeners to refer all serious questions to the church and so insure themselves against error. *The Play of the Weather* consists of a single sustained judgment scene, the moral of which proves to be that Jupiter's decrees may not be questioned, since, however arbitrary they may appear, they are based on the needs of the whole community and not on those of any interest group. Both plays reflect their author's authoritarian presup-

6. *Five Pre-Shakespearean Comedies,* ed. F. S. Boas (London, 1934), p. 86. Subsequent references to the plays in this edition are cited as "Boas."

positions: a final unchallengeable authority exists in both church and state, which absolves and indeed interdicts ordinary citizens from seeking to judge for themselves.

Much closer to Jonsonian justice would be that of *Gammer Gurton's Needle*. Here the Bayley, appealed to by the villagers for help in sorting out their disputes, mixes hard peasant sense with comic sportiveness in his dispensation. The *agent provocateur* of the play, Diccon the Bedlam, remains obdurately impenitent for his misdeeds. He will take no blame at all for the beating suffered by Doctor Rat: "hath not such an old fool wit to save his ears?" he inquires scornfully (Boas, V.ii.229). The Bayley agrees with Doctor Rat that Diccon should be punished for his mischief, but regards the suggested penalty, hanging, as rather too severe; he proposes that he himself be entrusted to devise a milder penance, so that the matter may "end with mirth among us all, even as it was begun" (V.ii.263). The penance he comes up with seems unlikely to disturb Diccon's digestion: Diccon is to swear, by Hodge's breech, never to refuse a free drink, never to offer money twice in payment of the same debt, and never to think that Hodge is a gentleman—in short, to do by way of shrift precisely what his rascally spirit has prompted him to do all along. The damage resulting from Diccon's pranks has been slight enough, more the product of the villagers' unruly passions than of Diccon's plotting. Mirth has been engendered in us, if not in the angry rustics. And Diccon himself, for better or worse, remains incorrigible. Comic justice acknowledges all this and measures its penalties accordingly, waiving any punishment more grievous than a pot of ale.

Court plays such as *The Arraignment of Paris* and a few of Lyly's comedies end with tribunals in which a god or goddess interposes in the affairs of the earthly characters, awards favors or renounces tribute in return for specified propitiations. Here, as in Heywood, the appeal is to the sacred authority of the crown, or of the mythic personages who symbolize it. Since power rests by definition with the gods, who are by definition good, the use of it can sometimes aid in solving a problem; it can never itself become a part of the problem. By the time Jonson's career was under way, Shakespeare had also written a number of comedies terminating in judgment scenes, in which a Duke or Prince presides over the reuniting of splintered families or sundered lovers, sometimes accompanying his acts with appropriate moral reflections. But

Shakespeare tends to shun sentencing and punishing. The closing lines of *Much Ado About Nothing* expressly refuse to entertain punitive designs against the play's chief mischief-maker, for to do so would mar the spirit of festivity, while the judicial fourth act of *The Merchant of Venice* is followed by a fifth filled with terrestrial and celestial music, as if to tease us out of all remembrance of legalism, punishment, and crime.

To Jonson such Shakespearean casualness did not come easily. Questions of justice seemed to demand careful accounting rather than offhand theatrical dispatching. Shakespeare scarcely concerns himself with the legitimacy of his dukes and princes; he simply assumes it. Jonson tends to ponder the credentials of his judges and magistrates, investing them with legal power but not necessarily equivalent moral authority. In *Every Man in his Humor* Judge Clement possesses the official status of a justice of the peace, but also the madcap personality of a Simon Eyre. It is the former that allows him to settle the confusions among the dramatis personae, but the latter that confers on his judgments their humanity and corrective wisdom.

In *Every Man out of his Humor,* exceptionally, no tribunal is convoked, nor does any character pass formal judgment on any other. The playwright's lieutenant, Macilente, maneuvers his companions into situations that will bring their humors into conflict, so that they may then cancel each other out. He does so, however, without any plenary session. When the last fool has gazed at his folly and abjured it, Macilente finds himself alone on the stage (except for the Interlocutors of the Induction) face to face with Queen Elizabeth, whose radiant presence has the power to dispel his own humor, envy. Justice here operates through essence rather than action. Elizabeth need say nothing at all; simply the thing she is suffices to dissolve Macilente's eccentricity. From this point Jonson was probably prompted to follow the path that led toward the resolutions of his next two plays, in which the search for authority takes on exceptional urgency. *Cynthia's Revels* and *Poetaster* both manifest a deep uneasiness with the imperfections of ordinary justice, a longing for something absolute which will sanction good men—including the poet in his role as social critic—and reprove bad. Both plays envisage justice lodged in a high tribunal of such unimpeachable purity that all doubt and dissent become blasphemous.

Cynthia's Revels (1600), despite its alluring title (its subtitle, actually) must be reckoned Jonson's most punitive, least festive play. Cynthia's court itself, both in the sense of her royal residence and of her judicial sessions, exists largely in order to ferret out and reprove the insignificant courtlings whose imbecile antics occupy the greater bulk of the action. The masque of the final scenes exists to bring them to justice in a suitably ceremonious manner. "The Goddesse mind," we learn from Cynthia's chief handmaiden, Arete,

> . . . holding true intelligence, what follies
> Had crept into her palace) . . . resolv'd
> Of sports, and triumphs, under that pretext,
> To have them muster in their pompe, and fulnesse:
> That so shee might more strictly, and to roote,
> Effect the reformation shee intends.
>
> (V.v.40–46)

We are informed, thus, by a character whose name guarantees her perfect virtue, that the masque and its revels are only a pretext, their true purpose being to expose and reform the court parasites, at Cynthia's instigation. Yet the justice of the revels, on any impartial view, proves to be a totalitarian farce.

The masque presents two quartets of fools, the he-fools and the she-fools, under the auspices of Mercury and Cupid, garbed as their corresponding virtues—self-love, for example, appearing as "natural affection" or "allowable self-esteem," and impudence as "courage" or "manly audacity." Having admired the spectacle, Cynthia bids the masquers unmask, only to register shock when she sees who they are. The creatures who stand before her have no right to enter the presence at all, much less to do so concealed beneath "the seeming face / Of neighbour-vertues." "Who would have thought," asks Cynthia hotly,

> that PHILAUTIA durst
> Or have usurped noble STORGES name?
> Or with that theft have ventred, on our eyes?
> Who would have thought, that all of them should hope
> So much of our connivence, as to come
> To grace themselves, with titles not their owne?
>
> (V.xi.57–65)

The wrathful speech could hardly be more disingenuous. Since the idea of the revels originated with Cynthia herself, the courtlings have had no say at all in the fashioning of the device, much to their annoyance. The script has in fact been written, the parts assigned, the properties prescribed, and the whole performance supervised by Cynthia's deputy, Crites, who received his commission from Arete, and who a moment ago has been lavishly praised for his share in the entertainment. Nor is the praise at any point withdrawn. Crites continues to be heaped with credit for having placed the rest, like pawns, in an untenable position, and they, in turn, are excoriated for their presumption in occupying it. The judgment, moreover, which befalls them for this symbolic usurpation remains unconnected to anything they have done in the course of the play. Earlier, we have heard much about such matters as Hedon's and Anaides' detraction of Crites, but it is not for this that they are now brought to the bar, nor for anything related to it. The same applies to the quirks of the other foolish characters. A pretty comic confrontation might have been based on the fools' insolence to Cynthia at the revels—they have been drinking the waters of self-love, and a tinge of lèse-majesté would fittingly climax the history of their impudence. But they are allowed no such self-possession. Instead, they are peremptorily divested of their personalities and flattened into emblems before being transfixed with judgment. The sentence itself perpetuates the emblematic mode, putting them through a series of grotesque postures—confession, recantation, and palinode—in which they renounce such irrelevancies as monkeys, lap dogs, and parakeets for pets. The whole operation gives the impression of an elaborate frame-up, in which a predestinarian god first deprives his creatures of their free will, and then overwhelms them with punishment—not for having sinned, but for being by nature sinful. Like sin, authority itself is a matter of essence, as Cynthia makes plain: "To men, this argument should stand for firme, / 'A Goddesse did it, therefore it was good" (V.xi.25–26).[7]

At first sight, justice in *Poetaster* (1601) seems to crackle with comparable high tension, the court of Augustus replacing that of Cynthia as princely domain and high tribunal. On closer view, however, it discloses

7. As Allan H. Gilbert has shown, in "The Function of the Masques in *Cynthia's Revels*," PQ, XXII (1943), 211–230, the conceit of the vices disguised as virtues belongs to a tradition going back to Plutarch. But the fact that Jonson drew on such a tradition does not, unfortunately, insure that he integrated it successfully into his play.

a multitude of humanizing touches. The process of judgment actually commences in Act IV, with Caesar's angry dismissal from court of the participants in the sacrilegious banquet. In the last act it proceeds to his pardoning of Gallus and Tibullus for their part in the banquet, a clear indication that his decrees, unlike Cynthia's, are neither infallible nor inflexible. During the subsequent discussion, Horace does not hesitate to reprove Caesar with some asperity for an unworthy remark, and Caesar, in reply, gratefully kisses the rod. Unlike Cynthia's pronouncements, then, Caesar's may be challenged, and challenged sharply. A moment later, when Virgil appears, Caesar places him in the highest seat, thus enthroning poetry, in the person of its most illustrious practitioner, on an eminence superior to that of the head of state. In *Cynthia's Revels,* the poet took his bearings exclusively from the goddess, and steered his course by her. Caesar, here, takes his bearings from the poets, and acknowledges them as his tutors and preceptors. Finally, the present court must suffer itself to be interrupted: Caesar himself defers his pastime to listen to outcries from braying fools like Lupus. Wise as he is, Caesar remains an earthly monarch, capable of being corrected, importuned, and misinformed. His aides are earthly too; none is invested with the a priori perfection of a Crites or an Arete, nor do the fools who appear for judgment belong to a race of inferior beings as do their counterparts in *Cynthia's Revels,* where a goddess gazed down from an infinite height on vermin ("this knot of spiders"—III.iv.88). Caesar's court, then, forms part of a human community, and the lives of Roman citizens impinge on it as the lives of the denizens of Gargaphie do not on Cynthia's.

As before, the finale unfolds in two distinct phases. First comes the glimpse of serene amity among the members of the elite band around the throne, then the widening of focus to include the lower orders who appear in litigation. In the first phase Caesar eulogizes poetry and describes its sacred mission to purify and edify Rome; Horace and the rest deliver their "dooms" of Virgil; Virgil arrives and reads from his work in progress, the *Aeneid.* So much illustrates the close and frank relations that ought to obtain, in an ideal state, between poets and sovereigns. Next comes the discordant irruption of Lupus, with his charges of treason against Horace, the counterjudgments imposed on him and his underlings by Caesar, and finally, as a sportful coda, the arraignment of the poetasters. Judgment emerges directly, here, from what the characters do, not merely from what they are. Instead of the charges against them being trumped up by the court, as in *Cynthia's Revels,* Lupus and his hangers-on have themselves trumped up the charge against Horace, and deserve severer treatment than they receive. Nor are their personalities annulled in the course of the proceedings; on the contrary they are permitted to express themselves with unbridled energy and impertinence. Caesar himself deals with the accusation of treason, ordering the informer whipped and Asinius Lupus the tribune fitted with a pair of asses' ears— to punish him for what he has done by exhibiting him for what he is.

The mock trial of the poetasters which follows, concocted by Gallus, Tibullus, and Maecenas, brilliantly fuses historical realism with satirical fantasy. On the one hand it draws on archaeological detail found in the annalists and chroniclers: the praetor, the reading of the charge, the administering of the oath, the formal pleas of the defendants, the lictors, the jurors, the urns, and so forth. At the same time it disdains mere literal reconstruction. Tucca is treated in a manner similar to Lupus, fitted, by Caesar's orders, with a pair of vizards, "That he may looke bi-fronted, as he speakes" (V.iii.435). Caesar himself thus rises to the occasion, and invents poetic variations on the judicial theme. Horace having administered emetic pills to Crispinus, the atmosphere grows progressively more surrealistic, as Crispinus vomits up the hard words in his vocabulary. Virgil, as physician, prescribes a "strict and holsome dyet" of readings (l. 536) to restore him to linguistic health. That no comparable purgation is ordered for Demetrius has rightly been taken by critics to reflect Jonson's sterner verdict on him: to purge him would be pointless, since his offense consists not in the misuse of talent but in the absence of it. Both are at length ordered into penitential costume (Demetrius into a fool's coat and cap, Crispinus into a "robe" that presumably has a similar meaning), and they are instructed to wear them in sign of atonement. Tibullus, finally, makes them swear never again to defame Horace, and Virgil concludes by dissolving the court.

We have, then, an extensive burlesque of legal procedure, held firmly in the realm of fantasy by grotesque details. Yet it succeeds in rendering more fine-grained judgments than the law could arrive at, and it also punishes according to an old Roman statute the detraction from which Jonson felt he suffered at the hands of his rivals, and for which he could not otherwise win redress in Elizabethan England. The intricate judicial machinery helps fix a final valuation on poets and poetasters, both as men and as men of letters, stressing the equivalence of the judgments: those who are good poets are also good men; the wretched poetasters prove as humanly contemptible as their verse is derisory. As in *Cynthia's Revels,* the emphasis falls more on judgment than festivity, yet festivity of a kind appears in the high-spirited prank of the purge. There has been another sort of festivity in the Act IV banquet scene, where the spectacle of poets and courtiers mimicking the gods in their least admirable activities—their carousals, their frivolities, their amorous dalliances—arouses intense conflict in Jonson. On the one hand he has Caesar denounce it as impious and unnatural, which it is not, and on the other he has Horace and Maecenas defend it, against the snooping tribune, as a harmless pastime, "bred, of noble wit" (IV.vii.42), which, with reservations, it may be allowed to be. It is as though Jonson could not make up his mind about the experience, but had to repress the pleasurable side of it by labeling it subversive, through Caesar, and then go on to show a scene of authorized mirth in the inner circle of the establishment, where the festive spirit is expressed not in eating and drinking but in administering a vomit.

Sejanus his Fall (1603), Jonson's first tragedy, which intervenes between *Poetaster* and *Volpone,* presents a justice as deformed and craven as that of *Poetaster* was healthy and self-sustaining, and some of the pessimism aroused by the sight of the Roman Senate surrendering its independence to a tyrant seems to carry over into the comedy that follows. The *scrutineo* of Venice, which in *Volpone* (1606) must decide the issues of crime and punishment, operates more autonomously than the Roman Senate, but hardly more clearsightedly. Both plays contain a pair of trial scenes in which justice itself, as men practice it, is arraigned and found guilty. The first such scene in both cases shows true justice betrayed. Toadies twist the facts to serve their own ends, blacken the innocent, and drape themselves in the mantle of public service. In the second scene, a truth of sorts emerges, and a kind of wild justice is enacted, but little thanks are due the agents of the law in either case. The fourth *avvocatore* of *Volpone* spends his time on the bench pondering the suitability of the newly rich Mosca as a son-in-law; it is in fact the sight of the two about to enter into a marriage bargain that precipitates

Volpone's decision to uncase: "Nay, now, / My ruines shall not come alone; your match / I'll hinder sure: my substance shall not glew you, / Nor screw you, into a family" (V.xii.85–88). In previous plays, judicial integrity alone sufficed to perceive the truth, and led to its disclosure. Here the disclosure comes about through judicial corruption. It is hard to imagine a more searching irony or one which more effectively defeats our wish to see justice triumph. Jonson's enigmatic treatment prohibits our knowing *what* has triumphed, and licenses nearly any interpretation of the nature of the guiding force behind events, including Celia's and Bonario's belief that heaven has intervened.

Perhaps, on balance, we are entitled to take comfort from the fact that the truth, for whatever reason, has prevailed, and that malefactors will be energetically dealt with. In its final moments the court does manage to achieve a certain stature. Its one unmistakably venal member falls silent, while its most vigorous inquirer into truth takes over as spokesman. We do not find ourselves disposed to contest the first magistrate's summing up, or most of his sentences. The banishment of Voltore, the confinement of Corbaccio to a monastery with the transfer of his estate to his son, the pillorying of Corvino, with compensation for Celia— all these seem beautifully appropriate. Given the nature of the case, a certain degree of stringency becomes fitting; the crimes of the three *captatores,* however comic, have never appeared other than odious. We conclude, therefore, that in the brief altercation between Mercy, as represented by Celia and Bonario, and Justice, as represented by the court (ll. 104–106), it is right that Justice have the last word. If the court has shown itself inept at uncovering truth, so has Bonario. If the magistrates seem too ready to condemn, the virtuous seem too eager to forgive. The *scrutineo* is not the palace of heaven, and cannot act as though it were. What we are meant to feel, no doubt, is that somehow justice has spoken through its imperfect instruments, that its institutions maintain a claim on our allegiance, however flawed their agents. Worldly justice may be shortsighted and easily abused, but it is all we have.

If we blink at the harsh dooms inflicted on Volpone and Mosca, we do so not for any judicial impropriety but for their fierceness as poetic retribution. Here, exceptionally, Jonson seems to forsake the mode of comic sentencing for the kind of penalties an actual court might impose. Perhaps he was aiming to capitalize on the widespread reputation for rigor of the Venetian courts, in which, according to a contemporary witness, "Alwaies the Advocators [i.e., the *avvocatori*] doe propounde that punishment which to that sort of offence doth seeme most sharpe and grievous, their office and duty being more to incline to severity than to mercie."[8] Jonson acknowledges his departure from comic custom, moreover, in both dedicatory epistle and Epilogue, in the one attempting to defend, in the other to offset, the play's stringent judgments. The dedication announces his intention of rebuking slanderers who claim that rascals always get off lightly in comedy. In fact, affirms Jonson, it has always been *"the office of a* comick-Poet, *to imitate justice"* (ll. 121–122). "Imitate," here, we may take in a fairly strict mimetic sense: Jonson wishes to give a taste of what justice, in the chill world, can be like when it takes its job seriously. On the other hand, he also simplifies and theatricalizes the actual judicial procedure of Venice, according to which the "advocators" did not themselves render judgment but merely forwarded evidence to the Senate or the Forty. The Epilogue reminds us that we have been at a comic feast, and requests our indulgence as a way of mitigating the sternness of the court.

> THE seasoning of a play is the applause.
> Now, though the Fox be punish'd by the lawes,
> He, yet, doth hope there is no suff'ring due,
> For any fact, which he hath done 'gainst you;
> If there be, censure him: here he, doubtfull, stands.
> If not, fare jovially, and clap your hands.

It lies in our power, then, to rescue the prisoner from his hard fate, or at least to soften it. If the play has insisted on equity, we are bidden to be equitable in our turn and not repay with ingratitude the rogue who has diverted us so well. Volpone has infringed the law, and the law has exacted its forfeits; he has pleasured us, and we must be ready with our rewards.[9]

8. From Lewkenor's translation of Gasparo Contarini, *De magistratibus et republica Venetorum* (1599), p. 91, quoted in Richard H. Perkinson, "'Volpone' and the Reputation of Venetian Justice," *MLR*, XXXV (1940), 17.

9. Edward B. Partridge, *The Broken Compass* (New York, 1958), pp. 104–111, comments interestingly on the feeding image in this play, but speaks only of its predatory aspects ("the one gross act which dramatizes man's insatiable greed," etc., p. 110). But the feeding is more than mere rending and devouring. Volpone's

With *Epiceone* (1609), Jonson moves decisively away from the rigors
of formal judiciary. The only court convened in this play consists of the
barber Cutbeard and the exbearward Otter, acting under instructions
from Truewit. No monarch or tribunal confers legitimacy on the proceedings, which derive such sanction as they possess wholly from our own
concurrence in them. They come about because Morose, driven by the
noise of his house to the law courts to investigate the possibilities of a
divorce, returns horrified by the even greater clamor there.

> . . . there is such a noyse i' the court, that they have frighted mee home,
> with more violence then I went! such speaking, and counter-speaking, with
> their severall voyces of *citations, appellations, allegations, certificates, attach-*
> *ments, intergatories, references, convictions,* and *afflictions* indeed, among the
> Doctors and Proctors! that the noise here is silence too 't! a kinde of calme
> mid-night!
>
> (IV.vii.13–19)

Morose thus rejects the aid of the law, since it means mixing with the
world on the world's terms and suffering its impertinencies and redun-
dancies. But he reckons without his "friend" Truewit, who succeeds in
bringing the law to him privately at home, in the persons of the disguised
Otter and Cutbeard. Of these two Truewit predicts to his accomplices,

> Clap but a civill gowne with a welt, o' the one; and a canonical cloake with
> sleeves, o' the other: and give 'hem a few termes i' their mouthes, if there
> come not forth as able a Doctor, and compleat a Parson, for this turne, as may
> be wish'd, trust not my election.
>
> (IV.vii.43–48)

And so it proves. The upshot of Morose's determination to preserve his
privacy is that he has inflicted on him an aggravated version of what he
has fled from: hubbub and jargon and professional pretentiousness,
pedantry and vain ceremony, and no decision. The mock proceedings,
moreover, an ear-splitting verbal duel between the two pseudo lawyers,

---

enticements to Celia have nothing gross or gluttonous about them; they are designed
to appeal to the fancy. Similarly with the exotic culinary experiments devised by
Sir Epicure Mammon. Such fantasies as that of the shrimps swimming "In a rare
butter, made of dolphin's milke, / Whose creame do's looke like opalls" (*Alchemist*,
IV.i.160–161) evoke a whole realm of complex sensuousness. They contain a poetic
dimension that powerfully enlists our own imaginative participation.

succeed in executing a judgment on him more delicately condign than anything he might have received from a bona fide court.[10]

It can hardly be accident that this hilarious burlesque of legality occurs in the play which also contains Jonson's most forthright statement of the link between comedy and feasting, and his most explicit disclaimer of the role of judge. Jonson has never gone so far in granting the public its privilege of liking and disliking, and in allowing this priority over the author's rights: "Our wishes, like to those (make publique feasts) / Are not to please the cookes tastes, but the guests" (Prologue, 8–9). Surprisingly, in a play written for the select theater of the Whitefriars, he rejects the exclusiveness of coterie drama, but nevertheless promises fastidious palates that if they deign to approach, they will find welcome and satisfaction. The play, like a well-planned meal, will cater to varied tastes, and pleasure all. Moreover, its abundance is such that its auditors will eat "A weeke at ord'naries, on his broken meat" (l. 27): the jests of his play will furnish good table conversation for days.

With comparable emphasis, Truewit in the first scene discards his attempted role as moral supervisor, once Clerimont has made it plain that serious advice on serious matters is unwelcome: "Talke me of pinnes, and feathers, and ladies, and rushes, and such things: and leave this *Stoicitie* alone, till thou mak'st sermons" (I.i.64–66). Disclaiming any wish to improve men against their will, Truewit adopts from this moment on an amused defense of the foibles of polite society—of the arts of seduction, feminine adornment, and style and artifice as against the merely natural. It is in his role as arbiter of elegancy, capable of transmitting society's code without being intimidated by it, that he takes command of the finale, which effectively judges not only Morose but, more crushingly, Sir John Daw and Sir Amorous La Foole. These two have been ripening toward deflation all day, starting out as harmless eccentrics and ending, through their very shapelessness and flaccidity, as

10. "Justice," says Enck, "is reduced to a mock disputation in bad Latin. Not only does the law receive an abstract rebuke, but Otter and Cutbeard in playing lawyers look like lawyers and, in this isolated house, are lawyers. . . . The interest lies in watching how closely the pretense parallels the real, how closely a noisy babbling becomes, while it comments on, a stern tribunal" (*Jonson and the Comic Truth,* p. 144). It becomes a stern tribunal because it substitutes for one and performs the offices of one.

serious social disrupters. They are the only characters to be publicly exposed and scolded before being contemptuously dismissed. But exposure constitutes their only punishment. There will be no emblematic donning of motley, or singing of ballads, or reciting of palinodes, for these two. Found wanting by society's rules for self-preservation, too stupid to play the social game without blundering, they are simply chased away as social pests, while more seriously disagreeable characters—the collegiate ladies—remain unrebuked. In a world where appearances count, those who "wound reputation" must be drummed out of town. The fact that the world's standards can only be shifting and unstable does not mean that they are worthless and can be discarded. It means that they enjoy only such provisional authority as men choose to grant them.

Society itself is jocularly exposed in the final moments. When Epicoene's peruke is plucked off to reveal "her" as a boy, when Cutbeard and Otter shed their gowns to become barber and bearward once more, the revelation extends potentially to everyone in the cast, and to us as well. "Nearly everyone in the play is epicene in some way," E. B. Partridge has demonstrated,[11] and this is not only figuratively but literally true. Not only Epicoene, but all the players on the Whitefriars stage are boys in disguise. The collegiate ladies, were their perukes removed, would also prove transvestites; Daw and La Foole would have their deficient masculinity exposed one more time; and the amphibious Otters would be seen to be as interchangeable in body as in marital role. The would-be Turk and commander of his household, Morose, would once again proclaim himself no man in such an unveiling, and so, too, would the trio of courtly wits, with their skittish and unstable attitude toward women. Wherever our gaze turns, it pierces beneath the highly wrought disguise to the larval condition of Epicoene. As we look further, we see an analogous condition in our friends, our neighbors, and ourselves. All are actors engaged in a masquerade, improvising various identities, sexual or professional, on the indeterminate basis supplied by nature. Whether we are ladies repairing our beauty, gentlemen promoting a reputation for gallantry, or doctors, lawyers, or parsons dependent on our gowns and a few learned terms, we all are striving to fashion masks for ourselves

11. *The Broken Compass*, p. 162.

that vastly elaborate on the simple basis of age, sex, or previous condition of servitude. In these circumstances, recognizing that we are what we can make ourselves appear, our best course is to adopt Truewit's advice and improve nature consciously, playing our chosen roles with as much generosity and panache as he does.

The Alchemist (1610) carries the subversion of justice a step farther, and forecloses even more sharply on the possibility of transcendent standards. It also introduces for the first time the discomfiting element of interested judgment. Truewit we gladly endorse in his role as legislator because of his impartiality. His successor Lovewit—the similarity in names points to a similarity in function—never pretends to detachment, but involves himself in a serious conflict of interest from the moment of his arrival on the scene. By the time of the final reckoning, he has profited handsomely from the circumstances he has been called on to help arbitrate. Unlike Truewit, who keeps the pot of the action boiling vigorously all day, Lovewit affects it only twice, both times inadvertently —once before the play begins, when like the god of second causes he withdraws, leaving his house with his manservant Jeremy, and again when he unexpectedly returns, bringing on the catastrophe. But instead of preserving his distance from the confidence game being promoted in his cellar, he joins it by accepting Jeremy's suggestion that he take the rich widow Dame Pliant for his wife. Having won this toothsome prize, he defends it by beating away the gulls who flock back to the house seeking their vanished fortunes.

The gulls themselves, as usual with Jonsonian characters in such straits, show neither remorse nor penitence, but only fury at the scoundrels who have fleeced them. Appearing to reclaim their investments, they retire, according to their different dispositions, with curses, threats, or bluster. Not one has learned from the experience, and the main defect of the implicit judgment on them is that it leaves them as benighted as it finds them. Dol and Subtle, ignominiously eluding the constables through a rear window, learn what they already know, that there is little honor among thieves. Surly, to his sorrow, learns that he has cozened himself "With that same foolish vice of honestie" (V.v.84). He has played the part of the just man, reluctant to take unfair advantage of a mere stroke of fortune, preferring to "deserve" Dame Pliant after respecting her honor in the garden, and expecting her to choose him rationally over his rivals, as reward for his chivalry. But this is to place his faith in a justice that everything about her, beginning with her name, proclaims more fanciful than castles in Spain. Gamesters who refuse to cash in on their own luck must be content to lose, and comic justice wastes few regrets on them.

For it is chance, more than choice, which shapes the outcome of this play, and chance, an amoral force, has small patience with any but its own successful votaries. The final disposals stem from the random conjunction of Lovewit's position with his temperament. In his taste for sport he resembles Clement or Truewit; he has a sweet tooth for a jest: "I love a teeming wit, as I love my nourishment" (V.i.16). Wit, for Lovewit, contains both pleasure and sustenance, as it does for the scapegrace young men of *Every Man in his Humor,* and as—in our capacity as spectators to a comedy—it should for us. As accidental owner of the house that harbors the cozening, Lovewit does not scruple to lay claim to the fruits of the cozening. He also chooses to protect this investment by pardoning his servant Jeremy: in return for the tangible benefits of a rich wife and a trunkful of booty, he adopts, in effect, the ethos of the cozeners, and makes it that of the play.[12] The result, however, is an uneasy conscience. He has sullied his innocence, Lovewit admits, in becoming accessory after the fact to such a cheat. At the same time he appeals to the audience not to judge him harshly, predicting that with the aid of his plunder he may somehow redeem himself, though how this is to be accomplished remains mysterious. Face, then, makes sure of the audience's favorable verdict by insuring its complicity; he enlists us in the ranks of the profiteers. He has, he says, escaped the fury of the gulls and his knavish comrades, yet the final decision rests with us.

> . . . I put my selfe
> On you, that are my countrey: and this pelfe,
> Which I have got, if you do quit me, rests
> To feast you often, and invite new ghests.
>
> (V.v.162–165)

12. "He appears a more prosperous version of the knaves, and his habits in discourse link him with them," observes Enck, correctly (*Jonson and the Comic Truth,* p. 160).

Jonson has addressed us from the outset as "Judging Spectators," request-ing "justice" for himself and "grace" for the actors.[13] Now Face swears us in as jurors—the term "countrey" designating the jury—and pleads for "grace" of an unusual kind. The jury is being invited, as Lovewit was invited, to share the spoils. If we will judge leniently and acquit the rascal, we are promised our cut in the form of a feast, the feast to be a renewal of the comedy itself. Lovewit's banquet will be ours on condition that we agree to wink at certain irregularities in the procure-ment of it. The fact that we "naturally and unthinkingly" applaud at the end of the speech produces "one of Jonson's most effective and devastating strokes,"[14] since it seals our guilty acquiescence before we have had the chance to reflect or consult our consciences.

More explicitly than in *Epicoene,* then, Jonson here shifts responsibility for final judgment onto us, and encourages us to follow the line of least

13. "Fortune, that favours fooles" (Prologue, 1–2), we may note, has been "wished away" only in the playhouse, not in the play. In the play Fortune is very much in evidence, and she distinctly does not favor fools. She bestows her blessings on the wits who can court her boldly enough, and leaves the fools in the lurch. In the playhouse, things are different. Neither the author nor the actors there care to entrust themselves to her cruel whims. They wish their merits to be recognized, their talent, skill, and hard work to be appreciated, or at least they wish themselves salvaged from rebuke by "grace." So Fortune is banished from the relations be-tween stage and spectators, only to return as the presiding deity of the plot, and regent of the relations among the dramatis personae.

14. Alan C. Dessen, *Jonson's Moral Comedy* (Evanston, Ill., 1971), p. 134. Paul Goodman, "Comic Plots: *The Alchemist,*" in Barish, *Ben Jonson,* p. 116 (originally published in *The Structure of Literature* [Chicago, 1954]), sees Face and Lovewit as "universal characters," "the witty and the urbane," "not involved in a particular intrigue," and hence able to step outside the play to address the audience directly. "The comic talents, the knaves or shrewd fools . . . are in a certain sense 'like the audience'; they have a cleverness that anyone might wish for himself." Again, "To be named 'Face' is to be a universal wit and to survive." Doubtless it is true that as between Face and Subtle, Face is the more resourceful, more adaptable in emergencies, and less prone to discouragement. But he is deeply "involved in a particular intrigue," and Subtle's histrionic talents are more than sufficient to inspire envy. The crucial difference would seem to be that Face belongs to the household on a permanent basis, whereas Subtle is only a bird of passage. This difference of circumstance outweighs Face's superior versatility. If Face and Lovewit do become "universal wits" at the end, they do so too casually, too off-handedly, to allow us to feel that this has been their destined role from the start.

resistance, rather than pursue the toilsome path of principle. We are to practice no stricter an accounting than we would wish for ourselves had we been clever enough to carry off such a stunt. As the Jonsonian equivalence between comedy and feasting comes into sharp focus, comedy loses much of its corrective sting, and the dispositions of the finale amount to a dividing up of the spoils of knavery. Only if we wish to be reckoned among the gulls will we protest too loudly.

Bartholomew Fair (1614) brings us to a further point in this overthrow of justice and its replacement by comic permissiveness. In the lunatic Troubleall, demented former officer of the petty court of Pie-powders, who wanders up and down demanding what warrant others have for their actions, Jonson travesties the craving for sanctions, the longing for official endorsement, that has haunted him since his earliest plays, and shows it to be hopeless, witless, impossible of fulfillment, and a stage on the road to madness if persisted in.[15] In the crackbrained Justice Overdo, who labors to make himself indistinguishable from fools and madmen, Jonson shows that the dedication to justice, even in a Justice, may coexist with folly. *Summum ius,* in fact, *summa iniuria.* Can justice consort with common sense? The play leaves room for doubt. This time the one authoritative and binding contract is that drawn up between author and audience. In the articles of the Induction, the poet acknowledges his obligation to provide mirth, in exchange for the spectators' pledge not to demand it in inappropriate forms. Both parties concur in the central assumption that the quest for mirth is legitimate, and that justice exists to further it, not to obstruct it. Corrective justice, within the play, proves to be largely the property of fools, madmen, and hypocrites. One by one the disciplinarians succeed in interfering with the king's peace, and so—by an apposite stroke of retribution—end in the stocks. Each of them embodies some objective in itself legitimate: Overdo, the need to maintain civic law and order; Busy, the need to restrain

15. Ray L. Heffner, Jr., "Unifying Symbols in the Comedy of Ben Jonson," in Barish, *Ben Jonson,* pp. 133–146 (originally published in *English Stage Comedy,* ed. W. K. Wimsatt, Jr., *English Institute Essays 1954* [New York, 1955]), discusses the play acutely from this point of view, focusing on the figure of Troubleall. See also the virtuoso analysis by Jackson I. Cope, *"Bartholomew Fair* as Blasphemy," *RenD,* VIII (Evanston, Ill., 1965), 127–152, of the dominant themes of "legalism" and "antiquated severity of judgment" in the play (p. 134).

carnal appetite; Wasp, the need to regulate aimless pleasure-seeking; and Troubleall, the need for adequate sanctions. But each pursues his purpose with such blind and punishing passion as to make the cure worse than the disease. Each behaves as though pleasure and justice were radically antithetical and irreconcilable, and each, after an interval in the stocks, ends a second time more the object than the agent of justice. In earlier plays, authority emanated from the top down, from Augustus, for example, through Virgil to Horace and Maecenas, and from them to the humbler citizens who pressed into the chamber in the final scene. Each judicial act reaffirmed the integrity of the judges, the rightness of their jurisdiction and the standards being applied. In *Bartholomew Fair,* the governors are all mad, and justice is left to sprout from odd corners of the earth. When it does, it reveals its official spokesmen to be frenzied enemies of the pleasure principle by which the playwright himself has agreed to be judged. As in *Epicoene,* the climactic moment is an unveiling, and a lesson in the arbitrary nature of our categories of identity. When the puppet Dionysius lifts his skirt to reveal his sexual nonentity, he heaps ridicule on all fundamentalist distinctions between male and female, righteous and unrighteous, saved and damned—perhaps even between animate and inanimate—showing, with Rabbi Zeal-of-the-Land Busy to witness, that our personages are artful constructs of our own, infusions of our own free spirits, our fair or foul vapors, into the blockish stuff of nature. A second unveiling, that of the Justice's wife spewing drunkenly into a basin as a member of the Fair's impromptu brothel, reinforces the lesson by eliminating social as well as sexual categories from the realm of the preordained. The only division that seems to survive intact is that between fools and rogues.[16]

More markedly than in *The Alchemist,* we conclude with indulgence, and with the wits free to carry off the spoils of their roguery. Quarlous has so managed matters that though his rival, Winwife, has won Mistress Grace for a wife, he, Quarlous, has won her as his ward, and also secured as his own wife the rich widow Dame Purecraft. These new arrangements accord nicely with our sense of fitness. It is proper that the booby Cokes be divested of his fiancée, Mistress Grace, with whom he has nothing in common, and that Justice Overdo be cozened of her as his ward, he

16. On this point see Harry Levin, "Introduction," in Barish, *Ben Jonson,* p. 49.

having purchased her, in conformance with the odious statute, from the Court of Wards, for the sake of her lands, and then bestowed her on the "wise gentleman" his brother-in-law, so as to keep her fortune in the family. It is right that Winwife marry Grace—in their fastidiousness and coolness, the two seem ideally matched—but acceptable, too, that he buy her from his comrade, Quarlous, without whose aggressiveness and energy he would not have won her. Quarlous and his widow, both unscrupulous fortune-hunters, thoroughly deserve each other; Quarlous now will fall heir to the unsavory pleasures he once horrendously outlined to Winwife, to be had from "ancient tripes" and "trillibubs."

In a world lacking unambiguous sanctions and pervasively tainted by self-interest, what affords pleasure to so many people while creating so few victims nearly takes on the character of miracle. The letter of the law may be a little the worse for wear, but its spirit has been much mended. The deed of wardship secured through fraud has at least as much validity as that obtained through an inhuman statute; the altered marriage license effects a truer union than the unaltered original; and the espousal brought into existence by the chance stroke of a madman's pen far outdoes in fitness the contract arranged by "friends" and relatives.[17] Knave, fool, and judicial agent seem to have deserved about equally; the final dispositions, proposed by Quarlous and accepted by Overdo, envisage general amnesty. Not only will no punishment be inflicted other than what has come about of its own accord in the course of the day, but all the people will repair to a feast at the home of justice: none required to fast it out penitently in the court—much less in cages; none goaded into rushing furiously back into their houses; none beaten away or dismissed through back windows into rear alleys. All will partake of the promised supper, its festive nature emphasized by the presence of the little actors who have helped tame the disciplinarians, who will be brought along to resume their interrupted disports.

Bartholomew Fair thus strikes a delicate balance between the claims of poetic justice and the realities of a world in which clear sanctions are not to be found. It ridicules official justice more devastatingly than *The*

---

17. A puzzle remains: how, if Quarlous has stolen the license for his own marriage to Purecraft, does Winwife (legally) secure Mistress Grace for himself? He identifies himself at the end as her "kinsman."

Alchemist, yet at the same time more richly satisfies our sense of fairness. Jonson's last four plays, in their dealings with this theme, betray the collapse of coherence that led Dryden to dismiss them, terribly but rightly, as dotages. The first two parody judicial process almost frenetically, yet fail to make judgment an effective agency of plot resolution; the last two, products of Jonson's final years of sickness, heavily abandon the whole question. In *The Devil Is an Ass* (1616), we find a laborious travesty of justice centering on the figure of a bigoted magistrate, which is then casually dropped and replaced with a denouement that contains scarcely any element of judicial assessment. The bigoted magistrate himself, Sir Paul Eitherside, would seem to convey Jonson's settled contempt for the whole legal profession, and his deepening despair over its remoteness from true equity: Sir Paul makes the *scrutineo* of *Volpone* look like the court of Augustus. The chief fool of the play, Fabian Fitzdottrel, is virtually *talked* out of his folly—an amazingly undramatic and un-Jonsonian proceeding—while the archknave, Merecraft, lurks in a corner, forgotten by the others on the stage, neither exposed, rebuked, nor sentenced. The Epilogue subsequently informs us that "the Projector, here, is over-throwne," but we must take this on trust, for Jonson never shows it. Merecraft lapses into muteness, vanishing from the consciousness of the other characters, who take no further notice of him. It is hard to imagine what an actor could find to do with himself in the part in this scene, having been so disastrously struck down from hyperactive manipulator to ignored supernumerary. The weight of the finale shifts to a series of listless and mostly unearned conversions to virtue by which Jonson clumsily undoes the knots of the intrigue. Usually, Jonsonian characters are so ruled by their humors or vapors or *idées fixes* that they are for dramatic purposes defined by them; they cannot survive the extinction of their follies; the scene of judgment simply snuffs them out. For Jonson to resort to the resurgence of an original goodness to unravel his plot is to abandon both psychological coherence and theatrical consistency, especially in the present play, whose premise—that men now outdo the devils in vice—would seem to forbid a sentimental resolution more strictly than ever. But by the time the action reaches its final moments, Jonson's attention has been totally captured by the prospect of the guardians of virtue promoting moral rearmament among the rest; as a result, the play's whole massive history of gullibility and knavery, instead of crystallizing in a scene of summary correction, slides unnoticed into Lethe.

The Staple of News (1626) manages somewhat better. We return to a ringing (if uninteresting) restatement of the old comic moral when the knavish lawyer is circumvented by having his own tactics turned against him: "To cheat the *Cheater* was no *cheat,* but justice" (V.iii.21). We have legalism bitingly parodied, and the preoccupation with it exposed as a species of madness, in the figure of the miser Penniboy Senior, who runs amok after losing his money and tries his dogs for plotting to cozen him. Penniboy's stinginess forms part of a syndrome of derangement that includes a perverse streak of self-punishment and a fixation on justice.[18] He boasts of his pinched existence, of the truly horrid fate of being "one that never made / Good meale in his sleep," of eking out his days "Like an old hoary Rat, with mouldy Pye-crust" (II.i.15–18), of turning over to his cook the dainties sent him as gifts, not to be cooked but to be appraised and sold for cash value. He prides himself on a compulsive punctuality and a fanatic frugality, cursing the cook for a single lateness, and his porter for spending sixpence once every seven years on sack, when the same sum, invested over seventy years, would eventually have compounded to more than twenty-five pounds. From time to time, to gloss his obsession, he explains that he is a "just man," who "loves justice still." Once again, as in *Bartholomew Fair,* the pursuit of justice involves an element of the maniacal, of punitive fury and hatred of pleasure. Those who live by levying tolls and exacting forfeits, who impose rigid abstinences on themselves, who treat life as a series of things to be weighed, measured, and hoarded, are in revolt against nature, however they may be pleased to think themselves her servants, and nature avenges herself by rebelling in turn. Nature, as Penniboy has pointed out in an earlier tirade, has no need of silver dishes, gold chamber pots, or perfumed napkins, but still less does she need the gold and silver coins amassed

---

18. It was Edmund Wilson who first pointed out, with needless pejorative emphasis, the presence of the anal-sadistic complex—parsimony, orderliness, and stubbornness—in Jonsonian characters and in Jonson: "Morose Ben Jonson," in Barish, *Ben Jonson,* pp. 60–71 (originally published in *The Triple Thinkers,* rev. ed. [New York, 1948]). Psychoanalytic patterns suggest themselves with particular insistence for *The Staple of News,* where the neurotic component seems incompletely transmuted by the creative alchemy.

in his coffers. The precious metals need not, for him, be changed into vessels for food or excrement; he already treats them as surrogates for bodily processes.

As he concludes his inquest into his dogs' misdeeds, the jeerers storm in, to mock him for his bankruptcy and to be mocked and reviled by him in turn; the situation deeply gratifies his secret wish to be hated by all other men. But it is not Penniboy, a jeerer of purest alloy himself, who can rout the jeerers, but only his moderate brother, who scatters the crew and restores the miser's wits by returning his bonds and mortgages. At this point, in obedience to the morality design of the action, Penniboy Senior undergoes a conversion: he forswears his parsimony as his prodigal nephew has already forsworn prodigality. With all characters thus firmly enrolled under the banner of "liberality," it is left to the play's metallic heroine, Lady Pecunia, to conclude with a plea for the ideal of the golden mean. Now it is a striking fact that as between the two extremes of reckless squandering and insensate hoarding, only the latter is presented as pathological. The prodigal need only lose his money to be brought to his senses; his escapades amount to little more than schoolboy pranks. The fanaticism of the miser, by contrast, wells up from black depths of self-hatred and life denial, and must pass through an interval of near-suicidal madness before being purged. Justice, then, as embodied in this character, proves much more dangerous than its opposite, not only ridiculous but malignant, linked to a passion for counting and measuring, to a wish to hurt and be hurt, and a venomous hatred of pleasure in any form.

Further than this, in his dethronement of an admired ideal, Jonson could hardly go; his last two plays shelve the whole question. *The New Inn* (1629) forges once more the link between comedy and feasting, this time with considerable intricacy. It consists of a feast within a feast within a feast: first the festive repast spread for us by the playwright himself, as master cook, in the Prologue; then the meal of mirth provided by the Host of the Inn; finally the philosophical banquet arranged by the visiting lords and ladies. But Jonson invites his guests to the table almost threateningly; the Neo-Platonic symposium has little of laughter in it; and the whole operation reaches a disastrous anticlimax in the indignant "Ode to Himself," written out of Jonson's anguish at the play's failure. Jonson here invokes the image of the comic feast for the last time to express the fury of the chef whose choicest delicates have been hoggishly snuffled at and spurned. If the comic muse, in happy vein, can furnish rich fare, it is also capable, in incompetent hands, of proffering a beggarly ration of crumbs, a sour draft of lees, and if the spectators' perversity makes them choose the lees over the lusty wine, the acorns over the wheat, why, argues Jonson defiantly to himself, "Envy them not, their palate's with the swine" (l. 20). Both *The New Inn* and *The Magnetic Lady* (1632) abandon the judicial finale almost entirely, contenting themselves with babies exchanged in the cradle, girls disguised as boys, long-lost families miraculously reunited, and other well-worn bits of comic claptrap, resurrected for the occasion to compose a denouement. The element of appraisal and evaluation has nearly vanished.

Whether this reversion to an older dramatic mode may also be said to reflect the renewed Neo-Platonism of Jonson's later years is difficult to say. Jonson avoids implying that the final sorting out of the intrigues is due to the mystic operation of higher powers, and it is hard to see much connection between the austere Platonism of Lovell's "orations" and the disclosures from romance that come to unsnarl the plot of *The New Inn*. Oddly enough, the element of judicial assessment, which has evaporated from the finale, reappears in the inner sanctum of the Court of Love, where the speeches on Love and Valor stress the necessity for judgment over passion, and a character named Prudence, presiding from her "seat of judicature," awards favors and penalties to the participants.

It is evident that when we speak of justice in Jonsonian or any comedy, we refer not merely to the legal forms for rendering judgment, or even to the morality behind the decisions, but to an ordering principle which conducts the characters to destinations appropriate to their dramatic journeys. Justice decrees that a play play itself out to the end, that it stabilize and equilibrate its various elements before taking leave of them. Early in his career Jonson prefers the formal scene of arraignment, which permits him to pass character and event in review and sentence them— that is, assign meanings to them. We find that the major comic successes occur when he balances a skeptical treatment of legal process against an imaginatively conceived distribution of reward and punishment. The comical satires, with their overpowering tribunals, leave us slightly oppressed beneath the weight of so much machinery; so, in a different way, do the savage parodies of due process in *The Devil Is an Ass* and

The Staple of News. In the one case the law is too worshipfully invoked as a salvation, in the other too furiously repudiated as a cheat and a delusion; in the last plays of all it is too wearily disregarded. In the great middle comedies we find plenary justice executed through spirited improvisations on normal procedure, according to a logic of the spirit no actual court could even approximate. Such justice fosters our festive responses as well as our judicial approval; it enables us to relish the follies of the fools and the peculations of the knaves without making us feel that we are endorsing the inadmissible. O rare and absolute true Gulls! O rare musique out of discordes! O rare Ben Jonson!

Replication as Dramatic Strategy in the Comedies of Ben Jonson

LAWRENCE L. LEVIN

O NE OF THE PROBLEMS facing Renaissance dramatists was to incorporate the multiplicity of characters, scenes, and events inherited from medieval narrative into a unified, coherent dramatic mold.[1] In grappling with an evolving form, Elizabethan playwrights experimented with different ways of designing their plays, from the dominating presence of a single figure to the emphasis upon one central action or a moral choice. One of the most striking attempts to achieve dramatic unity, and a source of confusion at times, was the deployment of multiple plots which would interact in one way or other with the main line of action. In conjunction with this technique there developed a system of repetitive devices of varying complexity and scope which reached its fullest, most mature expression in the plays of Shakespeare. H. T. Price[2] and Paul Aldus[3] in their respective studies have shown how a close examination of practically any Shakespeare play will reveal the dramatist's use of analogue as a means of unifying the play and commenting upon charac-

---

1. See Madeleine Doran, *Endeavors of Art: A Study of Form in Elizabethan Drama* (Madison, Wis., 1954), p. 18. For a discussion of Elizabethan attempts at solving the problems of unity of action, see pp. 288–294.

2. "Mirror-Scenes in Shakespeare," *Joseph Quincy Adams Memorial Studies,* ed. J. McManaway et al. (Washington, D.C., 1948), pp. 101–113.

3. "Analogical Probability in Shakespeare's Plays," *SQ,* VI (1955), 397–414.

ter, action, and theme. In addition, both critics have shown how this method can help shed new interpretive light on particular scenes and passages that formerly were obscured. Shakespeare's plays, especially the great tragedies, abound with analogical correspondences. Often the basic patterns are established in the opening scenes and spiral outward, clarifying and underscoring central areas throughout the play. A complete study of any of his plays can hardly fail to show how this technique is an integral and important ingredient in Shakespeare's dramaturgy.[4]

However, remarkably little scholarship has been expended in tracing analogous patterns in the plays of Ben Jonson, Shakespeare's greatest dramatic rival. The paucity of criticism in this area would suggest that Jonson's approach to playwriting followed far different lines. T. S. Eliot, in his well-known comparison of Shakespeare and Jonson, put his finger on a central difference between these two dramatists when he observed that in Jonson the "emotional effect is single and simple. Whereas in Shakespeare the effect is due to the way in which the characters *act upon* one another, in Jonson it is given by the way in which the characters *fit in* with each other."[5] Jonson obviously is not concerned with character in the same way as Shakespeare. Instead of a psychological study of men seeking answers to existential questions in an open-ended universe, Jonson introduces predefined characters into a particular situation and watches their formulaic responses.

Despite these basic differences, however, Jonson does include action that functions in an analogous manner. *Volpone,* for example, contains several scenes that either mirror one another, underscore thematic values, or point the way toward future events. The Act I entertainment put on by Nano and Androgyno anticipates the degeneration of the various *captatores* and, in particular, Volpone's own debasement as he assumes various disguises. With each one he is lowered on the social and moral scale until eventually his spiritual sickness is matched by his real physical

---

4. For general studies which heavily emphasize this approach to Shakespeare's plays, see Harold C. Goddard, *The Meaning of Shakespeare* (Chicago, 1951); Maynard Mack, "The Jacobean Shakespeare: Some Observations on the Construction of the Tragedies," in *Jacobean Theatre,* ed. John Russell Brown and Bernard Harris, *Stratford-upon-Avon Studies* (New York, 1960), I, 11–42; Christopher F. Givan, "Thematic Doubling in Shakespeare's Plays," Diss. Stanford, 1971.

5. "Ben Jonson," in *Selected Essays 1917–1932* (New York, 1950), pp. 132–133.

infirmity.[6] Volpone as mountebank, one of his degrading disguises, also serves as an analogue. Scoto's sale of false elixirs mirrors Volpone's own deception of those to whom he sells a false hope of gold. Furthermore, the mountebank's eventual beating at the hands of Corvino anticipates Volpone's punishment at the end of the play. Similarly, the subplot, as Jonas Barish has brilliantly shown,[7] operates dramatically and almost exclusively to mirror themes germane to the main plot. In her lewd behavior Lady Wouldbe functions as a visual embodiment of what Corvino is attempting to make of Celia, and Sir Pol's sudden exposure mirrors Volpone's own unmasking and subsequent punishment.

Analogous action in *Volpone,* though richer than in the rest of Jonson's plays, still does not rival the complex interplay and thematic doubling found in Shakespeare. The distinctions between the two dramatists, then, seem to hold true. In the area of structural and thematic patterning Shakespeare presents many themes in an exploratory, complex, highly orchestrated manner; Jonson uses the repetition of one or two basic concepts in a theme-and-variations technique. Rather than include diverse, contradictory, and qualifying shades of perspective, Jonson states an initial thesis and reinforces it through varied repetition.[8]

In the area of plot construction, however, Jonson developed a rather idiosyncratic technique. The "Jonsonian formula," as Edgar Knowlton has suggested,[9] consists of an unsatisfactory fourth-act solution to the previously developed intrigue, in which the major characters come together followed by the development of renewed activity which eventually

6. Harry Levin, "Jonson's Metempsychosis," *PQ,* XXII (1943), 231–239.

7. "The Double Plot in *Volpone,*" *MP,* LI (1953), 83–92.

8. Recently, L. A. Beaurline has argued that one of the reasons for the structural differences between the plays of Shakespeare and Jonson was that the former, in his limitless range and rich harmonics, was satisfying the Renaissance notion of plenitude, whereas Jonson was attempting to achieve "limited completeness"—a characteristic, he claims, of later seventeenth-century literature—rather than exhaustive divergence. Beaurline further contends that, after *Volpone,* Jonson rejected "not only episodic or narrative form but subplot, overplot, and parallel plot as well" ("Ben Jonson and the Illusion of Completeness," *PMLA,* LXXXIV [1969], 55). For an unfavorable evaluation of Beaurline's thesis and argument, as well as the author's defense, see "Notes, Documents, and Critical Comment," *PMLA,* LXXXVI (1971), 121–127.

9. "The Plots of Ben Jonson," *MLN,* XLIV (1929), 77–86.

leads to a "more palatable solution" in the fifth act. According to Knowl-ton, in both Acts IV and V, and occasionally in Act III, "a considerable assembly of personages took place, entailing on the part of the dramatist watchful construction" (pp. 79–80).

In connection with this generally accepted theory, I would like to propose that Jonson utilized another recurrent structural technique, that of a central analogue, occurring primarily in Act IV, but sometimes in Act III or V, which reflected upon the play's catastrophe. Rather than incorporating a series of thematic incidents and ancillary characters that worked together to elucidate theme and character and built toward a particular climax in the manner of Shakespeare, Jonson fashioned one or two significant pieces of analogous action as a key structural block with a dual purpose: to help unify the play by bringing into focus theme, incident, and character, and to anticipate, in one way or another, elements of the denouement and conclusion. The following study will examine Jonson's particular method of construction from his earliest plays through his "golden" period and conclude with *The Staple of News,* his last play of substance.

The Early Plays

Each of the plays before *Volpone,* with the exception of *Every Man out of his Humour,* contains a central episode that somehow parallels or prefigures a later unraveling of the plot by a justice figure who is either a poet himself or a patron of the arts assisted by a poet-scholar. In *Every Man in his Humour* the key piece of analogous action is rather unobtrusively inserted in the center of the play, Act III, scene iii, in an encounter between Doctor Clement and Oliver Cob, the comic water-bearer.[10] Cob suddenly intrudes upon Clement and Lorenzo Senior, who are discussing the latter's "profligate" son, and demands a warrant for Bobadilla's arrest. In the ensuing dialogue, Clement reprimands Cob for misusing language and disparaging the use of tobacco, threatens him with imprisonment, and then lets him go after making provisions to deal with those who have actually broken the law by assaulting Cob. The analogous court scene ends with Clement advising Lorenzo Senior to forget his

10. A more detailed presentation of this section on *Every Man In* appears in my article, "Clement Justice in *Every Man in his Humour,*" *SEL,* XII (1972), 291–307.

relatively slight problems by drowning "them all in a cup of sacke."[11]

This brief action prepares the audience for the Act V catastrophe in two ways. Once again Clement holds court while various characters come before him with their complaints. (This scene could be staged so that it visually parallels the analogue.) At one point, as Clement questions Tib, Cob's wife, who also has been unjustly beaten, Bobadilla and Matheo suddenly break in upon the proceedings. Bobadilla, like Cob did earlier, accuses Giuliano of beating him; and when Clement eventually gets the facts straight, he punishes the offenders rather harshly through incarceration and the stockade.[12]

More significantly, however, the analogue is a specific foreshadowing of the final confrontation between Clement and the clever Musco. Like Cob in his disguise of complete innocence (and Bobadilla and Matheo, who pose as soldier and poet respectively), Musco, impersonating Clement's own legal clerk, comes before the Justice pretending to be something he is not. After hearing testimony from Musco and Giuliano, Clement sees Musco's guilt, terrorizes him with his quibble over the word "must" for abusing the law and misusing language (V.iii.117–122), and, after apparently rejecting Musco's appeal for mercy (equivalent to Lorenzo Senior's plea in the analogue), Clement rewards Musco's wit by granting him a complete reprieve. Although the comic resolution is yet to be fully effected, Clement prematurely celebrates his "carouse" to the "Heroick spirite" (l. 444) by downing another cup of sack.

In both the analogue and the Act V action, then, Clement is interrupted by a character misusing language and apparently contributing to social disorder through improper communication and deception. Clement chastises the errant characters and establishes a benign order over kinetic confusion. By creating an Act III encounter analogous to certain events in the last act, Jonson has subtly prepared the audience for the final

11. III.iii.139. *Ben Jonson*, ed. C. H. Herford and Percy and Evelyn Simpson, 11 vols. (Oxford, 1925–1952). All quotations from Jonson are from this edition, which will hereafter be cited as H & S.

12. In the Folio, Jonson, realizing the inconsistency of this severity with Clement's character, and, perhaps, in order to make the end of the play more harmonious with the Act III analogue of justice and mercy, amended this punishment so that the two foolish characters merely are excluded from the dinner celebrating the restoration of order.

resolution of some of the play's complexities. Once we have seen how Clement reacts in a given situation, we have a paradigm of what to expect when a similar set of circumstances occurs later in the play.

In *Every Man Out* Jonson temporarily puts aside the method of structural foreshadowing he had experimented with in *Every Man In* and substitutes a series of exposures beginning with Sordido's epiphany and repentance in Act III and lasting until all the foolish characters, including Macilente, have been divested of their particular humors. In *Cynthia's Revels*, however, Jonson returns to the type of structural design he had used in the earlier play, but with certain differences. Instead of a cryptic hint of the play's outcome buried in a mid-play scene of apparently little significance, Jonson shifts the analogous scenes to the last act. In this manner he strengthens the obvious parallels so that the long-awaited climax to the folly of the courtiers and the appearance of Cynthia is heightened. In both *Every Man Out* and *Cynthia's Revels*, Jonson makes it clear early in the play that the foolish and malicious individuals infecting society will be soundly punished at the appropriate time;[13] therefore he dispenses with the analogous pattern in *Every Man Out* and uses it in a different way in *Cynthia's Revels*. Finally, in *Poetaster*, Jonson brings this initial phase of his experiment in construction to a conclusion by synthesizing the mid-play episode from *Every Man In* with the techniques of dramatic intensity, inversion, and parallel incidents which he develops in *Cynthia's Revels*. With this over-all pattern in view, let us look at what Jonson has attempted in *Cynthia's Revels* and *Poetaster*.

Throughout *Cynthia's Revels* Jonson has used Moria (Folly) and the gallants and ladies of fashion to reflect the inversion of order and values in the court. Moria has clandestinely brought Philautia (Self-Love), Phantaste (Fancy), and Argurion (Money) into court and established herself as the direct antagonist and pseudo rival to Cynthia. In the first part of Act V, by seating Moria in the chair of state as she presides

---

13. In referring to the false courtiers in *Cynthia's Revels,* Arete tells Crites that

> This knot of spiders will be soone dissolu'd,
> And all their webs swept out of CYNTHIAS court,
> When once her glorious *deitie* appeares,
> And but presents it selfe in her full light. . . .
>
> (III.iv.88–91)

over the battle of "court-complement," Jonson makes the analogy between debased Moria and virtuous Cynthia more explicit and paves the way for the sudden downfall of Moria and her court at the height of their presumption. At the same time, the mock court scene serves as a visual symbol of the perversion of Cynthia's court. Furthermore, it anticipates both the dethroning of Folly by Cynthia-Wisdom,[14] which occurs in the final scene of the play, and the exposure and reformation of the false courtiers by Crites. Instead of a mid-play analogue, then, we have a double-barreled exposure of folly in which the initial overthrow of the false monarch (Moria) anticipates the later establishment of the true monarch (Cynthia) as well as the final method of exposure and correction (a deity assisted by Crites).

By the beginning of Act V the courtiers and the court ladies have all drunk from the fountain of self-love, thus exacerbating their already diseased condition. For this reason Mercury enlists Crites' aid in helping to reform the deviant courtiers through humiliation ("And punish, with our laughter"), thereby bringing them into line with the "better race in court," those who "haue the true nobilitie, call'd vertue" (V.i.30,31). The occasion which enables Mercury and Crites to curb the pride of the false courtiers comes when Mercury, disguised as a French courtier, unexpectedly accepts Amorphus' challenge in wooing "the ladie courtship" (Moria) in the four *most cunning weapons of* court-complement" (iii.97). Presiding over the principal contestants from the chair of state[15]

---

14. The contrast and confrontation between two individuals representing opposing values is part of the masque furniture, particularly as Jonson used it. In *Hymenaei* (1606) two female figures, Truth and Opinion, emerge identically attired from a perfumed mist to debate the institution of marriage. "Who art thou," Truth questions, "thus that imitat'st my grace, / In steps, in habite, and resembled face?" (ll. 693–694). Truth's opening lines challenging Opinion could well be thought, if not expressed, by Cynthia (Wisdom), particularly if Moria (Folly) were dressed in robes not dissimilar to Cynthia's in order to help underscore the mock court analogy. In *Hymenaei,* Truth eventually exposes and routs Opinion (false Truth), who, in the end, is garbed in a heavily folded robe of "gaudie *colours*" to show "what vncertainties shee euer holds . . . " (ll. 924–925).

15. Alexander C. Judson, *Cynthia's Revels,* Yale Studies in English (New York, 1912), p. 214, argues unconvincingly that Moria stands during the court duel instead of occupying a chair of state. Herford and Simpson, however, assume, correctly, that "state" here refers to a chair with a canopy over it.

and serving as the object of their addresses are Moria, followed by Philautia, then Phantaste. Completing this picture of inverted values are Hedon and Anaides, who act as judges over the proceedings, awarding prizes to the most accomplished courtier. The real judges, of course, are Mercury and Crites, who easily defeat and humiliate the false courtiers by beating them at their own game. As Mercury's "stickler," Crites exposes in uncompromising terms the ludicrous affectations of the courtiers and, after routing them, observes to Mercury that the exposure of vanity and affectation is far easier and less important than the real task—to bring about in the minds of the offenders humble acceptance and inward reformation.

Immediately following the victorious collaboration between the god Mercury and the mortal but "judicious" Crites, the goddess Cynthia, through Arete, calls upon Crites to join with her in exposing and punishing the false members of the court by writing a masque. Having established the inverted court of Moria as a kind of antimasque, Jonson initiates his own masque of Virtue and Justice (V.vi.), when Cynthia is splendidly ushered in by her attendants. In the formal and rather artificial dialogue between Arete (Virtue) and Cynthia, Arete's compliments to true virtue contrast with the earlier praise of Folly by the false courtiers. The two masques that take place in scenes vii and ix are another form of the mock court scene, but here we have the proto-antimasque and the masque combined, while at the same time the masque of Cynthia is juxtaposed with the mumming revelers. The nominal masques are actually a perversion of the virtuous climate ritualistically established by Cynthia and her entourage. Dressed to represent the virtue antithetic to their own vice, members of the false court attempt to make a mockery of Cynthia's revels, just as their own pseudo court attempted to undermine Cynthia's rule. In the first part of Act V the false courtiers had referred to the activities in their mock court as "sport."[16] Now the word takes an ironic twist when Cynthia's "sports," the evening masques, coincide with the vapid "sports" of the

16. The masque Jonson wrote for Lord Haddington's wedding in 1608 contains his first clear use of the antimasque, according to H & S (II, 276). Here, as a foil to Venus' majesty, is the *"Reuell"* of Cupid and his twelve male attendants who represent *"the sports . . . that accompanie* Loue" (ll. 159–160).

courtiers. From her own chair of state, Cynthia indicates that her "sports" (xi.2) comprise not only the revels but also the act of exposing and punishing those who would disrupt and debase the essential activities of the court. The participants in the antimasque are exposed when Cynthia causes the dancers to unmask, revealing in shocking contrast pure vice stripped from its disguise of antithetic virtue.[17]

Crites, who in the analogue had aided the god Mercury in exposing the courtiers in Moria's false court, has been equally responsible for bringing these members before Cynthia's censuring gaze for the final exposure and cleansing of the court. And though Cynthia demands that the poet-scholar "lance these vlcers growne so ripe" (xi.94), Crites attempts to effect the difficult task he had earlier mentioned in the analogue, that of convincing the offenders of their guilt and bringing about true inward repentance.

The play ends with the destruction of Moria's socially corrosive pseudo court. Self-knowledge replaces self-love, and the erring courtiers and ladies become the positive attributes which they had merely impersonated in the masque. Jonson has used the mock court scene not only as a mirror image of Cynthia's presence and values and as an anticipation of the final events of the play, but additionally as part of a double humiliation and exposure of court vices accompanied by an exaltation of the poet-reformer in league with an enlightened monarch.

Cynthia's Revels and *Poetaster* are companion plays in a number of ways, including their use of the "mirror scene": both contain a perverted court which is later contrasted with the true or ideal court. In *Poetaster* the banquet episode is the central event before Act V which functions similarly to the mock court scene in the earlier play.[18] The banquet,

17. The pattern is again similar to Jonson's early masque, *Hymenaei*, written only a few years after *Cynthia's Revels*. *Hymenaei* contains two separate masques, one for the men and one for the women. The first masque consists of eight men, four Humors, and four Affections, who draw their swords and attempt to surround the altar and *"disturbe the* Ceremonies" (l. 116). Hymen enlists the aid of Reason, who appears miraculously seated on top of a globe. Raising her sword against the rash intruders, who represent the base appetites and uncontrolled passions of man, Reason utters a censuring speech after which *"the* Humors *and* Affections *sheathed their swords, and retired amazed . . . "* (ll. 157–158).

18. That the banquet is central to Jonson's drama "in structure as well as intention" has been recognized recently by Gabriele Bernhard Jackson, who points

which takes place in the palace, is attended by men and ladies of the court masquerading as gods and goddesses in a kind of bacchanal. As Jupiter, assisted by Julia (Caesar's daughter) as Juno, Ovid presides over the motley, gaudily costumed assemblage composed, among others, of flawed courtiers and false poets (Ovid and Crispinus). In a hedonistic orgy where the laws of marriage and traditional social values are inverted, Ovid-Jupiter sanctions the new laws while Tucca suggests that he "that speaks the first wise word, shall be made cockold" (IV.v.42–43); and all agree. Thus, in the abusive, though playful, exchanges between Ovid and Julia, and in the carousing, the name-calling, the strutting, and posing, those who participate in this immoderate charade parody the mightiest of the gods, reducing them to Lilliputian insignificance and absurdity.

Finally, at the peak of Ovid's presumption, when he utters blasphemous statements concerning the Emperor (ll. 200–210), Caesar suddenly appears and pulls Ovid from his Olympian throne. Having been led by Lupus and Histrio to Ovid's revels, Caesar and Horace, exemplars of the true ruler and the virtuous poet, overturn the sacrilegious court of misrule and establish their own court. Despite Maecenas' and Horace's pleas for mercy, Caesar metes out harsh punishment to the leading offenders. Ovid and Crispinus are particular objects for Caesar's censure because they have betrayed their responsibilities as poets, trampling rather than exalting virtue.[19]

---

out that, although the banquet occurs in Act IV, the description of the feast itself is placed in the dead center of the play: Gallus' description of the banquet in IV.ii.21–24 is "preceded by 1612 lines of text and followed by 1607" lines; in terms of scenes, "Gallus' outline of the banquet occurs in the middle of scene 11" in a play that contains twenty-one scenes in all (*Vision and Judgment in Ben Jonson's Drama* [New Haven, Conn., 1968], p. 24).

19. Eugene M. Waith ("The Poet's Morals in Jonson's *Poetaster*," *MLQ*, XII [1951]) has argued that Ovid, dominated by his passion, is "the complete romantic lover" (p. 13), who is used by Jonson to demonstrate "the case of the morally irresponsible poet" (p. 15), in contrast to Horace and Virgil, "who are the true exemplars of the good poet" (p. 15). Jackson seconds this thesis and adds that Ovid has already "discredited himself privately among his companions" in the banquet scene, and the appearance of Caesar and Horace is necessary for his discomfiture "among his fellow poets" (*Vision and Judgment in Ben Jonson's Drama*, p. 25).

This centrally located banquet episode brings together most of the play's important characters and themes and ends in exposure, punishment, and an assertion of the "correct" values. Furthermore, it anticipates the alliance between Caesar and the true poet in Act V, when the poetasters and other erring court figures are exposed for the final time. Although the end of the play lacks a restoration of the correct norm as symbolized by the communal feast,[20] the arraignment serves an analogous, though unequivalent, function: it brings together the central members of the action in a formal and rather ritualistic purgation of particular ills accompanied by a reinforcement of community values.

The fifth act of *Poetaster* has been called an "appendage" because Jonson in the banquet scene had pronounced "his most impressive ethical judgments" and provided the necessary "correction of the principal characters."[21] In Act V, however, Jonson arrives at a final definition of the various themes—law, justice, poetry—which he has been developing and modifying throughout the play.[22] Here we discover that the corruption of manners and morals within the palace displayed and symbolized in the banquet scene is present again, but, by introducing Virgil into the court in the final act, Jonson achieves a harmonious trinity (Virgil, Caesar, Horace) with which to stifle the play's antagonists in a series of events that inversely parallel the banquet episode.

When Caesar welcomes Virgil to court in Act V, scene ii, he honors the ideal poet by seating him in a place superior to his own, saying,

> "Vertue, without presumption, place may take
> "Aboue best Kings, whom onely she should make.
>
> (V.ii.26–27)

20. Jonson deliberately shifts the communal banquet from the end to the middle of the play to emphasize the perversion of values in Augustus' court. Before the appearance of Caesar, the banquet is devoid of the true justice figures or controlling agents who traditionally "host" the final celebration; in this case they have been intentionally excluded from the revels and must crash the party in order to regain their positions of authority over vice and folly.

21. Oscar James Campbell, *Comicall Satyre and Shakespeare's "Troilus and Cressida"* (1938; rpt. San Marino, Calif., 1965), p. 129.

22. Waith observes that the poet's "moral obligations are brought out by Horace in the third act, by Caesar in the fourth act, and by Horace, Virgil, and Caesar in the fifth act" ("The Poet's Morals," p. 19).

In an ironic reversal of the earlier scene where the gods and goddesses were mocked by unworthy mortals led by the false poet Ovid and Caesar's scolding daughter, Jonson gives us another kind of "banquet," in which the idealized participants seek truth and virtue rather than the self-gratification which pollutes and destroys. Virgil, whom Horace has called a Jove-like being above the "moodes of common men" like a "heauenly bodie" (V.i.103,105), is "a rectified spirit," a being truly god-like in his humility, his words and deeds. Again we have a poet and the blood royal presiding over the court from the chair of state. However, instead of the false courtiers in their private, sacrilegious debasing of the gods accompanied by lewd behavior, we have the Jove-like Virgil in a private chamber reading from his *Aeneid,* where he has set down the affairs of gods and men with proper reverence—in the spirit of true poetry, which is to guide men to virtuous action.

The passage Virgil reads tells of Dido giving herself to Aeneas in a cave during a storm. Jonson selects this particular incident not only because it serves as an analogue to "the sort of love which has proved the undoing of Ovid and Julia," as Eugene Waith has indicated,[23] but because it reminds us of the disparity between Virgil and his account of the famous banquet held by Dido for Aeneas, and the banquet held by Ovid and Julia for corrupt members of the court. Furthermore, Virgil's depiction of tarnished Fame seems specifically to condemn the earlier banquet revelry when he reads that *"Shee was last sister of that Giant race, / That thought to scale IOVES court . . ."* (ii.82–83). Virgil continues cataloguing the evils of Fame but is cut short, at the mention of her destructive distortion of truth, by the intervention of Lupus and his officers, who proceed to arrest Horace and Maecenas for treason. For the second time in the play Lupus, after having been informed by an actor, has suddenly intruded upon court activities in order to stop treasonous behavior. In the banquet episode Lupus and Histrio had apparently triumphed, but in the present companion scene Caesar apprehends the truth and, in a reversal of the earlier episode, punishes the guilty accusers while exonerating and ennobling the accused. The whipping of Aesop, the false, informing actor, and the humiliation of the credulous Lupus

23. *Ibid.*

anticipate the final exposure of Crispinus and Demetrius, which had been foreshadowed in the previous banquet scene.

At the court tribunal presided over by Virgil under the watchful gaze of Caesar, the corruption which entered the palace in the banquet scene, and later even penetrated into the Emperor's court of law, is finally removed. For the second time in the play, a false poet is found guilty of perverting his office by a spokesman for true poetry and the virtuous poet. Crispinus and Demetrius are found guilty of denigrating Horace ("poet, *and* priest *to the* Muses" [iii.227–228]), just as earlier the revelers, particularly Ovid, had disparaged the true religion and mocked the gods. Horace, who had pleaded mercy for Ovid and Julia during the banquet confrontation, now is able to exercise his merciful nature by forgiving Demetrius' envy and by mildly punishing Crispinus. The play concludes, like *Cynthia's Revels,* with order restored and a reaffirmation of the necessary link between the sovereign and the poet-scholar in their attempt to preserve and enrich the state.

Volpone

Jonson obviously took delight in experimenting with the techniques of anticipation, inversion, and parallel incidents in his early plays. In *Volpone,* however, although retaining his central analogue device, Jonson uses analogous patterns in a more complex manner; the ending alone is anticipated in at least four different ways: the mountebank scene, the confrontation between Volpone and Lady Wouldbe, the exposure of Sir Pol, and the mid-play analogue. Jonson has varied his previous method of dramaturgy by expanding the reduplicative process in terms of the underplot and its dramatic and thematic interaction with the main plot.

The mountebank episode in Act II, for example, suggests a number of parallels with the fourth and fifth act trial scenes. The Scrutineo at the beginning of Act IV, scene v, has been informed of the truth of Volpone's imposture, just as Sir Pol at the opening of Act II, scene ii, has been given the truth by Peregrine about mountebanks being "lewd impostors" (l. 14); but both believe the disguise and simple lie, reject the discomforting truth, and fall prey to the obfuscating oratory of a Scoto or a Voltore. As Scoto, Volpone explains that he has been absent from Venice for eight months and now sets up his bank in *"an obscure nooke of the* Piazza" (l. 38) in order to have *"pleasure, and delight"* (ll. 71–72), for he has "nothing to sell" (l. 72). Correspondingly, in Act V, Volpone absents himself by feigning death and then appears later, disguised as a *commendatori* (a social degeneration for Volpone to an "obscure" court official) so that he can have "a rare meale of laughter" (V.ii.87). In Act V, scene xii, Volpone learns that he literally has nothing to sell when Mosca, masquerading as a gentleman, usurps his entire estate and existence. Finally, in the mountebank scene, the sudden arrival of Corvino and his beating of Volpone anticipate Volpone's exposure and punishment at the end of the play.

In addition to the mountebank analogue, two episodes in the subplot produce a comic foreshadowing of Volpone's final fate in the hands of the *Avocatore*.[24] The first occurs in Act II, scene iv, when Lady Wouldbe's verbal onslaught turns Volpone's successful scheme for making money into an unexpected nightmare. Volpone is forced to declare himself cured and to give up, momentarily, his gold, the price of admission (he gets no treasure from Lady Wouldbe), when in reality he gets sick for the first time: "Before I fayn'd diseases, now I haue one" (III.iv.62). This ironic *volte face* points to the poetic justice of Volpone's punishment when he is to be imprisoned and "crampt with irons" until he is "sicke, and lame indeed" (V.xii.123,124).[25]

The second subplot analogue is the humiliation of Sir Pol by Peregrine, which, according to Barish, anticipates the "mortification" of Volpone in the following ways:

The *mercatori* enlisted by Peregrine perform the office of the *avocatori* who pronounce sentence on Volpone, and the divulging of the pathetic notebook,

---

24. Both these analogues have been ably developed by Barish; my brief discussion is merely intended to remind the reader of his observations.

25. In addition, Volpone's anguished cries for help ("My good angell saue me" and "Some power, some fate, some fortune rescue me" [III.iv.115,126]) and his sudden mock-heroic rescue by Mosca, his "redemption," anticipate on another, farcical level the Act III, scene vii, attempted seduction of Celia by Volpone and her miraculous rescue by Bonario, who answers her cries to "iust God" (l. 266).

with its scraps from playbooks, becomes the burlesque substitute for the exposure of Volpone's will, in bringing on the disaster (p. 103).

By crawling into the tortoise shell, Sir Pol is "playing possum after the fashion of his model, Volpone, who has feigned death in the foregoing scene" (p. 103). And, of course, the final uncasing of Sir Pol from his tortoise disguise, his exposure and beating, foreshadow Volpone's final fate in Act V.

These three scenes, all specifically concerned with characters in the subplot, provide clear analogues to subsequent action: the mountebank episode parallels events in the fourth-act trial scene, while it and the other two suggest the eventual discomfiture of Volpone. At the same time, Jonson has included another preparative analogue that more obviously parallels parts of the court scenes, particularly those occurring in Act V; and it is in this scene that Jonson again supplies us with his central analogue signature.

The Act III bedroom scene between Volpone and Celia is justifiably famous for its dramatic action, the sweeping grandeur of Volpone's language, and the beautiful simplicity of his "lovely" but ironically grotesque song to Celia. Much has been written about this famous attempted seduction scene,[26] but no one has pointed out that this episode also serves as a central cipher for the play's equally famous catastrophe. In Act III Volpone leaves the security of his bed, throws off his disguise, and reveals a physically healthy but spiritually sick individual; spiritual love has been replaced by hedonistic sexual activity.[27] In a sudden effusive outburst, Volpone admits his deceptions to Celia, contending they were done out of love for her. On her own behalf, and as the representative of Christian virtue, Celia pleads for the preservation of her innocence, opposing Volpone's perverted religion, his bribes of gold, with an appeal to his "conscience," honor, and, finally, his humanity.[28]

26. For a particularly intelligent close reading of this scene, see Edward B. Partridge, *The Broken Compass* (New York, 1958), pp. 89–97.

27. Harriett Hawkins ("Folly, Incurable Disease, and *Volpone*," *SEL,* VIII [1968]) shows how this scene is the climax to a "series of anticipations followed by interruptions and frustrations" which torture Volpone (p. 339).

28. Celia's earlier protestations to Corvino and her cries for divine intervention immediately anticipate her treatment in the hands of the merciless, unheeding Volpone. Ironically, at the moment Celia calls for divine aid, after being com-

At the crucial moment, after Celia has appealed to Volpone's sense of justice and mercy (ll. 240–244) in preserving her innocence and has been denied, Volpone forces himself upon her in a lustful act. Celia's despairing and seemingly futile cry to "iust God"—an "appeal which Volpone, the worldly realist, immediately points out to be 'in vaine' " [29]— is miraculously and providentially answered by the sword-waving Bonario, who leaps out from where Mosca has hidden him and rages melodramatically:

> But that I am loth to snatch thy punishment
> Out of the hand of iustice, thou shouldst, yet,
> Be made the timely sacrifice of vengeance,
> Before this altar, and this drosse, thy idoll.
>
> (ll. 269–272)

Volpone has been caught in the act ("I am vn-masqu'd, vn-spirited, vn-done, / Betray'd to beggery" [ll. 278–279]) and exposed in the reality of his existence as a ravisher, a swine, a worshipper of false idols, and an utter impostor. Although Bonario is tempted to exact retributive vengeance on Volpone, he foregoes the role of justicer, trusting that sooner or later Volpone will "meet his iust reward" (l. 275). He does, however, give Mosca a few bloody blows before making his exit from the premises to reveal Volpone's "villainy" to the world.

Like most of Jonson's analogues, the seduction scene, rather than paralleling point for point the events of the last act,[30] suggests relationships and anticipates particular action. The dramatic confrontation between Volpone and Celia as representatives of different value systems is repeated in the Act IV and Act V courtroom scenes, where Christian innocence and virtue are placed on trial against the corrupted standards

---

promised by Corvino, Volpone suddenly leaps out of bed, miraculously cured by her "beauties . . . great worke" (ll. 146–147), and attacks her. Volpone is a perverse stand-in for Bonario, while Corvino, who has turned his back on his wife's anguished state, will again reject and prostitute her while publicly cuckolding himself in the next act.

29. Alan C. Dessen, "*Volpone* and the Late Morality Tradition," *MLQ*, XXV (1964), 392. See also his *Jonson's Moral Comedy* (Evanston, Ill., 1971), pp. 70–104.

30. The attempted rape and rescue analogue is perhaps not as tidy as Jonson's previous ones, possibly because he had anticipated the ending in so many other ways. But the analogue is suggestive and recognizably there nonetheless.

of Venetian society. In both instances Celia seems utterly beyond all hope of help, despite her repeated cries to heaven, when Volpone, as a result of Mosca's plotting and his own overweening nature, is suddenly defeated in a melodramatic eleventh-hour reversal. Only twice in the play, here in the third act analogue and in Act V, does Volpone publicly throw off his disguise and reveal his deceptions; and both times he and Mosca are punished in proportion to their respective ranks: Bonario's flashing sword of justice lacerates Mosca and causes Volpone to pray for his roof to fall and bury him in ruins, thus anticipating Mosca's perpetual whipping and Volpone's eventual tortured confinement. Volpone has indeed betrayed himself "to beggery" when the "iust reward" predicted by Bonario in the analogue is fulfilled, ironically, by the corrupt Scrutineo.

Furthermore, Bonario's melodramatic rescue of Celia, snatching her miraculously at the last moment from the jaws of destruction, matches the implausible sudden revelation and fortuitous conclusion of the catastrophe. Indeed, Bonario's rescue of Celia may anticipate the Act V statement of the first *Avocatore* when he says that the "knot is now vndone, by miracle" (1. 95). In a world as godless and corrupt as Venice, innocence and virtue cannot survive. Only through an unrealistic, last-minute, melodramatic reversal is justice imposed, evil punished, and virtue rewarded.

One interpretation of the catastrophe, then, is that Jonson must supply his own miracle because the world of the play (which mirrors the lamentable state of the real world) is so corrupt and unrepentant that vice and crime would otherwise go unpunished. More traditionally, the punishment at the end of the play is seen as an answer to Bonario's and Celia's perpetual cries to "iust God," or as a sign that representatives of evil like Volpone and Mosca will always eventually overstep themselves and cause their own downfall ("Mischiefes feed / Like beasts, till they be fat, and then they bleed" [V.xii.150–151]); and, indeed, this proposition operates with great regularity in Jonson's comedies.

Arguments have been made in support of these variant readings of the play in view of a catastrophe which intentionally deviates from the *"strict rigour of* comick *law."* [31] Despite his claim to have written

---

31. Ben Jonson's "Epistle" to *Volpone* in H & S, V, 20, l. 110.

Volpone in only five weeks, Jonson was a meticulous craftsman, and it is not by accident that at least three entirely different perspectives on the play emerge in the final act. Jonson, it would seem, intended multiple interpretations of his drama in order to give his audience, and the reader, food for reflection. By the same token, it is equally probable that he constructed the Act III analogue so that it, too, would support any one of the readings of the play suggested in the closing scene. Both the analogue and its correspondent climactic scenes unify the play and draw our attention to important philosophical issues through dramatic technique while successfully preserving the necessary ambiguity of the whole.

Epicoene

Jonson's attempt to create specific mid-play scenes that would reflect upon or anticipate events in the final act seems more obvious in the earlier plays, culminating with *Volpone,* than in the later plays, where this technique is, at times, more diffuse. In the four plays already discussed, there exists a single episode that clearly and specifically anticipates the play's catastrophe. In his next two comedies, *Epicoene* (1609) and *The Alchemist* (1612), Jonson shifts his emphasis from a single scene that anticipates the conclusion and in the fourth act of each play substitutes instead two separate pieces of action, both of which comment upon the central figure in the final act—Morose and Lovewit—and point to the play's ending. In *Epicoene* these two scenes deal with the manipulation of Captain Otter by the wits, which leads to his confrontation with Mrs. Otter, and the deception of Sir John Daw and his close friend Sir Amorous La Foole. In both cases the younger generation, Dauphine, Truewit, and Clerimont, exposes the follies of the old. Truewit is the apparent mastermind directing the duping of the two hapless knights, here and in the subsequent act, and both times the plot works to Dauphine's advantage.

The similarities between the exposure of Daw and La Foole in Act IV and the action involving Morose in Act V are part of Jonson's replicative plan. Truewit manipulates the disguised Otter and Cutbeard as he did the earlier plot against Daw and La Foole. The *"tragi-comoedy"*

(IV.v.31) directed by Truewit in both acts deals essentially with the distribution of comic justice. Significantly, it is Dauphine who administers the *coup de grâce* of comic justice to Daw and La Foole, and later to Morose. In Act IV Daw and La Foole, separated from everyone in locked closets, are a humorous extension of Morose's own isolation and irrational behavior, which reaches a climax in his antisocial behavior in Act V. Similarly, Dauphine's methodical disarming of Daw and La Foole, his corporal chastisement of them and their own willingness to be dismembered and mutilated, anticipates Morose's self-mutilation (his admission of impotence)[32] and his eventual chastisement by Dauphine.

After the two knights have been stripped of their swords, Morose rushes in with both weapons in his hands; but in Act V, scene iv, he is forced to disarm himself and confess his impotence before the devastating critics of "society," the Ladies Collegiates, who previously had witnessed the humiliation of Daw and La Foole. All three have shown their lack of manhood before the Collegiates, who have been the agents conferring or denying manliness to the various characters in the play. Morose's public confession of impotence, "I am no man, ladies" (V.iv.44), equates him with the "emptie caskets" (IV.vi.57), Daw and La Foole, and reinforces Dauphine as the rich "mine of vertue" (l. 58) in the eyes of the ladies. The blindfolds worn by the two knights in their isolation so that they can be beaten parallel Morose's blindness to Epicoene's true nature as well as to Dauphine's key role as master manipulator and distributor of the final comic justice. La Foole's ingrained cowardliness, accompanied by his fear of the supposedly enraged Jack Daw, forces him to accept any condition his opponent is willing to impose upon him in order to be free from an actual confrontation: "I'll stand to any conditions" (IV.v.230). Similarly, at the end of the play Morose gives Dauphine a carte blanche to free him from his abortive marriage to Epicoene: "Make thine owne conditions. . . . I will subscribe to any thing, and seale to what thou wilt, for my deliuerance" (V.iv.173–174, 198–200). Dauphine's revelation of Epicoene's true identity not only destroys Morose, who remains speechless, but comes as the final blow to

---

32. In IV.iv. Morose had wished for mutilation and castration in his desperation to rid himself of Epicoene: "Would I could redeeme it with the losse of an eye . . . a hand, or any other member" (ll. 7–8).

Daw and La Foole, who failed to learn their earlier lesson and required another exposure when their fates became inextricably linked with Morose's through the web spun by the three wits.

Although the initial gulling and exposure of Daw and La Foole clearly anticipate the later exposure of Morose, the play's central event, the revelation of Epicoene's true sex, does not seem to be adequately fore-shadowed; "her" identity remains a mystery to the audience until the final moments of the play. Practically the only hint we have concerning Epicoene's true sex is "her" name and that of the play,[33] so that the revelation of Epicoene as a disguised male comes to the audience as a complete surprise. However, in keeping with his strategy of analogous action, Jonson has given us a parallel case that anticipates the play's sudden reversal in the actions of Tom Otter and his wife who, as Ray Heffner has observed, "burlesque the main action"[34] and thus comment upon Morose and Epicoene. In a recent article, Mark Anderson has attempted to show how Mrs. Otter with her "dominance, courtly ways, excessive chatter, and identification with the Ladies Collegiates belie[s] the so-far-apparent nature of the Silent Woman and foreshadow[s] her first metamorphosis."[35] But as far as I can determine, no one has observed the extent that Mrs. Otter foreshadows Epicoene's *second* metamorphosis from female shrew to female impersonator.[36]

A number of critics have commented upon the inverted relationship between Tom Otter and his wife and their contribution to Jonson's insistent exposure of ladies of fashion (or those aspiring to fashion) and certain marital situations. Mrs. Otter, related to La Foole "by the mother

---

33. For an enlightening discussion of the "epicene" nature of the play, see Partridge, *Broken Compass*, pp. 161–170. Among other things, he points out that specific classical allusions made by Morose about Epicoene, her own change in character in Act III, and her new name of Morose indicate her masculine function (p. 167).

34. Ray L. Heffner, "Unifying Symbols in the Comedy of Ben Jonson," in *English Stage Comedy*, ed. W. K. Wimsatt, Jr. (New York, 1955), p. 87.

35. "The Successful Unity of *Epicoene*: A Defense of Ben Jonson," *SEL*, X (1970), 358.

36. Beaurline has observed that the entire group of hermaphroditical fools (the Collegiates, La Foole, Daw, Otter, and Mrs. Otter) "prefigures the true identity of Epicoene; they massively and exhaustively suggest the various changes that Epicoene undergoes" ("Ben Jonson and the Illusion of Completeness," p. 59).

side," is the "most masculine, or rather *hermaphroditicall*" (I.i.79–80) of the "mankind generation," the Ladies Collegiates. Though the Otters are discussed briefly before their first appearance, in Act III, scene i, we learn that Captain Otter is the "subject" of his "Princesse" who, having married down in social class, provides him with a half crown a day for "maintenance." But the ultimate reversal of roles, and the scene most illuminating for its anticipation of the play's denouement, occurs in Act IV, when Captain Otter is baited by the three wits to deprecate his wife, after which he is physically beaten by her in Punch and Judy fashion.

In Act IV, scene ii, the parallels between Captain Otter and Morose are made explicit: Otter has married for money; Morose has married to prevent Dauphine from getting his money—both have made a bad bargain. Otter, in his invective against his wife and marriage ("Wiues are nasty sluttish *animalls*" [l. 56]) protests that "I ha' not kist my *furie*, these fortie weekes" (ll. 79–80); similarly, Morose has yet to consummate his marriage to the Silent Woman (heaven forbid!). In general, Otter's masculinity is dissipated by a domineering wife, so that he exists on a symbolic level with Morose.[37] Furthermore, the inverted model of the Otters, with Mrs. Otter adopting the masculine function and Otter suffering under her "tyrannie," is a visual embodiment to Morose of his own situation and a hint at Epicoene's identity, for Mrs. Otter, according to her actions and the way she is described, is essentially a man disguised as a woman. In one of the funniest and most devastating moments of the play, Captain Otter anatomizes his wife, contending that her teeth, eyebrows, and hair are artificial ("Euery part o' the towne ownes a peece of her" [ll. 94–95]) so that she "takes her selfe asunder still when she goes to bed, into some twentie boxes; and about next day noone is put together againe . . ." (ll. 97–99). At the close of this speech, Mrs. Otter attacks her husband, there is a martial call to arms, and, at the height of the noise and confusion, Morose suddenly appears. Descending *"with a long sword"* (according to the stage directions), he menacingly

37. In discussing the significance of the Otter name, Robert Knoll (*Ben Jonson's Plays* [Lincoln, Nebr., 1969]) reminds us that the Elizabethans not only considered otters neither fish nor beasts, but also believed the male was capable of bearing young; thus the subjugated member of the pair, male or female, assumed the female role (p. 111).

approaches Mrs. Otter as she vows to make Otter an "example" for be-traying her, and exclaims that "I will haue no such examples in my house, lady OTTER," "your examples are dangerous" (ll. 120-121, 123-124), before he puts the noisy fools to rout.

Although this episode exists clearly within the thematic and dramatic contexts of the play, we can see retrospectively how Jonson has created a structural foreshadowing of the play's conclusion. Mrs. Otter, verbally stripped of her feminine parts by Captain Otter, is another Epicoene who has assembled *his* disguise from various "boxes." Whether the Silent Woman is in reality a shrew or not is less important than the fact that Morose views her as no better than Mrs. Otter. To him Mrs. Otter's "examples are dangerous," not only because they function as a parallel case, but because her behavior furnishes a precedent that eventually leads to his own emasculation by Epicoene in Act V, where the battle between the sexes, parodied by Otter and his wife, reaches a stormy climax, for it is there that Otter's statement that "euery part o' the towne ownes a peece of her" (which is an echo of Morose's earlier agony regarding Epicoene—"I haue married his [Cutbeard's] citterne, that's common to all men" [III.v.64-65])—becomes a painful reality for Morose before Dauphine wins the game by changing Epicoene's sex to match her behavior:

O my heart! wilt thou breake? wilt thou breake? this is worst of all worst worsts! that hell could haue deuis'd! Marry a whore! and so much noise!
(V.iv.148-150)

In Act IV, scene ii, as we have seen, Morose had rescued Otter, driving his wife away by shaking his sword (his masculinity) at her; but when Mrs. Otter discusses his behavior with the Ladies Collegiates, she de-scribes him as a madman and a sexual pervert: "he came downe with a huge long naked weapon in both his hands, and look'd so dreadfully! Sure, hee's beside himselfe" (IV.iii.2-4). To the Ladies, who keep apart from their husbands and refrain from having children (natural sexual-ity), Morose's assertion of masculinity is unnatural and not to be tolerated[38] (the image is one of isolation and the anticommunal act of

---

38. In IV.vii., at the end of the gulling of Daw and La Foole, Morose repeats this scene and more desperately tries to reassert himself in his own house (which is presently under siege from within) by apparently brandishing *two* swords which, in fact, represent the sloughed-off masculinity of Daw and La Foole.

masturbation). Appropriately, then, just as Daw and La Foole willingly give up their weapons in Act IV, Morose is symbolically castrated in Act V and reduced to the impotent male whom the Collegiates seek in a husband.[39]

In *The Silent Woman* Jonson deviates somewhat from his earlier method of foreshadowing the conclusion on a one-to-one basis. However, once we have established Jonson's particular technique as a concrete part of his dramatic strategy (and his approach does indeed vary from play to play), the method of construction in each individual drama becomes more apparent, and the play's over-all plan becomes more accessible to analysis on this basis. In *Epicoene* Jonson has again foreshadowed the final act in the previous one, and though we may be shocked at the play's unusual and unexpected denouement, we can see in the study if not in the theater how Jonson has hinted at his transvestite bombshell.

The Alchemist

The Alchemist and *Volpone* have much in common, particularly their method of organization around various characters duped in their quest for quick money. Furthermore, there is a similarity between the roles of Bonario and Surly. Surly's background as a gangster and swindler hardly qualifies him for the role of reformer,[40] but, like Bonario and Celia, he is established by Jonson as a voice of truth in a corrupt world. In Act IV Surly, like Bonario, is ostensibly used to save the heroine from the coils of the would-be ravisher. Again, Jonson provides a kind of justice figure, one who is capable of discovering the truth, routing the knaves, and saving the day. But as in *Volpone,* the "savior" is unsuccessful. The discomfiture of Surly is similar to the courtroom scene in *Volpone* when the *captatores* are all in league against the only represen-

---

39. La Foole and the Ladies Collegiates tell Epicoene she should follow Mrs. Otter's example in learning how to treat a husband, and Haughty says that Centaure "has immortaliz'd her selfe, with taming of her wilde male" (IV.iii.27–28).

40. See Judd Arnold, "Lovewit's Triumph and Jonsonian Morality: A Reading of *The Alchemist,*" *Criticism,* XI (1969), 158–168.

tatives of truth. In both cases Jonson shows the helplessness of truth and honesty in a society where virtue is routed and fools and crime triumph.

More central to our study of Jonson's method of analogous construction is the fact that Surly's fourth act behavior inversely anticipates Lovewit, who in Act V appears as his counterpart. Although Surly's attempts to bring the rogues into line are unsuccessful, he does anticipate Lovewit's real power to discover truth and order the action. Surly and Lovewit are both gallants and wits who have the ability successfully to deceive the other characters in pursuing their own selfish ends. Both are helped to the widow Pliant by Face and by assuming the Spanish Don disguise, and both attempt to break up the "venter *tripartite.*" Surly and Lovewit are justice figures, not only in their ability to expose the knaves and effect the traditional comic reformation, but also in their efforts to gather evidence in order to build an effective case against the criminals. Once the two rationalists arrive at the truth, they cause the action to take an unexpected, dramatic turn: Surly throws off his disguise and is driven out by the gulls; Lovewit disguises himself to win Dame Pliant, then unmasks and drives out the gulls. To Face, both are forms of the plague, although the protean trickster manages to elude the disease of "houseless poverty" that eventually faces Dol and Subtle in their return to the streets. In throwing off the Spanish disguise and suddenly confronting Subtle and Face with their villainy, Surly anticipates Lovewit's unexpected early homecoming and his own attempts at breaking up the conspiracy. The question raised here is why does Lovewit succeed where Surly has failed so miserably?

If Surly fails because he is guilty of deception by appearing to be altruistic while acting out of purely selfish motives—hustling Dame Pliant for himself—then Lovewit should experience a similar fate. But Lovewit, unlike Surly, does not suffer from the "foolish vice of honestie" (V.v.84); thus he is able to succeed where Surly has failed.[41] In terms of the values of the play's milieu, Surly is unsuccessful, not because he practices a mild form of deception, but because he momentarily suspends his dishonesty. In addition, despite the many similarities between Surly and Lovewit, there is a basic difference that helps to account for Surly's

41. For a more elaborate discussion of this point, see Dessen, *"The Alchemist: Jonson's 'Estates' Play,"* RenD, VII (1964), 47–48.

discomfiture, and that is his role as a humorless "reforming zealot," a type for whom Jonson had nothing but distrust and, at times, contempt.[42] But even here Jonson constructs an analogy between Surly and Lovewit. In Act IV, Surly, dressed as a Spaniard and true to his arrogant, ill-tempered nature and name, has angrily exposed and denounced as impostors the members of the "venter *tripartite*." According to Jonson, a true justice figure should be devoid of anger and malice, but Surly in his fit of righteous indignation is the incarnation of wrath and madness in his railing against Subtle and Face.

In contrast to Surly is Lovewit, who in Act V also appears disguised as a Spanish lover. But by having him wear the stage clothes of the mad Hieronimo ("HIERONYMO's old cloake, ruffe, and hat" [IV.vii.71]), Jonson parodies Surly, drawing attention to his particular form of madness and his unsuitability as a figure of justice.[43] Although Lovewit uses the Spanish disguise not to confront and expose the knaves or for "retribution or ordering or education, but to cash in on the spoils available from the activities of the rogues,"[44] he is himself a parody of Hieronimo in his role as prime mover of the subsequent action. He writes his own play, as it were, casting himself as hero, assisted by Face; and in this role he exploits, manipulates, and disposes of the wits as well as the gulls and brings about a form of comic justice that is as controversial as Hieronimo's own brand of tragic justice.

The second piece of analogous action in Act IV also anticipates a climactic moment in the last act by using a similar twist of inversion. When the nearly completed philosopher's stone is destroyed in a tremendous explosion (attributed to Mammon's subversion of the necessary righteous environment), Face announces the bad news to Subtle and Mammon:

42. Arnold is one of the more recent critics to make this observation, "Lovewit's Triumph and Jonsonian Morality," pp. 158–160.

43. According to Jonson's model, Seneca, the "sword of justice is ill-placed in the hands of an angry man"; and anger itself is a passion akin to madness "for it is equally devoid of self control . . . " (*L. Annaeus Seneca Minor Dialogues Together With the Dialogue On Clemency*, trans. Aubrey Stewart [London, 1889], p. 73). H & S, in a note to *The Staple of News*, indicate Jonson's indebtedness there to Horace's *Epigrams*, where he says " 'Ira furor brevis est' " (X,291).

44. Dessen, *Jonson's Moral Comedy*, p. 131.

O sir, we are defeated! all the *workes*
Are flowne *in fumo:* euery glasse is burst.
Fornace, and all rent downe! as if a bolt
Of thunder had beene driuen through the house.

(IV.v.57–60)

Subtle pretends to faint at this devastating piece of information, Face exclaims that he will never "be mine owne man againe" (l. 70), and Mammon, while admitting the justness of his punishment, curses himself for his "voluptuous mind" (l. 74).

The scene ends with Mammon, like the legacy hunters in *Volpone,* pouring more money into the coffers of the wits while receiving another blow to his dreams of gaining the all-powerful "stone." Subtle and Face congratulate themselves for their extraordinary cunning and set off to bilk the disguised Surly and gain Dame Pliant for Face. The "venter *tripartite"* at this point has reached a high-water mark of success and solidarity. True to the nature of comedy, however, the rogues are allowed to reach a peak of prosperity and security before their fortunes are suddenly reversed and they lose all they had hoped to gain. At the end of scene v, Subtle expresses the sheer excitement, pleasure, and relief of the successful trickster, wishing he and Face would be as light "as balls, and bound / And hit our heads against the roofe for ioy . . ." (ll. 98–99). Here, as in *Volpone,* the exuberant language of the characters carries a rational meaning that is apart from its emotional context. At this point Face and Subtle have bounded as high as they can go, and through the laws of Jonsonian comedy, as with those of nature, they will only crack their "heads against the roofe" and come hurtling painfully back to earth by attempting to rise higher.

This preceding action is now treated ironically in its mirror scene, Act V, scene iv, when the enterprise of Subtle, Face, and Dol is destroyed in reality by the sudden, unexpected (explosive) return of Lovewit, who sets up his own cozening shop. Face, who in the earlier charade had claimed that he "ne'er must hope to be mine owne man againe," now finds that he must subordinate himself to Lovewit and have his "part [fall] a little" (V.v.158). Dol, no longer the sister of an English lord but the Queen of Fairies (a step up the hierarchical ladder), is deeply involved in exploiting another gull, Dapper, before the explosive climax of the scene. Although Subtle, Face, and Dol seem to be working together, as they had earlier, the return of Lovewit, the audience knows, has served to undermine the triple partnership and create a new team—Face and Lovewit.

In the Act IV analogue, the three wits deceived Mammon by staging a show (Dol plus the explosion) for his benefit, pretending that their work was destroyed and they were out of business, temporarily, at least. In the Act V mirror scene, Lovewit and Face stage their own show to deceive the deceivers and put Subtle and Dol permanently out of business. While Subtle and Dol have been planning to double-cross Face and steal away with the goods, Face and Lovewit have worked out their own double cross, which comes as a tremendous shock when Face informs his former partners that the *"indenture tripartite"* has been dissolved. Face's revelation is punctuated by the knocking of law officers who have come to arrest Dol and Subtle; the rogue's warning ("Harke you, thunder" [V.iv.137]) provides a verbal link to the "bolt of thunder" of Act IV. When Mammon's hopes had been shattered in the analogue, Subtle had fallen down in a feigned swoon; now that the enterprise of Subtle and Dol had been itself destroyed, the two conspirators must make their escape by tumbling over the backyard wall in a final and real ignominious fall from success and prosperity to failure and poverty.

In Act IV, scene v, Mammon had felt justly punished for his own "base affections" and Subtle had irreverently questioned the universal workings of justice:

> Hangs my roofe
> Ouer vs still, and will not fall, ô iustice,
> Vpon vs, for this wicked man!
>
> (IV.v.78–80)

Now, much to his chagrin and sorrow, Subtle discovers the strange and untimely way justice has of coming from an unexpected quarter at what should be the moment of triumph. Most ironic and unacceptable of all, of course, is the realization that Face, whom Subtle now sees as an agent from hell, is the chosen instrument of justice. This is the last we see of Subtle and Dol. Through this scene, Face and Lovewit have initiated their purge of the opposition, and the play hereafter surges rapidly to its conclusion as the gulls, including Surly, prove no match for the new partnership.

Jonson's method of construction in *The Alchemist* is consistent with that of the other plays. In Act IV he has depicted the cunning and deceit of the "venter *tripartite*" and their secure self-satisfaction at the peak of criminal success, while indicating their imminent downfall, which occurs in a fifth-act companion scene where the earlier significant action is ironically commented upon and reversed. In addition, the Act IV appearance of Surly in disguise anticipates Lovewit in a number of important ways (as gallant, perceptive onlooker, justice figure, initiator of subsequent action, and savior of Dame Pliant), prepares for Lovewit's later parody of the humorless, "mad" Surly, and signals the eventual triumph of selfishness and dissimulation over truth and justice. The distinction here, however, is somewhat blurred because Surly *is* interested in Dame Pliant for himself, and perhaps Dame Pliant is better off in the hands of the gallant Lovewit than those of the gamester and "sour moralist" Surly. Nevertheless, these complications are part of Jonson's plan, for, as in *Volpone* and *Bartholomew Fair,* the audience is trapped into identifying and siding with the cleverest of the rogues against their victims.

Bartholomew Fair

In *Bartholomew Fair* Jonson again provides his preparative analogue watermark. Here the stocks episode in Act IV presents a forum for exposure which suggests the final outcome of the play as well as the means by which it is effected. Throughout the play, Wasp, Busy, and Overdo, representatives of education, religion, and justice, have perverted their functions and become objects of ridicule rather than respect. In Act IV, scene v, by placing these three "enemies" of the Fair in the stocks for disturbing the peace, Jonson provides a dramatic emblem for the abandonment of moral, spiritual, and judicial responsibilities by tainted, but hubristic, leaders who have themselves subverted the social order. But in addition to its thematic and climactic functions, the stocks episode also anticipates particular features of the final act.[45]

45. Richard Levin recognizes this feature when he points out that the stocks episode not only "visually" links the three sternest critics of the play together, but it also "suggests a temporary resolution to their quarrel with the fair, preparing

In the first place, the scene with Busy, Overdo, and Wasp in the stocks foreshadows their Act V conversion, reformation, and silence through exposure. In both cases the three would-be reformers, shackled by their own self-deception and folly, renounce their proper roles and leave the Fair, and, by implication, society at large, without appropriate guidance. The cacophonous dialogue between the three in the stocks continues the vapors contest, a symbol of irrational man, while anticipating the puppet show which itself mirrors the earlier vapors combats. In a play as densely populated and complex as *Bartholomew Fair,* Jonson could hardly be expected to bring all the characters together in the traditional mid-play exposure or quasi solution to the intrigue, but in Act IV, scene vi, he does manage to effect the preliminary exposure and humiliation of three of the play's biggest fools[46] through the device of the pillory. In addition, the Act IV analogue anticipates the final metamorphosis and philosophical resolutions of the three authoritarian figures: Busy, no longer an active reformer, is "glad to be thus separated from the *heathen* of the land, and put apart in the stocks (vi.86–87); Wasp, "a halting *Neutrall"* (l. 112), refuses to take a stand, silently bowing out of the entire situation; and Overdo becomes "a Stoick i' the stocks" (l. 102) before hatching his irresponsible plan to give a blank warrant, the ultimate abdication of duty, to Troubleall. In Act V the three foolish authority figures not only receive exposure but undergo the type of change suggested by the analogue: Wasp, vowing silence and social isolation, resigns his office as tutor ("I will neuer speak while I liue, againe, for ought I know" [V.vi.103–104]); Busy miraculously converts, resigns his role as "reformer" [47] and becomes a spectator rather than a participant; and Overdo stoically accepts his own abdication as Judge to the questionable moral, and legal, authority of Quarlous.[48]

---

us for their permanent submission in the next act" (*The Multiple Plot in English Renaissance Drama* [Chicago, 1971], p. 213).

46. Cokes is exposed in his folly throughout the Fair but undergoes no transformation whatever; Littlewit, like Overdo, is silenced in V.vi. when he discovers that the "green madam" is his wife, but, unlike Overdo, he gives no indication of insight or reformation.

47. Jonas A. Barish, *Ben Jonson and the Language of Prose Comedy* (Cambridge, Mass., 1960), p. 238.

48. Appropriately, Overdo is a certified Justice of the Peace, whereas Quarlous was an Inns of Court dropout (he was never called to the bar).

Throughout the last half of the play two major props have been on stage, Ursula's booth for roasting pigs, a symbol of the vices harbored there, and the stocks, emblematic of the judicial corrective force opposed to vice. In Act IV, scene vi, the two arenas merge when Troubleall, Knockem, Whit, Edgworth, and Quarlous either enter or emerge from the pig booth, and Wasp, Overdo, and Busy are placed in the stocks. This scene recapitulates major themes of the play—Troubleall's "warrant," Quarlous' alliance with the underworld figures, the vapors, and the stealing of Cokes' marriage license by Edgworth for Quarlous' "sport" (l. 28), to mention a few. At the same time, significant plans are laid, by Overdo, Quarlous, and Dame Purecraft, which will effect the play's catastrophe: Overdo, taking pity on Troubleall's distracted state, vows to be merciful and ease his conscience; Dame Purecraft decides to desert Busy and marry Troubleall; and Quarlous decides to disguise himself as Troubleall.

The sudden intrusion by Troubleall in the Act IV analogue, his freeing of Busy and Overdo from the stocks in an apparent restoration of the Fair's "norm," anticipates the denouement, when Quarlous, now disguised as Troubleall, accompanied by Dame Purecraft and befriended by Overdo, miraculously sets straight the confusion caused by Overdo and brings about an approximation of the conventional comic reestablishment of order and communal harmony. The sudden conversion of the three "lawgivers" in Act V is as improbable and unexpected as their sudden freedom from the stocks, but, as the analogue seems to suggest, though Quarlous-Troubleall has providentially stepped in to save the day, the three institutional spokesmen have been silenced, and the vices which inhabit the Fair, symbolized in the pig-booth-stocks juxtaposition, are now led by Quarlous, the self-seeking opportunist.

In a sense, the boozing can held by Troubleall in Act IV, scene vi (ll. 130–131), representing the eradication of rational controls and necessary societal discriminations, is passed to Quarlous-Troubleall in Act V, scene vi, when he entreats Overdo to invite the denizens of the Fair to his house for a communal feast, where they will see the rest of the puppet play and "drowne the memory of all enormity in . . . [Overdo's] bigg'st bowle" (V.vi.99–100). Quarlous could be suggesting, as most commentators agree he is, that Overdo take a more reasoned, humane, and balanced response to life: "remember you are but *Adam*, Flesh and blood! you

haue your frailty, forget your other name of *Ouerdoo*" (ll. 96–98). However, in agreeing to "drowne the memory of all enormity," Overdo is
closing his eyes to the true crimes perpetrated at the Fair. By inviting
the fairgoers, including Ursula, Knockem, and Edgworth, to his home,
Overdo is perpetuating the evils satirized throughout the play, many of
which will now emanate from the house of justice itself. In the end, then,
the play's three notorious representatives of the institutions of education,
religion, and justice are silenced and rendered as ineffectual as if they
were indeed placed in the stocks, while the fools and criminals, good-
natured though they may be, are allowed to prosper unchecked, like
Face in *The Alchemist*. Thus the "comic resolution" of *Bartholomew
Fair,* as suggested by the Act IV analogue, shows the triumph of vice
over the Fair's nominal and enlightened leaders. The visual link with
the analogue is further heightened (in addition to the clothing worn by
Troubleall) if the three "lawgivers" are placed by the stocks or arranged
so that the audience is reminded of the thematic parallel. Then we can
realize even more vividly the irony of the justice figure celebrating his
own exposure and deflation by drinking not to affirm his role as protector
of the microcommonwealth, but to escape from his humiliation and
responsibilities.

Later Plays

Although only two years separate *Bartholomew Fair* from *The Devil
Is an Ass* (1616) and ten years intervene between the latter and *The
Staple of News* (1626), these last two plays represent a decline from the
golden plays of Jonson's middle period. In these dramas Jonson, perhaps
writing intuitively rather than cerebrally, brings together elements successfully utilized in earlier plays and mechanically sets them into rather
superficial, unrelated, and often meaningless activity.[49] The analogous
action in these plays is less complete in detail, correspondence, and suggestiveness: the exposure and discomfiture of the foolish characters by
occurring at the end of Act IV detract from the effectiveness, even

49. Knoll, *Ben Jonson's Plays,* p. 168. For an attempted defense of Jonson's later
plays, see Larry S. Champion, *Ben Jonson's "Dotages": A Reconsideration of the
Late Plays* (Lexington, Ky., 1967), pp. 22–44.

the necessity, of Act V, making it, in the words of Herford and Simpson, "a gratuitous piece of futility" (II,163); and the "fresh cheat" is introduced in a final act which lacks the satisfactory complex denouement of the comic masterpieces. In *Volpone,* for example, Jonson had used the premature exposure of the manipulators and the fresh cheat of the Act IV trial scene conspiracy in order to build toward a supreme, albeit controversial, denouement, so artfully had he manipulated his materials. But by 1616 Jonson seems to have retained only the bones of his once-successful formula, without the skill or energy to flesh it out.

It would appear from the number of parallel scenes and their symmetrical arrangement in these two later plays, however, that Jonson was still quite adept at arranging the mechanical parts of his drama, although at the same time he had sacrificed the meaningful and substantial relationship between parts that characterizes his major comedies. In both *The Devil Is an Ass* and *The Staple of News* Jonson carefully weaves interconnected scenes and episodes into a rather complicated fabric, but the force of the analogous action is dissipated by a multiplicity of events, and, in *The Devil Is an Ass* particularly, the dramatic design is wrenched by a failure to conclude the play in a manner consistent with its own established limits.

Despite the obvious and subtle flaws in these plays, Jonson still constructs parallel episodes which help to anticipate the conclusion. In *The Devil Is an Ass* the ending is prefigured in two ways which are reminiscent of Jonson's replicative technique. In the first place, Wittipol in Act IV has already succeeded in soundly outwitting Meercraft and Fitzdottrel, and now that he is on the side of virtue and justice there is every reason to suspect he will triumph over evil, and these particular individuals, again. In effect, as other critics have commented, the play is essentially over by the end of Act IV.

A second foreshadowing of the final unmasking of Fitzdottrel's folly of feigned possession is the Act V exposure, humiliation, arrest, and imprisonment of Pug, who, like his master, has counterfeited in order to achieve destructive ends. Throughout the play Jonson has indicated a clear link between Pug and Fitzdottrel,[50] but in Act V these thematic and

---

50. Fitzdottrel is first depicted as a comic Faustus with Pug as his Mephistopheles —both show themselves to be asses: Pug is deceived by the disguised Trains, who

dramatic parallels reach a head; Pug's behavior and treatment clearly foreshadow what happens to Fitzdottrel in the last part of the play. Early in the act Pug is forced to feign madness by making incoherent utterances in order to keep Ambler from arresting him for having stolen his clothes, but Pug is eventually arrested, rejected by Fitzdottrel as an "infernall counterfeit," and imprisoned. Fitzdottrel, who has taken and squandered Mrs. Fitzdottrel's fortune, is also forced to talk gibberish and appear possessed (at Pug's urging) in order to recoup his losses to Wittipol and his wife.

The dramatic moment toward which events have been building throughout the play, particularly during the last act, comes at the moment when Shackles enters and announces that Pug was in truth a devil. Fitzdottrel, overjoyed that he did indeed raise the devil, throws off his feigned possession (*his* "infernall counterfeit") in order to "shame the *Feind"* and reveals his own duplicity and that of Meercraft. However, though the catastrophe has been prepared for by the Act IV exposure of Fitzdottrel and by Pug's ultimate humiliation in Act V, there is no clear indication of the form the denouement will take. Jonson's scheme of dramatic anticipation is partial and unsuccessful in this case.

The deployment of an unexpected denouement accompanied by "poetic justice in the fifth act when a disguise is removed to the discomfiture of the foolish and the sinful characters"[51] is a recurrent device in Jonson's stagecraft. However, in *The Devil Is an Ass* this formula is more closely adhered to in the fourth-act exposure of Fitzdottrel. Jonson's fifth-act technique lacks the element either of inevitability or surprise and appears, instead, to be a facile device used by the playwright to conclude the play abruptly while making a final satiric thrust at

---

takes the ring in Act III just as Fitzdottrel is taken in by Wittipol, disguised as a lady of fashion, and relieved of his wife and property. Throughout the play Fitzdottrel beats Pug for manifesting his own essential folly.

51. William A. Armstrong, "Ben Jonson and Jacobean Stagecraft," in *Jacobean Theatre,* ed. John Russell Brown and Bernard Harris, *Stratford-upon-Avon Studies* (New York, 1960), I, 59. According to Armstrong, frequent changes of scene do not appear in Jonson's best plays; therefore, he concludes that it is "one of the several signs of his declining powers in *The Devil Is an Ass* that he should begin to avail himself of a free and easy convention which he had previously eschewed" (pp. 56–57).

witchcraft and the concept of demonic possession.[52] Despite Fitzdottrel's exposure as "an *Asse,* in spight of prouidence" (V.viii.154), the land and his long-suffering wife are returned to him in the end. This unexpected and unwarranted conclusion in which the satiric butt is rewarded in the end without undergoing contrition, repentance, reformation, or enlightenment is not anticipated by the preceding analogous action, nor is it consistent with Jonson's other comic resolutions.

Most of the failings of *The Devil Is an Ass,* particularly its organization, are shared by *The Staple of News.*[53] The denouement in the later play, however, is more adequately worked out than its predecessor, and in many respects this is a better play. The action that most clearly resembles Jonson's technique of analogue occurs in two pairs of parallel episodes. The first set of scenes (III.i. and V.i.) is linked by the devious, manipulating lawyer Picklock who, in both episodes, pretends to be helping Penniboy Junior when he is actually acting out of self-interest to fleece him of his money. Picklock's confession of duplicity in Act III prepares for his function as the "fresh cheat" in Act V—and in both episodes the visual-symbolic display of clothing is significant. In Act III, scene i, at the Staple, Fitton and Cymbal are stagemanaged by Picklock and told to wear impressive robes of their office in order to greet Pecunia, one monarch to another, as it were. The next scene opens with the grand entrance of Penniboy Junior, dressed in all his much-heralded finery, triumphantly leading in Pecunia and her colorful entourage. In sharp opposition to this scene of success and affluence is Act V, scene i, when Penniboy Junior appears dressed in rags,[54] divested of Pecunia, stripped of his wealth, and deserted by the leeches who surrounded him

52. On the topicality of Jonson's play—its relationship to James I and witchcraft —see the important article by G. L. Kittredge, "King James I and *The Devil is an Ass,*" *MP,* IX (1911), 195–207.

53. See Dessen, *Jonson's Moral Comedy,* p. 241, and Richard Levin, *Multiple Plot,* pp. 184–191. Levin finds fault in the "overall design" as well as the organization of the last act, but he warns us not to be blinded to "the integrity of the design itself" (p. 191). For a defense of the play's construction, see Champion, *Ben Jonson's "Dotages,"* pp. 44–75.

54. An insightful discussion of the metaphysical significance of clothing in *The Staple of News* appears in Partridge's article, "The Symbolism of Clothes in Jonson's Last Plays," *JEGP,* LVI (1957), 396–400.

when he was rich. The significant difference between the last act here and in *The Devil Is an Ass* is that Penniboy Junior has learned a lesson from his humiliation and will later successfully prove his virtue in a dramatically enacted situation.

Although this ironic contrast in setting and the parallel function of Picklock are dramatically effective, they do not constitute a substantial structural foreshadowing of the last act. In Act III, scene i, when Cymbal dons his robes, the "Staple gowne," and waits in "state" to greet Pecunia, we have a type of mock court scene where the Staple represents the potential, if not real, power in the land to influence public opinion for good or ill. The Staple backed by Pecunia's wealth is a substantial threat to the stability of the state. In *Cynthia's Revels* Jonson had used the mock throne scene as a foil to set off Cynthia's cleansing court of virtue, and in *Poetaster* he had done a variation on this theme, but in *The Staple of News* he fails to provide a parallel episode, and the Staple office, like Subtle's alchemical works, disappears in *fumo,* though without the corresponding correlative "explosion" that Jonson had provided in *The Alchemist.*

In the second set of scenes (III.iv. and V.iv.) the action takes place in Penniboy Senior's house. It involves two types of madness, a farcical trial scene that is immediately preceded by the legalistic maneuvering and subsequent defeat of Picklock, and the concommitant restoration and elevation of Penniboy Junior by his father. In Act III, scene iv, Penniboy Senior, an ailing miser, becomes suddenly invigorated when Cymbal pushes the magic "money" button by offering to divide half his projected profits with him. Like Volpone leaping out of his bed after Celia, Penniboy Senior, warming to his favorite subject ("[This righteous indignation] Puts life in man" [l. 45]), jumps out of his chair and launches into a mad and bitter harangue against human nature and its thriftless habits: "Who can endure to see / The fury of mens gullets, and their groines?" (ll. 45–46). Jonson's stage directions throughout Penniboy Senior's speeches here indicate the change in his tone from vehemence, to impassioned anger, to near madness; and the scene ends in confusion and Cymbal's jeering as he is unceremoniously escorted from the madman's house.

In this episode Jonson has portrayed the hoarder of money (as he had earlier in *The Case is Altered* and *Volpone*) as a sick, mentally deranged individual, one whose humors are obviously unbalanced. In Act V, scene iv, we are shown what can be more absurd and irrational than a wealthy miser, and that is a miser who has lost all his money. Having expended his energies in the acquisition and maintenance of wealth, Penniboy Senior is without any inner resources once that outlet is removed. The mock trial of his two dogs (the "prisoners"), who are accused of driving Pecunia and her servants away by befouling their clothes, and the subsequent taunting by the Jeerers is the farcical purgatory in which Penniboy Senior must dwell until Penniboy Canter returns to restore his wits after his "short madnesse" (V.vi.14) by returning Pecunia to him. Penniboy Senior has been so chastened by the experience, and so affected by his brother's speech on the proper treatment of Pecunia, that he, like Penniboy Junior earlier, experiences a sudden conversion, frees his dogs, and gives his "house, goods, lands" (l. 55) and Pecunia to his reformed nephew.

The failure of the denouement in *The Staple of News* is that of the play as a whole: the pieces are there, we are given some excellent moments, but parts of the design are missing and others are poorly executed. The false resolution at the end of Act IV is not as damaging as that in *The Devil Is an Ass,* because the fresh cheat is more organically a part of the over-all design, and the combat waged in Act V between hypocrisy (Picklock), virtue (Penniboy Canter), and "repentant prodigality"[55] (Penniboy Junior) gives us a catastrophe more credible than the sudden conversion of Penniboy Senior, thus tending to make the play's resolution more acceptable. The denouement is weak, however; and despite Jonson's careful attempts to unify the plot and present a balanced, symmetrical play, the occasional lapses in organization (the Staple scenes, for example) and dramatic strategy (the allegorical confusion and didacticism) make for a less successful play than those of the previous decade.

The preceding discussion of Jonson's comedies has attempted to show how he fashioned a form of analogous pattern into a conscious repetitive principle of dramatic construction. Throughout his career Jonson experimented with different and sometimes unique methods of playwriting,

55. Champion views the play in these terms, *Ben Jonson's "Dotages,"* p. 69.

but at the same time his characteristic techniques of dramaturgy are clearly stamped on practically every one of his plays. Most studies of Jonson's dramatic corpus, in fact, trace lines of progression and continuity from the early through the late works while affirming the essential originality and inventiveness of each play. In *Every Man In* Jonson had tentatively tried to create a mid-play scene that suggested a final ordering of the play's action. Whether he felt this method was too mechanical, unnecessary, overly subtle, or inappropriate for his next play, we can only speculate. It seems clear in studying his early plays, however, that Jonson was trying different methods, some conventional, some new, in order to find a mold that best suited his particular form of social and ethical commentary.

In *Cynthia's Revels* and *Poetaster* Jonson began to feel more secure with the method of analogous action and obviously took delight in experimenting with foreshadowing, inversion, and parallel incidents. In both plays a central scene, Moria's court and Ovid's banquet, is ironically matched by a later mirror-like scene in which the forces unleashed, and partially corrected, by the initial episode (itself a summary point) are checked permanently by an idealized counterpart. Here, and in *Volpone* and *Bartholomew Fair* as well, Jonson has constructed one central analogue that relates to important themes while suggesting, often in general outline rather than through congruent detail, the final outcome of the play. In *Volpone,* the Act III analogue appears to support several possible interpretations of the play's ending, while the stocks episode in *Bartholomew Fair* suggests a less festive reading of the final events of the play and makes for a more pessimistic interpretation of the play as a whole than most critics would accept.[56]

In *Epicoene* and *The Alchemist* the analogous action is more "darkly" interwoven into the fabric of the play, but it is there nonetheless. *Epicoene* is a special case because of the nature of the denouement, although even here Jonson does hint at it. The events surrounding the exposure of Daw and La Foole repeat themselves in Act V and comment upon the character of Morose. Similarly, in *The Alchemist,* the Act IV appearance of Surly anticipates, in part, Lovewit's later behavior. The

---

56. For a less festive interpretation of the play see Dessen's chapter on *Bartholomew Fair* in *Jonson's Moral Comedy,* pp. 138–220.

companion scenes representing the apex and nadir of the "venter's" fortunes indicate a different and perhaps more sophisticated handling of the type of situation found in the court and banquet episodes of the earlier plays.

The last two plays considered in this study represent, most critics agree, a weakening of Jonson's dramatic skills. It is not surprising to find, therefore, that with this breakdown in constructive power Jonson departed from the relatively lucid lines of his idiosyncratic method of dramatic analogue. Instead of the taut design and clear focus characteristic of the previous plays, Jonson retained vestigial elements of his technique in an essentially mechanical and inconclusive form largely devoid of substance. Here, as in other matters of construction, *The Devil Is an Ass* and *The Staple of News* are indeed "similar in kind and inferior in quality to the great plays." [57]

In the most distinguished era of English drama, Jonson, along with his rival, Shakespeare, was considered foremost among his country's leading dramatists. Throughout the ages Jonson has been acclaimed for his originality and his brilliant constructive skill. Dryden's famous comment about admiring Jonson but loving Shakespeare (*Essay of Dramatic Poesie*) certainly reflects the judgment of history, for over the years Jonson has fallen on hard times, his reputation intact but his works seldom read. In the past two decades, however, interest in Jonson has increased, and recent studies, though perhaps confirming Dryden's observations, have helped awaken a new generation to an appreciation of rare Ben's art. An understanding of Jonson's dramatic strategy of replication provides further evidence for our evaluation of Jonson as an original literary artist whose technical skills we cannot help but admire.

57. See Knoll, *Ben Jonson's Plays*, p. 167, about *The Devil Is an Ass*.

Language as Theme
in The Dutch Courtesan

DONNA B. HAMILTON

J OHN MARSTON'S *The Dutch Courtesan* is primarily a play about lan-
gauge, what it can do and what it cannot do. In the process of exploring what language can do, Marston loads the play with examples of
the foolish being taken in by the subtle and the clever, of the lover and
his beloved exchanging their vows of faithfulness, and of the intelligent
and the witty enjoying each other's conversation. The central actions,
however, in both the main plot and the subplot, demonstrate how the
irrational and the foolish render language helpless and ineffectual. In all
cases, whether communication is proceeding or not, the quality of a person's speech bears a direct relationship to his moral and intellectual
capacities.

Marston's interest in the correspondence between language skills and
moral stature is rather like that of Ben Jonson, who in his *Discoveries*
says, "Wheresoever, manners, and fashions are corrupted, Language is.
It imitates the publicke riot. The excess of Feasts, and apparell, are the
notes of a sick State; and the wantonnesse of language, of a sick mind." [1]
Jonas Barish, in his superb study of Jonson's prose, expands on this comment: "A man's speech, in short, the faculty that distinguishes him from

---

1. Ben Jonson, *Works*, ed. C. H. Herford and Percy and Evelyn Simpson, 11
vols. (Oxford, 1925–1952), VIII, 593.

the brutes, provides the truest index to his disposition and his moral health. Corruption of speech implies corruption of thought and feeling." [2] These words can serve well as a guide to reading much of *The Dutch Courtesan;* most obviously, Freevill's attempts to reform the hypocritical Malheureux, whose "wantonnesse of language," or inability to achieve a unity between words, feeling, and truth, indicts him almost from the moment he steps on the stage.[3] But while Marston shares Jonson's method of revealing moral qualities through the language of his characters, he does not share Jonson's technique of plot development.

In a Jonsonian comedy obsessions, suspicions, and misconceptions keep the characters from understanding the motives of others and from being understood themselves. The quantity of verbal errors or misunderstandings increases as the speed of the action increases, until all explodes in chaos. In *The Dutch Courtesan* the content of the verbal errors varies, but there is no real increase in their number as the play proceeds. The plot complication is not, as in Jonson, a natural outgrowth of the verbal disorder, but a device which Freevill conspicuously attaches to the ongoing action and openly calculates in order to reduce the quantity as well as to change the quality of Malheureux's verbal and moral waywardness. The unity of Jonson's method merits the praise which we all give it; Marston's method in *The Dutch Courtesan,* on the other hand, has often been considered unsatisfactory. Madeleine Doran, comparing the structure of *The Dutch Courtesan* to other tragicomedies whose "problems are realistically viewed" but whose "endings are not," emphasizes that while Marston does not evade the "psychological-moral problem of Malheureux," nevertheless "the solution is wholly contrived. His rescue is effected by the most incredible devices of intrigue and disguise on the part of his friend Freevill." [4] We might allow that the devices of intrigue and

2. *Ben Jonson and the Language of Prose Comedy* (Cambridge, Mass., 1960), p. 90.

3. I doubt that Barish would agree with my reading, however. Commenting briefly on *The Dutch Courtesan,* he concludes "that the idiom Jonson worked out as a symbol of moral incoherence has become a piece of incoherence pure and simple, a furious raving or perpetual motion of words signifying nothing" (p. 283).

4. *Endeavors of Art* (Madison, Wis., 1954), pp. 367, 369. For similar objections, see John Peter, *Complaint and Satire in Early English Literature* (Oxford, 1956), p. 246; and John J. O'Connor, "The Chief Source of Marston's *Dutch Courtezan*," *SP,* LIV (1957), 514–515.

disguise are not realistic; yet those devices do serve to dramatize some of the limitations of language in effecting individual and social reform.

Freevill's efforts to cure Malheureux of his moralistic rigidity and hypocrisy are based on the assumption that both he and Malheureux are basically men of reason and judgment, despite their differences in opinion and despite Malheureux's deviation from what Freevill considers to be an intelligent way of viewing man's nature. For three and a half acts, Freevill tries to change Malheureux through the art of persuasion, first by joking and teasing, then by taunting and insulting, and finally by denouncing unequivocally Malheureux's hypocritical habit of adopting extreme moral positions. In the middle of Act IV, announcing that he will now force Malheureux to feel his errors, Freevill dons his disguise and works out Malheureux's punishment and salvation on a physical level, not merely because it is a comic convention but because Malheureux has been proven incapable of responding to intellectual arguments and verbal confrontations. On the level of the subplot, Cocledemoy follows the same pattern in his assualt on Mulligrub. In bringing the plots to a close in this manner, Marston masterfully succeeds in making the conventional comic devices of intrigue and disguise serve the play's themes.

Language can reveal moral inadequacies and it can express truth, but it has no effect if the erring individual cannot recognize its meaning or importance. Perhaps the most interesting reflection of Marston's realistic sense of the power and limitations of language can be found in his ability to write a play based on moral issues and then to go on to label it as "Slight hasty labors" in which "We strive not to instruct, but to delight." [5] In doing so, Marston seems to imply that drama, like conversation, has its limits in effecting change. Yet language can provide other rewards and pleasures beyond the strictly moral. And Marston is not about to close himself or his audience off from all that is good and

---

5. Together with this disclaimer in the Prologue to *The Dutch Courtesan* is the Induction to Marston's *What You Will:*

> Music and Poetry were first approv'd
> By common sense; and that which pleased most
> Held most allowed pass: your rules of art
> Were shapt to pleasure, not pleasure to your rules.

Professor Doran refers to the scarcity of such claims in her chapter "Moral Aim," in *Endeavors of Art*, p. 93.

entertaining and touching and clever in the creative use of language. Thus, for the fullness of Marston's insight, we must turn to the play itself.

When the play begins, Marston introduces the leading characters for the main plot and the subplot, Freevill and Cocledemoy, as men who enjoy being heard and to whom others listen with pleasure.[6] Freevill, relishing the style of his storytelling as much as its content, starts his explanation of how Cocledemoy stole Mulligrub's goblets by announcing, "In most sincere prose, thus."[7] When he finishes, the audience knows not only the direction of the subplot but also that Freevill is a witty fellow whose speech is a mark of his intelligence and sense of humor. In Freevill's second set speech of the scene, in which he praises the courtesan, he again calls attention to the style of his performance when he concludes by demanding jokingly, "Give me my fee," pointing both to his skill with words as defense lawyer for the courtesan and to his sense of the comedy implicit in such a defense. Likewise, in the subplot, Marston focuses on Cocledemoy's style when, in the play's second scene, Mary Faugh scolds him for being "the foulest-mouth'd, profane, railing brother." Undaunted by her accusation, he announces, "I'll make an oration," and proceeds in ironic praise of the merciful bawd who "lives by others' pleasure, and only grows rich by others' rising," concluding his case with the lawyer's formal *"Dixi."* This fun with language immediately sets Freevill and Cocledemoy off as men who are justifiably sure of themselves and of their ability to entertain. However, once Freevill undertakes the more serious task of reforming Malheureux, he finds himself less successful.

Refusing at first to take either himself or Malheureux too seriously, Freevill attempts to diminish Malheureux's moralizing by countering his sentences with humorous antithetical quips. For Freevill, lust is not a "deadly" sin but a "lively" one, not a "head" sin but a "middle" one, not a "daily" vice but a "nightly" one (I.i.68–73). Malheureux's appeal to Freevill's "health and strength and name" is answered by Freevill's rhetorical tour de force as he builds the case for the bawd in parody of

6. Among the many critics who discuss the other numerous connections between the two plots are M. L. Wine, ed., *The Dutch Courtesan*, Regents Renaissance Drama Series (Lincoln, Nebr., 1965), p. xxi, and Philip J. Finkelpearl, *John Marston of the Middle Temple* (Cambridge, 1969), pp. 214–216.

7. Quotations are from Wine's edition.

Malheureux's seriousness. When Malheureux consents to visit Franceschina on the grounds that "The sight of vice augments the hate of sin" (I.i.153), the disgusted Freevill, in recognition of Malheureux's habitually thoughtless and unconscious manner of using words, parrots the commonplace expression: "The sight of vice augments the hate of sin! Very fine, perdy!"

When the two friends reach Franceschina's, Freevill continues his effort to expose Malheureux's hypocrisy by suggesting that there may be discrepancies between what Malheureux says and what he means. Freevill first attacks him for calling Franceschina a whore: "You may call her a courtesan, a cockatrice, or . . . a suppository. But whore! Fie! 'tis not in fashion to call things by their right names" (I.ii.97–100). While the speech satirizes Franceschina's corruption, it also marks Malheureux's lack of perspective and his inability to make any subtle distinctions in judging another's quality, an inability which is reflected in his impulsive and conclusive manner of speaking. Freevill's suspicions that Malheureux is only "one of a professed abstinence" (I.ii.109–110) rather than one of strong conviction are proven true as he now overhears Malheureux's reactions to the passions which Franceschina has aroused within him. Malheureux, struggling to find the words to justify his new feelings, does a *volte-face:* "No love's without some lust, no life without some love" (I.ii.143). But contrary to what might have been expected, Malheureux's new naturalistic position does not rid him of his hypocrisy. To Freevill he can still turn the face of the moralist: "A wanton lover you have been" (I.ii.152). Repeating word for word Malheureux's excuses for his new behavior, Freevill calls attention to the emptiness of Malheureux's words and dismisses him with contempt: "Go your ways for an *apostata!*"

Marston interrupts Freevill's campaign to cure Malheureux by introducing the scene in which Freevill and Beatrice restate their lovers' vows, another situation which tests Freevill's judgment and ability to adapt language to situation. Freevill drops the teasing and caustic prose that he has been using to counter Malheureux's hypocritical sentiments expressed in blank verse, and shifts to blank verse himself, a medium which can also be made suitable for the poetic ceremony of wooing his lady. Beatrice's reply in like style indicates that her feelings are in harmony with his. Moreover, that the two lovers are conscious of having selected

a particular medium for a particular kind of communication is suggested by Beatrice's return to prose when the wooing scene is over: "I
take you and your word, which may ever live your servant" (II.i.58–59).[8]
The changes in style which Marston employs become a comment on the
perfection of communication which can be achieved through flexible
and sensitive use of language, talents which are available only to those
of integrity.

After Freevill sings to her, Beatrice describes what she has to offer to
their partnership in terms of her virtue, intelligence, and ability to communicate. Although incapable of "a mistress' compliment, / Forced dis-
courses, or nice art of wit," this naturally gentle and moderate Beatrice
can provide him all that "Unsullen silence, unaffected modesty, / And
an unignorant shamefastness can express" (II.i.12–17). Beatrice reminds
Freevill that her "simplicity" does not mean that she is "void of skill,"
that is to say, of reason. If Freevill does not think of Malheureux at this
point, the audience surely does, for Malheureux's resistance to compre-
hending plain speech and uttering reasonable explanations sets him
quite apart from these lovers. To emphasize his inferior ability to understand a love-relationship, Marston will bring him on stage after Beatrice's
exit to utter his well-known lament on the "free-born birds" who "Carol
their unaffected passions." Although Freevill admits that his love for
Beatrice is also passionate and "extreme" (II.i.50–52), the unity of feeling
which their conversation expresses is an assurance that their love is firmly
based. The audience is invited to share Beatrice's opinion of Freevill:
"I judge you all of virtue, and our vows / Should kill all fears that base
distrust can move" (II.i.25–26). The wooing scene adds considerably to
Freevill's credentials as Malheureux's reformer, bestowing more authority both to his efforts at verbal and intellectual confrontation with
his friend and to his later decision to try other tactics.

The evidence which will provoke Freevill's decision to forsake verbal
confrontation accumulates rapidly as Malheureux returns to the stage
following the meeting between Beatrice and Freevill. That Malheureux

8. In an unpublished University of Wisconsin dissertation, "Prose in the Plays of
John Marston" (1967), Paul A. Rathburn discusses the various prose styles in *The
Dutch Courtesan* and the dramatic effects Marston achieves by alternating prose and
verse, pp. 202–227.

is becoming increasingly disoriented morally and rationally is shown by his "free-born birds" speech in which lust appears to him as love, his former standards become impersonal "national custom," and virtue seems an unnatural quality.[9] Continuing his verbal efforts to cure his friend's confusion, Freevill drops his earlier teasing and joking and tries another style of persuasion, this time describing the physical and moral destruction which results from association with such as Franceschina. He interrupts the series of warnings with a sarcastic challenge: "Yet since thou art in love" and "Yet since you needs must love." Oblivious of Freevill's tone, Malheureux mistakes the warning for an acceptable rationalization, considering the satisfaction of his passion "unavoidable" (II.i.140). As a newly reformed spokesman for true love, Freevill knows that passion is natural to man and that it can be controlled. His frustration with trying to reason Malheureux into a more tenable position finally explodes: "But since you needs must love, you must know this: / He that must love, a fool and he must kiss!" (II.i.142–143). At the end of the first act Freevill had already guessed that Malheureux had the makings of a fool in him: "Of all the fools that would all man out-thrust, / He that 'gainst Nature would seem wise is worst" (I.ii.160–161). Now Freevill is even more certain, for when a man "needs must love" to the point of forsaking other standards, he has lost control over his reason, has become obsessed, and is reduced to the level of a fool. The label "fool" becomes particularly fitting for Malheureux if the term is used to designate a condition of abnormality and stupidity made obvious primarily by inadequacy in language expression and comprehension. When language and reason fail, as they do in Malheureux when Freevill tries to explain how natural passions can be controlled, the only means left for a cure is that traditionally used on the fool, a physical reprimand. Consequently, Freevill feels compelled to initiate a course of action that will culminate in Malheureux's nearly being executed at the gallows.

In the midst of all of the complications of the plot which draw the

---

9. Because Finkelpearl has analyzed this and several more of Malheureux's speeches to demonstrate Marston's skill in "showing how people are trapped and deceived by their own language" (*John Marston of the Middle Temple*, p. 204), I will not treat them in detail. His comments would be helpful to anyone who finds the play's emphasis on language interesting.

play to a close, the emphasis on language is maintained. Ironically, the value of being true to one's word is the ploy that Franceschina uses to dupe Malheureux into agreeing to kill Freevill: "had ick not made a vow . . . So long as Freevill lives, I must not love" (II.ii.153, 164). And after the fake quarrel between Malheureux and Freevill has been publicly staged, Freevill pauses briefly to deliver to his friend the last heated appeal to his mind:

> Cannot thy virtue, having space to think
> And fortify her weakened powers with reason,
> Discourses, meditations, discipline,
> Divine ejaculatories, and all those aids against devils—
> Cannot all these curb thy low appetite
> And sensual fury?
>
> (IV.ii.7–12)

With Malheureux's refusal to respond, Freevill announces the only course of action which is now available to effect a cure:

> Now repentance, the *fool's whip, seize thee!*
> Nay, if there be no means I'll be thy friend,
> But not thy vice's; and with greatest sense
> *I'll force thee feel thy errors to the worst.*
>
> (IV.i.31–34; italics mine)

All is now ready to give the fool Malheureux the chance to "feel" what he has been unable to comprehend intellectually.[10] His offhand report to Franceschina of killing Freevill brings the unexpected arrest by the officers hidden in the curtains. His denial of guilt is useless: "Thy own lips say thou liest" (V.i.49). Knowing and being able to communicate the truth are crucial to him, but what he knows as truth proves false when Freevill cannot be found at Shatewe's. When Freevill finally stops the execution of Malheureux by removing his disguise, he explains to him that his technique has been calculated "to *force* you from the truer danger" (V.iii.43; italics mine). Malheureux acknowledges his own shortcomings, the efficacy of Freevill's method, and his own reform:

---

10. Finkelpearl comments on these lines: "Freevill has hit upon a method of education particularly appropriate for a Stoic to whom it was a fundamental tenet that the senses cannot furnish any useful knowledge" (*ibid.*, p. 211).

> I am myself. How long was't ere I could
> Persuade my passion to grow calm to you!
> Rich sense makes good bad language.
>
> (V.iii.61–63)

Marston allows Malheureux's concluding ambiguous remark to point in two directions. On the one hand, it recalls Freevill's original intention, to cure Malheureux's "bad language" with the "rich sense" or reason of skillful verbal discourse. But for a figure so morally and intellectually debilitated as Malheureux, whose use of "bad language" has been amply demonstrated, only physical experience, giving the senses rich stimulation, can cure him.

The technique of using language as a moral yardstick is sustained elsewhere in the play by creating characters who share either the virtues of Freevill or the vices of Malheureux. In a category with Freevill and Beatrice are Crispinella, Tysefew, and Cocledemoy, all unusually adept in communicating what they wish as well as in assessing what they hear. And with Malheureux we find Caqueter and the Mulligrubs, who, lacking these qualities, use language dishonestly, carelessly, even foolishly to achieve selfish personal ends. An exception is the comically dangerous Franceschina, whose shrewd conversation and quick perception of the weaknesses of others are enlisted to promote her wicked practices. Combining the worst vices of the play, uncontrolled passion and reason put to evil purposes, Franceschina must remain in prison at the play's end because she is unfit to join the newly reformed society.

The interrelationship of language and virtue that Marston dramatizes in the cure of Malheureux is stated most directly by Crispinella. Her crisp lucid prose, her comments on virtue, love, and marriage, and her concern for speaking well invite comparison with Malheureux's. Her very presence in the play is an assurance that the rational, the honest, and the free can exist in a flawed society. Her independence is possible because she knows her own mind, she refuses ever to be dishonest, and consequently she is never confused:

> I consider nature without apparel; without disguising of custom or compliment, I give thoughts words, and words truth, and truth boldness. She whose honest freeness makes it her virtue to speak what she thinks will make it her necessity to think what is good.
>
> (III.i.35–39)

There is no counterpart to Crispinella in the source.[11] Marston introduces her after the main issues of Malheureux's hypocrisy have been raised. What Marston dramatized first by way of a negative example can now be set forth positively. Through her wit she effectively exposes Caqueter, another of the play's fools. The more she teases him into revealing about the borrowed ring that he pretends is his own, the farther he moves from the truth. Near the end of the play she compares his shortcomings to the inadequacy of much communication:

His discourse is like the long word *Honorificabilitudinitatibus:* a great deal of sound and no sense. His company is like a parenthesis to a discourse: you may admit it, or leave it out, it makes no matter.

(V.ii.22–25)

A more complicated statement about the relationship of words to reality is made in the scene in which Crispinella and Tysefew attest to their love for each other by means of wit-combat (IV.i). While the wit-combat gives the appearance that they are quarreling, the reality is that they are in love. Neither lover takes the conversation seriously, but both are serious about their love. Love precedes the language which follows merely as an external formality. There is a sense here both of the inadequacy of direct speech and of the advantage of understatement. There is no confusion of incident or of values; feeling and intellect are in harmonious agreement. In the context of a satiric comedy, the fact that these skeptics can fall in love makes even more convincing and acceptable the reform of Freevill and his steadfast love for Beatrice. Moreover, the contrast in wooing styles, the one being poetic and romantic and the other satiric and witty, emphasizes the contrasts in personalities at the same time that it furnishes another illustration of the variety of ways in which truth can be communicated, provided that those doing the communicating know what they are about.

Of all of the sounds of the play, those made by Cocledemoy have remained the most memorable over the years. While literary critics have often been offended by his coarse manner, theatrical history attests to his continuing popularity on stage; Cocledemoy was made increasingly more prominent by excising the main plot and elaborating the subplot.[12]

11. O'Connor, "The Chief Source of Marston's *Dutch Courtesan*," p. 512.
12. See Wine, *The Dutch Courtesan,* p. xiii.

Hearing words spoken on the stage can produce a more balanced effect than merely reading Cocledemoy's speeches to oneself. His self-consciousness about his language drains off any moral offensiveness that his diction might otherwise have and places the emphasis on his style, which the audience is encouraged to compare to the starkly different styles of Freevill, Malheureux, Franceschina, Crispinella, and the Mulligrubs. The predominant feature of his style is the rude biting vocabulary common to Marston's verse satires: "I rail at thee, my worshipful organ-bellows that fills the pipes, my fine rattling, phlegmy cough o' the lungs and cold with a pox?" (I.ii.20–22). His conversation is also crowded with nonsense words ("catastrophonical," II.i.190; "flumpum pumpum," IV.iii.6); his homemade Greek (*"Hadamoy key,* dost thou frown, *medianthon teukey?"* IV.iii.10); and impertinent Latin (*"tempus praeteritum,"* I.ii.11; "catafugo," IV.iii.1). Yet despite its coarseness and conglomeration of foreign words, his jargon proves far more comprehensible and more pleasant to listen to than Franceschina's irregular mixture of accents, a difference which emphasizes Cocledemoy's superiority over her, despite the fact that they both inhabit the stews. Cocledemoy's language entertains the audience, Franceschina's words "alienate." [13] His verbal virtuosity is an effective complement to his ingenious methods of gulling Mulligrub and provides a central link between him and Freevill, his counterpart in the main plot. Both utilize their superior understanding of language in their efforts to expose fools. In contrast to Cocledemoy's verbal and physical flexibility, the Mulligrubs' obsession with broadcasting their righteousness and intelligence serves only to assure the audience that these are the areas in which they are the most deficient. Mistress Mulligrub, concerned that she "must bear a brain for all" (III.iii.27–28), wonders about the origin of her vocabulary—"Methodically! I wonder where I got that word. Oh! Sir Aminadab Ruth bade me kiss him methodically! I had it somewhere, and I had it indeed" (ll. 53–56)—and in the process reveals the low state of her morals.

The suggestion that an irrational atmosphere renders language helpless is also repeated on the level of the subplot. Just as Freevill eventually pursues a physical means to bring down Malheureux, so must Cocle-

13. *Ibid.,* p. xix.

demoy, whose railing is as ineffective in changing Mulligrub's ways as are Freevill's warnings and explanations to Malheureux. As each reformer takes up the physical techniques of manipulation and disguise, Marston has him remark on this decision to complement language with a physical device. Freevill will disguise himself as a knave to bring down the "fool's whip" on Malheureux (IV.ii.31–38). Cocledemoy challenges his wit and decides, "My scurvey tongue will discover me: must dissemble; must disguise" (II.i.201–202). But just as Crispinella and Tysefew do not take seriously their wit-combat, neither are these clever fellows confused about their own physical or moral identities. Their physical disguises become an amusing parody of the verbal expression of destructive hypocrisy. When truth is a delight and the motive for disguising, the disguise does not offend, as Freevill explains to Beatrice:

> the delight
> And satisfaction which we all have got
> Under these strange disguisings, when you know,
> You will be mild and quiet
>
> (V.ii.61–64)

He adds, "Where pleasure hath some profit, art is sweet" (l. 73).

With these words by Freevill, Marston raises quite explicitly the issue of the relationship between instructing and delighting. We are not surprised at the suggestion that good art should edify after discerning the seriousness with which Marston explores moral issues throughout the play. As though illustrating the theory that art can be a vehicle for instruction, Marston brings the main plot to a conclusion with an announcement by the reformed Malheureux of the lessons he has learned: "He that lust rules cannot be virtuous" (V.iii.67). But just as Marston has indicated the limited effect of words alone in reforming Malheureux, so does he now, in bringing the subplot to a close, seem to turn away from emphasis on the didactic function that the language of his play can serve. Following the reluctant confession of Mulligrub, who promises to forgive Cocledemoy for his pranks in exchange for his own release, Cocledemoy removes his disguise and explains his behavior: "honest Cocledemoy restores whatsoever he has got, to make you know that whatsoe'er he has done has been only *euphoniae gratia*—for wit's sake" (V.iii.133–135). Whether the audience benefits from the moral or not (and the playwright will never know just how much effect his words have had), there still remains *euphoniae gratia*—pleasant sound for the sake of wit, language enjoyed for its own sake. The final result of the sensitivity to language which *The Dutch Courtesan* cultivates is perhaps that of making the audience more responsive to the strength of the artist's own linguistic achievement. And it is probably out of considerable confidence in the value of his art that Marston at the end of the play asks his audience to indicate in their applause the contentment of their "pleas'd minds."

Hieronimo in Decimosexto:
A Private-Theater Burlesque

JOHN REIBETANZ

CRITICAL OPINION has not been kind to *The First Part of Hieronimo*, an anonymous play first published in 1605. This play, which centers on the Spanish court immediately before the events chronicled in *The Spanish Tragedy*, has suffered damnation through both contemptuous neglect and overt hostility. The body of criticism which has grown up around *Hieronimo* is as cadaverous as Andrea's ghost, amounting to little more than the play's 1200 lines; and nearly all of it is as belligerent as Revenge himself. At the turn of the century, when German critics trained their sights on the play to battle over its attribution to Kyd, *Hieronimo* was always the main casualty on both sides. K. Wiehl wrote that Kyd could not possibly have been the author of *Hieronimo*, for "One obtains here by no means . . . the impression of a poetic creation, so much as one of bare doggerel, in which conscious and purposefully wrought art . . . is nowhere to be observed." [1] G. I. Sarrazin argued in favor of Kyd as the author, but admitted that *Hieronimo* was less satisfying than *The Spanish Tragedy:* "The plot unfolds at a more precipitous pace, the dialogue is more hasty, cruder, less artful, [and] the diction is more bombastic and tasteless." [2] Across the sea,

---

1. "Thomas Kyd und die Autorschaft von *Soliman und Perseda, The First Part of Jeronimo,* und *Arden of Feversham,*" *Englische Studien,* XLIV (1912), 345–346.
2. *Thomas Kyd und sein Kreis* (Berlin, 1892), p. 56.

F. S. Boas denied Kyd's authorship of this "crude melodrama" and labored to "lift once and for all the incubus of *The First Part of Hieronimo* from off his reputation," observing mournfully that "Fortune could scarcely have taken a more crushing revenge upon the dramatist than by doing her best to sink his reputation beneath this *damnosa hereditas*." [3] Arthur Freeman has dubbed the work an "abortion," "whatever hack turned out the version." [4] The play's most recent editor, Andrew Cairncross, departs from this uncharitable line of thought. Cairncross argues that *Hieronimo* is the first section of a two-part play by Kyd, the latter section being *The Spanish Tragedy;* he finds many traces of Kyd's genius in *Hieronimo,* and suggests that the "brevity and corruption" of the play result from the quarto's having been a memorial transcript. [5] I shall offer a different interpretation: that *Hieronimo* is a full-blown theatrical burlesque of *The Spanish Tragedy,* written for and initially performed by child actors sometime between 1599 and 1604. [6] The discussion that follows first will show how plausible it is that such

3. *The Works of Thomas Kyd* (Oxford, 1901), pp. xliv, xlv, xiv.

4. *Thomas Kyd: Facts and Problems* (Oxford, 1967), pp. 177, 176.

5. "Introduction" to the Regents Renaissance Drama edition of *"The First Part of Hieronimo" and "The Spanish Tragedy"* (Lincoln, Nebr., 1967), p. xiv. All references to *Hieronimo* are to this edition. Cairncross acknowledges that the two-part play theory is an old one, held in the nineteenth century by Sidney Lee and Hartley Coleridge. It is grounded in Henslowe's record of six performances of a "comodey of Jeronymo" (variously phrased) in 1592, three of them on days immediately preceding performances of "Jeronymo" (*Henslowe's Diary,* ed. R. A. Foakes and R. T. Rickert [Cambridge, 1961], pp. 16–19). Scholars have noted that this practice of consecutive performance was followed for the first and second parts of two-part plays, and have identified the "comodey of Jeronymo" as *The First Part of Hieronimo,* postulating that this work was the first half of Kyd's two-part play. The many serious reasons for doubting their identification are listed by Boas (*Works of Thomas Kyd,* pp. xli–xliv) and Freeman (*Thomas Kyd: Facts and Problems,* pp. 175–177), and the widely held conclusion that *The First Part of Hieronimo* was written well after 1592 is to my mind entirely convincing.

6. This view was advanced more briefly in Appendix II of my doctoral dissertation, "The Two Theatres: Dramatic Structure and Convention in English Public and Private Plays," Princeton 1968, now being prepared for publication. Chapters Three and Five of the dissertation study the development of burlesque and other styles in private-theater drama between 1599 and 1605.

a burlesque would have been welcomed on the private-theater stage at that time; and it will then explore *The First Part of Hieronimo* as a parody of *The Spanish Tragedy,* in particular, and of public-theater dramaturgy in general. Viewed in this light, *Hieronimo* emerges from a full critical reading as a work of deliberate, comprehensive, and sometimes very deft comic art. If not from anonymity, its benighted author can be redeemed from perdition.

The early history of *The Spanish Tragedy* provides ample evidence that the fashion of one age is the joke of the next. More popular than any other play at the start of the seventeenth century (though parodied even then on the private stage), Kyd's tragedy had become an object of widespread derision and had passed into eclipse long before the century was over. When Pepys went to see a rare performance of it in 1668, his reaction was common: "Their play was a bad one, called 'Jeronimo is Mad Again,' a tragedy. Here was some good company by us, who did make mighty sport at the folly of their acting, which I could not neither refrain from sometimes, though I was sorry for it."[7] In fact, long before the Restoration, Ben Jonson could not refrain from "mighty sport" at the expense of the play either, though he was probably not sorry for it. In the Induction to *Cynthia's Revels,* Jonson characterizes the theatergoer who esteems *The Spanish Tragedy* as one "whom it hath pleas'd nature to furnish with more beard, then braine" (ll. 206–207),[8] and he casts like aspersions in the Induction to *Bartholomew Fair.* So in *Every Man in his Humour,* when the foppish gull Matheo pulls a quarto from his pocket and praises it as "well penned," "excellent," and "the best you ever heard," the victimized book turns out to be *Go by Hieronimo* (II.iii.126–141). Unlike some of Jonson's other opinions, his attitude toward *The Spanish Tragedy* was typical: many of his fellow playwrights also voiced their objections through disparaging references and parodies. Birdlime, in Dekker and Webster's *Westward Ho,* spoke for a whole generation when he compared a woman to a play: "If new, very good company, very good company, but if stale, like old *Ieronimo:* goe

---

7. *The Diary of Samuel Pepys,* ed. H. B. Wheatley (London, 1905), VII, 316–317.

8. Ben Jonson, *Works,* ed. C. H. Herford and Percy and Evelyn Simpson, 11 vols. (Oxford, 1925–1952), Vol. IV. All further references to Jonson's plays are to this edition.

by, go by."[9] The allusion becomes more biting when one recalls the earthy associations that "stale" conveyed in the seventeenth century.

When dramatists parodied *The Spanish Tragedy,* they centered their attention on two kinds of situation in the play: those which were rather grotesque, like Andrea's ghostly monologue or the discovery of Horatio's body, and those in which Kyd had pulled out all the fantastical stops of his infamous rhetoric. Take-offs of both kinds abound in plays performed during the first decade of the seventeenth century.[10] Beaumont creates a witty and representative *reductio* of Andrea's prologue in *The Knight of the Burning Pestle,* for instance, when he has Rafe enter *"with a forked arrow through his head"* and begin: "When I was mortall, this my costive corps / Did lap up Figs and Raisons in the Strand."[11] The long speech that follows supplements the ludicrous visual effect by continuing to fit absurdly mundane objects and characters into the heroic framework. Chivalrous feats of arms jostle with apprentices' activities on Shrove Tuesday; Rafe draws inspiration for his knightly prowess from a shoemaker's daughter ("the blacke thum'd maide"); and the sting of Death is sadly transmogrified ("Death caught a pound of Pepper in his hand, / And sprinkled all my face and body ore"). This series of incongruities reaches its climax in Rafe's dying words: "I die, flie, flie my soule to *Grocers* Hall." Beaumont drowns the grandiose language and cadences and the intense characters of *The Spanish Tragedy* in a sea of commonplaces—a practice followed by nearly all those writers who chose to parody melodramatic incidents from the play. Accordingly, Lording Barry shifts the hanging of Horatio from Hieronimo's bower to Ram-Alley, in his play of that name: Boucher, the disappointed suitor of a Ram-Alley widow, hangs himself in front of her house. The successful suitor and then the widow discover him at once, and mouth successive variations on the speeches of Hieronimo and Isabella ("This place was made for pleasure not for

9. *The Dramatic Works of Thomas Dekker,* ed. Fredson Bowers (Cambridge, 1953–1961), II, 342.

10. Nearly exhaustive lists of *Spanish Tragedy* parodies are given by Freeman (*Thomas Kyd: Facts and Problems,* pp. 131–135) and Boas (*Works of Thomas Kyd,* pp. lxxxiii–lxxxiv, xc–xcvi).

11. Ed. Cyrus Hoy, in *The Dramatic Works in the Beaumont and Fletcher Canon,* gen. ed. Fredson Bowers (Cambridge, 1966–), I, 85.

death" becomes "This place was made to pleasure Cittizens wiues, / And not to hang vppe honest Gentlemen"). Their passionate attentions prove uniquely moving, causing Boucher himself to jump up: "Zeart a man had as good be hangd outright, / As to indure this clapping." [12]

Playwrights who parodied the highly rhetorical rather than the grotesque incidents of *The Spanish Tragedy* cultivated either this kind of bathos or, conversely, an even more inflated style, one which would amuse through exaggeration rather than reduction. The anonymous author of *Wily Beguiled* subjects Hieronimo's speech at the start of Act III, scene vii, to just such a treatment. He assigns a clever variation on the lament to Lelia, the heroine of this light comedy. Lelia has hardly the motive and the cue for passion that Hieronimo has; her love life is merely undergoing a temporary setback—yet she complains to her Nurse in these words:

> What sorrow seiseth on my heauy heart?
> Consuming care possesseth euerie part:
> Heart-sad *Erinnis* keeps his mansion Here,
> Within the Closure of my wofull breast;
> And blacke despaire with Iron Scepter stands,
> And guides my thoughts, downe to his hateful Cell.
> The wanton windes with whistling murmure beare
> My pearcing plaints along the desert plaines,
> And woods and groues do eccho forth my woes,
> The earth below relents in Crystall teares,
> When heauens aboue by some malignant course
> Of fatall starres are authors of my griefe. [13]

Excesses of allegory, alliteration, and pathetic fallacy all operate here to drive Hieronimo's passionate bombast and cosmic comparisons—completely uncalled for by this situation, anyway—over the brink into absurdity.

Of all the plays which contain parodic allusions to *The Spanish Tragedy,* Jonson's *Poetaster* and Marston's *Antonio and Mellida* stand out for the fullness of their satires. Each takes a step toward sustained burlesque by devoting part of a scene to a lampoon that encompasses

---

12. *Ram-Alley,* ed. Claude E. Jones (Louvain, 1952), p. 66.
13. Prepared by W. W. Greg (The Malone Society Reprints; Oxford, 1912), ll. 817–828.

several different aspects of Kyd's tragedy. Act V of *Antonio and Mellida* opens with the stage direction *"Enter* Balurdo, *a* painter *with two pictures, and* Dildo." [14] The dialogue that follows weaves a close and clever burlesque around the famous "Painter Scene," with its search to express the inexpressible through visual emblems. On the heels of this travesty, two other characters enter and launch into a version of the stichomythic conversation between Lorenzo and Balthazar at the opening of Act II, scene i—a favorite target for satirists. Like Balthazar, Marston's Alberto can find no answer to the problems of unrequited love, so he ends the conversation by breaking into yet another burlesque: first he echoes the lament of Hieronimo that *Wily Beguiled* also parodied, and then he exits on a couplet like Hieronimo's after the bloody denouement of *The Spanish Tragedy*. As Hieronimo said, "And gentles, thus I end my play: / Urge no more words, I have no more to say," and ran to hang himself, so Alberto says to Feliche: "Farewell, dear friend, expect no more of me; / Here ends my part in this love's comedy" (V.i.65–66)—a very appropriate echo, since Feliche has just told him to go hang himself. The speech also marks the end of Marston's part in this tour de force of travesty. Stepping out of his main dramatic action for the better part of a scene, he has played the role of a skillful theatrical juggler and held up various aspects of *The Spanish Tragedy* to quick comic scrutiny: its emblematizing (one thinks of the rope or the bloody handkerchief), its amatory stichomythia, its cosmic bombast.

In Act III, scene iv, of *Poetaster,* Jonson creates a similar collage out of the Lorenzo-Balthazar stichomythia, the traditional cry of "Vindicta," the murder of Horatio, and Lorenzo's coercion of Pedringano. But Jonson's burlesque of *The Spanish Tragedy* is also notable for the context in which he places it. This scene takes satiric aim not just at Kyd but at the whole tradition of popular dramaturgy. The parody begins with an initial distinction between public-theater plays and those performed "on the other side of *Tyber*" (III.iv.194), and proceeds to jibe at the "dolefull straine," "amorous vaine," "furie," "thunder," and other hallmarks of the "rumbling plaier" found on the public stage. The characters recite brief examples of each hallmark, and fully half of these examples

14. Ed. G. K. Hunter, Regents Renaissance Drama edition (Lincoln, Nebr., 1965).

come from *The Spanish Tragedy:* Kyd's play is the main butt because Jonson obviously finds it most representative of the entire tradition of public-theater dramaturgy. Nor was Jonson alone in this view. Private-theater playwrights who parodied *The Spanish Tragedy* focused on those elements of the play that were most typical of the public-theater emphases that they themselves were rebelling against. The "huffing" style, and the emphasis on narrative detail and physical spectacle in *The Spanish Tragedy,* as well as the often pathetic empathy which the play evoked, were central features of a technique that was to be rejected and ridiculed.[15] It is no accident, then, that all of the parodies mentioned in this article come from plays written for the private theaters, for it was there that dramatists had such an ax to grind, particularly during the period of intense theatrical rivalry at the turn of the century. In fact, parody of *The Spanish Tragedy* was a pastime associated almost exclusively with private-theater dramatists and the university wits with whom they shared so many prejudices; public-theater plays rarely refer to *The Spanish Tragedy,* and never parody it.[16]

15. These developments are explored in greater detail in Chapter Three of the author's doctoral dissertation, "The Two Theatres." But notice how Joseph Hall singles out some of the same stylistic traits in his satire of the public-theater playwright:

> When he conceiues vpon his fained stage
> The stalking steps of his great personage,
> Graced with huf-cap termes and thundring threats
> That his poore hearers hayre quite vpright sets.
> . . . .
> There if he can with termes Italianate,
> Big-sounding sentences, and words of state,
> Faire patch me vp his pure *Iambick* verse,
> He rauishes the gazing Scaffolders.

(*Virgidemiarum* I. iii, in *The Collected Poems of Joseph Hall,* ed. A. Davenport [Liverpool, 1949], ll. 15–18, 25–28.)

16. University satires of Kyd may be found in the Parnassus Plays, ed. J. B. Leishman (London, 1949), esp. pp. 184, 332–333, 334–349, and Thomas Tomkis' *Albumazar,* all Cambridge plays; and in *Narcissus, A Twelfe Night Merriment* performed at Oxford in 1602. The exception to my statement about public-theater plays is Jonson's *Every Man in his Humour;* but this play was written before the private theaters reopened, pioneered techniques that Jonson used on the private stage as soon as the opportunity presented itself, and was calculated to appeal

Before *The First Part of Hieronimo* can enter the scene, one more piece of theatrical background needs to be put in place. When productions resumed at private theaters in 1599–1600 after a lapse of almost a decade, two unique circumstances exerted great pressure on the form of the plays that were written for those theaters. The first of these was the emergence of a new breed of dramatists. In contrast to their public-theater colleagues, they were avowed men of letters, building or hoping to build literary reputations.[17] These writers jumped at the chance to display their dramatic talents before an audience more select and sophisticated than the spectators who frequented the Rose or the Globe; that they found this audience at Paul's and Blackfriars is evident from the many references in their plays to "Select and most respected auditors" possessing "Quicke sight, and quicker apprehension."[18] As a result, a new awareness of dramatic form evolved on the private stage. Playwrights who cherished their literary identities developed a dramaturgy with an equally self-conscious form. This tendency emerged most defiantly in parodies of public-theater fare: the structure and conventions of public-theater drama were subjected to numerous take-offs, culminating in the sustained corrosion of Beaumont's 1607 burlesque, *The Knight of the Burning Pestle.* Of course, these playwrights wove the new formal awareness into the fabric of their plays in more subtle and varied ways, developing, for instance, the kind of drama that Beaumont and Fletcher were later to perfect; but parody was the most obvious manifestation of the formal revolution which they were enacting.

The second force contributing to this revolution was one which might at first have seemed a dead weight. At a time when Burbage and

largely to the segment of the public-theater audience that later patronized the private houses. For private-theater satire of revenge tragedy, see especially Marston's *The Malcontent* and his *Antonio* plays.

17. Alfred Harbage notes that no more than two-fifths of the popular repertory was composed by men with pretensions to learning, even if Heywood is included in this group—a dubious association. On the other hand, four-fifths of the private-theater repertory was composed by such writers (*Shakespeare and the Rival Traditions* [New York, 1952], p. 101).

18. These quotations are from the Prologues to *Antonio and Mellida* and *Cynthia's Revels*, respectively.

Alleyn were dazzling audiences with their mimetic skills, these dramatists had to write for child actors. No matter how experienced the
children might become, the range of portrayal that a playwright could
depend on would be relatively limited. Satire, the stylized humours
plays, and court comedies were a good bet; but to demand sustained
mimesis of a heroic part, for example, was to run the danger of
grotesque, unintentional farce. At first, the private theaters played it
too safe: they tried to revive the hopelessly outmoded allegory of *The
Contention between Liberality and Prodigality* or the Lylyan style of
The Maid's Metamorphosis, and soon found out that "if your house bee
haunted with such *hobgoblins,* 'twill fright away all your spectators
quickly." [19] Then, they seem to have discovered a happy congruity between the boys' skills and the playwrights' predilections for self-
conscious artifice. If the demands of certain dramatic situations made
it clear to an audience that the actors were only boys, these situations
could be used for deliberate effect. They could burlesque public-theater
practices and call attention to theatrical technique by turning the stage
action back upon itself. Private-theater playwrights now saw the possibility of a style "in which the author, consciously using child actors for
a special effect, will keep his audience consciously aware that they are
watching children imitating adults." [20] *The Wisdom of Doctor Dody-
poll,* for example, uses this awareness in concert with its parody of

19. Induction to *Cynthia's Revels,* ll. 197–198.
20. R. A. Foakes, "John Marston's Fantastical Plays: *Antonio and Mellida* and
Antonio's Revenge," *PQ,* XLI (1962), 230. Here and in his latest book (*Shakespeare: The Dark Comedies to the Last Plays* [London, 1971], esp. pp. 63–75),
Professor Foakes has argued convincingly for a burlesque interpretation of Marston's
work; and I have profited much from his acute insights on private-theater
burlesque, and those of Anthony Caputi (*John Marston, Satirist* [Ithaca, N.Y.,
1961]). But as Foakes acknowledges in a recent article ("Tragedy at the Children's
Theatres after 1600: A Challenge to the Adult Stage," in *The Elizabethan Theatre
II,* ed. David Galloway [Toronto, 1970], pp. 37–59), burlesque was far from being
the only dramatic contribution of the private theaters. For a detailed study of other
and later developments, see Chapters Three to Five of the dissertation referred to
earlier, "The Two Theatres." Two particularly illuminating discussions of private-
theater technique are Arthur Kirsch's "*Cymbeline* and Coterie Dramaturgy," *ELH,*
XXXIV (1967), 285–306, and Michael Shapiro's "Children's Troupes: Dramatic
Illusion and Acting Style," *CompD,* III (1969), 42–53.

public-theater conventions. In Act III, the mad Prince Alberdure mistakes a peasant for his love, Hyanthe; the boy who plays the peasant is obviously wearing a full stage beard:

ALBERDURE

Hyanthe. ô sweete *Hyanthe,* haue I met thee?
How is thy beautie changed since our departure?
A beard *Hyanthe?* ô tis growne with griefe,
But now this loue shall teare thy griefe from thee.

PEASANT

A pox on you: what are you?[21]

We may conjecture that the peasant's angry words chart his reaction to an attempted embrace by Alberdure, as well as to a tug on his beard. But even without this supposition, the whole situation is an uproarious take-off (perhaps literally) of the stage beard and ultimately of the typical boy-girl disguise conventions. The original production would have added another comic turn—when the peasant was played by a (beardless) boy. This aspect of the burlesque receives more prominent treatment in a later confrontation between the two characters, after Alberdure has recovered his wits:

ALBERDURE

Why tellest thou me of madnesse?

PEASANT

You were little better than mad euen now sir,
When you gaue me such a twitch by the beard.

ALBERDURE

I can remember no such thing, my friend.

PEASANT

No sir, but if you had a beard your self you wold.

(ll. 1185–1189)

The boys call attention to the fact that they are boys. The art is to display the art, for comic effect.

---

21. As prepared by M. H. Matson and checked by Arthur Brown (The Malone Society Reprints; Oxford, 1964), ll. 1007–1011.

At this point Hieronimo, like Revenge, can finally awake and "reveal his mystery" to us. To begin with, we can tell that *The First Part of Hieronimo* was written for child actors from the way it too exploits them for comic effect. The primary vehicle for such comedy is Hieronimo himself, and in fact the many references to his size only become meaningful when one considers the play in this light. No playwright would give his main character lines like "As short my body, short shall be my stay" (iii.103) and "My mind's a giant, though my bulk be small" (iii.114),[22] or would have other characters castigate him as "a little pygmire marshal" (x.46) "very little longer than thy beard" (x.35), if the aim were not to burlesque by calling constant attention to the diminutive actor. These allusions culminate in the appropriately short, punning epilogue with which Hieronimo ends the play:

> . . . My arms
> Are of the shortest; let your loves piece them out.
> You're welcome, all, as I am a gentleman;
> For my son's sake, grant me a man at least;
> At least I am.
>
> (xiii.10–14)

Though the actor who played Hieronimo was apparently the shortest in the troupe, his fellows were "little eyases" too. Hieronimo reveals this in the battle scene, when he looks at the combatants and boasts, "Why, I could whip all these, were their hose down" (xi.140). One does not make such statements about actors who are grown men; at least, one did not on the seventeenth-century stage, before the *Marat/Sade* era. But the other players in *Hieronimo* give away the game themselves, as well. The villainous Lazarotto confesses that he has "no hope of everlasting height" (iii.60) because "I have mischief / Within my breast, more than my bulk can hold" (iii.6–7). Notwithstanding such wickedness, Horatio resolutely asserts that "I have a heart thrice stronger than my years" (i.9) and begs that the King "Let not my youthful blush impair my valor" (i.11). The King seems almost convinced, replying that he would even choose Horatio for an important diplomatic assignment "were he not so young" (i.61). References like these provide compelling proof that *Hieronimo* was written for one of the children's companies.

---

22. See also vi.65 and vi.87, where he styles himself "little Hieronimo."

The anonymous author took full advantage of the satiric potential inherent in an all-child cast. Supplementing the allusions I have just mentioned, many passages in *Hieronimo* intensify the stress on the actors' size, either to exploit the innate comedy of such a situation or to burlesque public-theater practices. No sooner has the play opened, centering on the ceremonies which make Hieronimo Marshal of Spain, than the little actor finds himself in an awkward tableau designed to call attention to his "pygmire" stature. When the King confirms his title, Hieronimo kneels and says:

> My knee signs thanks unto your highness' bounty;
> Come hither, boy Horatio; fold thy joints;
> Kneel by thy father's loins, and thank my liege
> For honoring me, thy mother, and thy self
> With this high staff of office.
>
> (i.4–8)

The speech itself is rich in grotesque humor, as "boy Horatio" comes to kneel by the "loins" of his "father," boy Hieronimo; but it suggests a more ludicrous visual spectacle. The son dwarfs the father, who has shrunk even further by kneeling, and the hypallage of "this high staff of office" becomes literally true as the staff also towers over him. After Hieronimo has maintained this ridiculous position for some time, the King's words only serve to accentuate the disparities: "Knight Marshal, rise, and still rise / Higher and greater in thy sovereign's eyes" (i.20–21). We see that the Knight Marshal's ability to fulfill this injunction has rather well-defined limitations. This kind of self-conscious playing on the circumstances of production occurs frequently in *Hieronimo,* and it sometimes becomes an effective vehicle for satire of public-theater drama. An example of such usage has already been given here in the speeches of Lazarotto, referred to in the preceding paragraph. The stereotyped villains of popular drama were famous for such shocking admissions of their depravity. Aaron's words from *Titus Andronicus*—"Vengeance is in my heart, death in my hand, / Blood and revenge are hammering in my head" (II.iii.38–39)—found echoes in the lurid confessions of dozens of equally nefarious characters, each claiming primacy in the amount of evil that surged up in his black heart. The author of *Hieronimo* subjects the whole tradition to a *reductio* by putting a similar speech into the mouth of a child actor, even as he calls attention to the

actor's lack of "height" and "bulk." The "boiling bloody breast" becomes a tempest in a teapot, provoking anything but the customary
horror.

But the most sustained and vigorous use of this technique comes
toward the end of *Hieronimo,* when the author gives the *coup de grâce*
to a staple of the popular stage. Sidney had long before mocked the
practice of having "two Armies flye in, represented with foure swords
and bucklers,"[23] but stage battles still flourished in public-theater histories and tragedies. Certain to summon up an audience's adrenalin
and partisan sympathy, these scenes were the ancestors of the ubiquitous
barroom brawls in television Westerns. Private-theater dramatists liked
to think themselves above such crude devices, and steered clear of stage
battles even when they wrote for experienced adult actors who had
served time in numerous theatrical armies. The *Hieronimo* playwright
went a step farther, developing in scenes x and xi a consummate parody
of the convention. At the beginning of scene x, we read the following
stage direction: *"Enter* Balthazar, Alexandro, Villuppo, Don Pedro,
with soldiers, drum and colors." It would be wonderful if we could re-
capture the effect of this entrance on the play's original audience,
familiar with (and perhaps contemptuous of) the public-theater battle
scenes as they were. They had been warned of what was afoot by a
messenger who entered in scene viii to announce that "the Portugales /
Are up in arms, glitt'ring in steel" (ll. 81–82), and had heard a distant
drumming in scene ix. But surely nothing would have quite prepared
them for the spectacle which now confronted them, or would have
dampened their response to it. Decked out in all the cumbersome
accouterments of war, and marching to the beat of the drum, a fantastical troop of children files onto the stage; and Balthazar compounds
the absurdity by delivering a grandiloquent pep talk—another public-
theater chestnut—in which he says that thoughts of past tribute to Spain
"should raise spleens big as a cannon bullet / Within your bosoms."
Then, as these pint-sized soldiers *"march about,"* their Spanish counterparts enter and engage them—first in a contest of drum flourishes, and
then in a trading of insults on a very touchy subject:

23. "An Apology for Poetry," in *Elizabethan Critical Essays,* ed. G. G. Smith
(Oxford, 1904), I, 197.

BALTHAZAR

Thou inch of Spain;
Thou man, from thy hose downward, scarce so much;
Thou very little longer than thy beard;
Speak not such big words;
They'll throw thee down, little Hieronimo;
Words greater than thyself, it must not be.

HIERONIMO

And, thou long thing of Portugale, why not?
Thou, that art full as tall
As an English gallows, upper beam and all;
Devourer of apparel, thou huge swallower,
My hose will scarce make thee a standing collar.
What, have I almost quited you?

The boy who played Balthazar must have been one of the tallest in the company, turning his contest with Hieronimo into a hilarious Mutt-and-Jeff affair which would only be thrown into high relief by the symmetry of their speeches.

As the encounter escalates, another public-theater ghost is exorcised, the tradition by which champions on each side single out particular adversaries for the coming fight. In stichomythic half-lines, Lorenzo chooses Alexandro, who agrees; Rogero and Villuppo likewise agree, as do Horatio and Don Pedro. Andrea and Balthazar round out the chorus:

BALTHAZAR

Meet me.

ANDREA

I will.

BALTHAZAR

Single me out.

ANDREA

I shall.

ALEXANDRO

Do you the like.

LORENZO

And you all, and we.

ANDREA

Can we be foes, and all so well agreed?

BALTHAZAR

Why, man, in war there's bleeding amity.

Andrea's ostensibly innocuous question is a satiric master-stroke: the author adroitly calls our attention to the transparency of the emperor's suit of clothes, and the whole fabrication collapses. The tradition will be subjected to more blatant farce later in the battle, when the heroes meet with considerable difficulty in actually finding their adversaries (even to the point of sending out emissaries), and when Andrea and Balthazar lay a friendly wager "three wounds to one" (xi.67) which is the stronger warrior. At this earlier point, the parody also becomes more farcical. When Andrea tells his general to deliver a general defiance to the Portugales, the general disappoints our rhetorical expectations by uttering a bald four words: "Defiance to the Portugales!" This numbing anticlimax provokes a similar request from Balthazar to his general, and a similarly loquacious response: "Defiance to the Spaniards!" Andrea immediately drives the scene further into absurdity by disclosing his impatience, traditional but hardly warranted by those speeches: "Now cease words; / I long to hear the music of clashed swords."

We do not know exactly what this music sounded like when it came, but we may assume that it bore less resemblance to the "sweet air" of Ariel than to Malevole's "vilest out-of-tune" strains. The child actors were not experienced in swordsmanship, and their awkwardness must have been compounded if—as was probable—they wielded normal-sized weapons. The *Hieronimo* author complements this visual buffoonery with parodies of personification, anaphora, antanaclasis, synecdoche, parison, and other rhetorical devices of popular heroic drama. By skillfully combining the satiric potentialities of boy actors and well-timed comic dialogue, he renders impossible the partisan involvement which such battles generated on the public stage;[24] instead, he creates in scenes

---

24. We cannot even take the deaths of these characters seriously. As R. A. Foakes has written of Marston's characters, "Their grand speeches are undermined by bathos or parody, and spring from no developed emotional situation, so that we are not moved by them, and do not take them seriously enough to demand justice at the end" ("John Marston's Fantastical Plays," p. 236).

x and xi the fullest burlesque of the convention that has come down to us.

This kind of burlesque forms the backbone of *Hieronimo's* parody of *The Spanish Tragedy*. While other private-theater playwrights scaled down Kyd's inflated language and melodramatic incidents by hedging them about with commonplaces, the author of *Hieronimo* realized that he could effect a more basic reduction. Since he was writing a complete travesty of *The Spanish Tragedy,* and since most of Kyd's characters would appear on stage throughout his play, he could burlesque them most graphically by highlighting the scaled-down actors who played them. At its core, his *reductio* would be a literal one. Therefore, those frequent references to the actors' size in *Hieronimo* form a vital part of the arsenal with which the play deflates *The Spanish Tragedy*. Discussion will now focus on how this satiric weapon and others were trained specifically on *The Spanish Tragedy*—on its characters, its situations, and its rhetoric. But first, perhaps a short summary of "what happens in *Hieronimo*" would lend more coherence to examination of this widely unread work.

As mentioned earlier, the ceremony of Hieronimo's investiture as marshal opens the play. The Spanish nobles then decide to send Andrea on a diplomatic mission to Portugal, to demand neglected tribute; this decision triggers both a tearful departure scene between Andrea and Bel-imperia, and a scene in which the jealous Lorenzo plots with Lazarotto—"a discontented courtier"—to separate Andrea permanently from Bel-imperia by either promoting a rival lover, Alcario, or killing Andrea. Hieronimo and Horatio overhear this scheme and write a warning letter to Andrea, who is meanwhile rebuffed by Balthazar and the Portuguese. To facilitate his plan, Lorenzo dresses up Alcario as Andrea, and arranges a rendezvous for him with Bel-imperia; but Lazarotto, ignorant of this ruse, jumps the gun and kills the disguised Alcario instead of Andrea. Lorenzo manages to have Lazarotto executed at once so that their scheme will remain a secret, while Hieronimo and Horatio rejoice that no harm has come to Andrea—who apparently did not receive their letter. There follows another lachrymose leave-taking scene, as Andrea parts from Bel-imperia to do battle with the Portuguese. In the skirmishes which were described above, Balthazar kills Andrea and is captured by a mournful Horatio and a delighted

Lorenzo. The play ends with Andrea's funeral, a brief but amusing appearance to Horatio of Andrea's grateful ghost (escorted by Charon and Revenge), and the short epilogue by Hieronimo.

The ridiculous picture that Hieronimo presents in the epilogue is no worse than his demeanor anywhere else in the play. We might expect Kyd's main character to bear the brunt of any take-off, and the *Hieronimo* author does not disappoint these expectations. As F. S. Boas wrote, this Hieronimo "sinks into a buffoon. His opening words . . . strike a grotesque note, which is repeated in every scene where he appears." [25] Although Boas was hardly cognizant of or sympathetic to the author's overriding purpose, his estimate is a just one. The author carries out this grotesque travesty by enlarging upon two basic premises. First, as we have seen, he logs great satiric mileage from assigning this role to the troupe's shortest actor. Secondly, he takes the hints of Hieronimo's approaching senility found in *The Spanish Tragedy* (such as his displays of emotional instability, or the King's readiness to indulge his whims) and dilates them into a rather endearing portrait of a first-class comic loony. Hieronimo's reaction to the King's trust in scene i provides an early example:

> Oh fortunate hour, blessed minute, happy day,
> Able to ravish even my sense away.
> Now I remember too—oh sweet remembrance!—
> This day my years strike fifty, and in Rome
> They call the fifty year the year of Jubilee,
> The merry year, the peaceful, jocund year,
> A year of joy, of pleasure, and delight.
> This shall be my year of Jubilee, for 'tis my fifty.
> Age ushers honor; 'tis no shame; confess,
> Beard, thou art fifty full, not a hair less.
>
> (ll. 22–31)

Hieronimo is mad againe! The "even" of line 23 must obviously be taken with a large grain of salt; and Hieronimo's inane lucubrations give the author an opportunity to caricature the often empty rhetorical balances and repetitions of *The Spanish Tragedy*. Nor does he miss the opportunity to underline the age discrepancy between actor and role, in the first of several pointed references to Hieronimo's "beard."

25. *The Works of Thomas Kyd*, p. xliii.

The relationship between Hieronimo and Horatio provides a platform for further parodic excursions. The adoring father of Kyd's tragedy, proud of his son's achievements and heartbroken at his loss, is here shaped by his senility into a doting dolt who will not leave off singing the praises of Horatio at every conceivable moment. Each gesture of his son, no matter how insignificant, provokes a new burst of rapturous adulation from Hieronimo. These indiscretions reach a ludicrous extreme in the battle scenes when, like a jack-in-the-box, Hieronimo pops out now and then to punctuate the fighting with an aria:

> Oh valiant boy; struck with a giant's arm
> His sword so falls upon the Portugales,
> As he would slice them out like oranges,
> And squeeze their bloods out. Oh abundant joy,
> Never had father a more happier boy.
>
> (xi.1–5)

So close is the son to the father in this play that poor Horatio only shows his face without Hieronimo in one short scene (ii); and Hieronimo never makes an appearance without Horatio close under his wing. In fact, the two often act like a kind of vaudeville comedy team, with the father making a somewhat stupid remark and the son chiming in with an equally inane echo. So in scene viii, when Lorenzo has Lazarotto carted away, Hieronimo directs an aside to Horatio—"Is not this a monstrous courtier?"—and a suitable reply follows: "He is the court toad, father." A similar exchange takes place in scene vii: after Andrea has narrowly escaped assassination, and we might be wondering why he did not heed the letter that Hieronimo and Horatio labored over for a whole scene, their monumental incompetence reveals itself by this route:

> HIERONIMO
>
> Horatio, 'twas well, as fortune stands,
> This letter came not to Andrea's hands.
>
> HORATIO
>
> 'Twas happiness indeed.
>
> (ll. 132–134)

The scene (vi) in which they compose this fugitive letter is their most farcical one. It is heralded by a stage direction which, like so many in

Marston's burlesques,[26] sets an unmistakably rollicking pace: *"Enter Hieronimo trussing of his points, Horatio with pen and ink."* Horatio begins on the wrong foot by folding the paper inappropriately, and Hieronimo reprimands him in terms calculated to relate much more closely to the play's first audience than to its Spanish setting:

> Fie! I am ashamed to see it.
> Hast thou worn gowns in the university,
> Toss'd logic, suck'd philosophy,
> Eat cues, drunk cees, and cannot give a letter
> The right courtier's crest?
>
> (vi.6–10)

Then, a second blunder by Horatio triggers another one of those ingenuous vaudeville exchanges:

> HIERONIMO
>
> . . . .
> Fie, fie, Horatio: what, is your pen foul?
>
> HORATIO
>
> No, father, cleaner than Lorenzo's soul;
> That's dipp'd in ink made of an envious gall;
> Else had my pen no cause to write at all.
>
> (ll. 12–15)

The author may here be guying a familiar figure from public-theater drama, the virtuous character who (like Kyd's Hieronimo or like Hamlet) is shocked and overwhelmed by his discovery of evil in the world; certainly, Horatio fits the mold of such a naïf elsewhere in the play, too.[27] More specific satire of *The Spanish Tragedy* comes when

26. Caputi notes several in *Antonio and Mellida:*

In Act II, scene i, the stage direction reads: *"Enter Forobosco, with two torches: Castilio singing fantastically; Rossaline running a coranto pace, and Balurdo; Feliche following, wondering at them all."* In Act III, scene ii, Castilio enters sprinkling himself with sweet waters. Later in the same scene Balurdo enters backwards, admiring himself in a mirror, and Flavia enters backwards, holding a mirror for Rossaline. And near the end of Act III, Antonio runs on stage, disguised as a sailor, and Mellida, disguised as a page, enters dancing (*John Marston, Satirist,* p. 141).

27. See iii.104 ff., for instance. In scene xiii, Horatio's response to the ghost seems to be patterned on Hamlet's.

Hieronimo begins to dictate his often nonsensical phrases to Horatio. He arrives by stages at the following opening: "Signior Andrea, 'tis a villainous age this, that a nobleman should be a knave as well as an ostler, or a serjeant, or a broker; yet I speak not this of Lorenzo; he's an honest lord." Hieronimo's failure to come to the point mocks the politic circumlocutions which his Kydian namesake had hidden behind, "*Pocas palabras!* mild as the lamb" (III.xiv.118). When he finally does utter the letter's sole literalism—namely, that Lorenzo "has hired one to murder you"—Horatio recoils in dismay, but Hieronimo defends his diction:

> Art thou a scholar, Don Horatio,
> And canst not aim at figurative speech?

Wisely, Horatio does not push the issue.

Although satire of Kyd's main character forms the central thread running through *Hieronimo,* the author by no means confines his caricature to the little marshal. Nearly the complete consort of *Spanish Tragedy* characters turns up in *Hieronimo,* humorously distorted as in a fun-house mirror. A quick glimpse at each main figure awakens respect for the broad range of the play's satiric portraiture. In each case, the author pinpoints an idiosyncrasy actually shown by Kyd's character, consistently exaggerates or overturns it, and develops it into a unique profile. The caricature of Andrea, for instance, has its roots in the twin vocations which he acknowledged during the opening monologue of *The Spanish Tragedy.* There, Minos was undecided whether to consign Andrea to an afterlife with the underworld's lovers or with its martialists. The *Hieronimo* author nearly solves this dilemma, creating an Andrea whose military prowess is more highly touted than convincing, and who fares better as the sweetest flower in Bel-imperia's garland (*The Spanish Tragedy,* I.iv.4) than on the battlefield. His first speech rings with bravado, in another imitation of Kyd's cosmic bombast:

> I will be heard like thunder, and as rough
> As northern tempests, or the vexed bowels
> Of too insulting waves, who at one blow
> Five merchants' wealths into the deep doth throw.
> I'll threaten crimson wars.

> (i.88–92)

But the only engagements which Andrea seems to enter into with alacrity are those with Bel-imperia, and in his military expeditions a considerable shadow falls between the motion and the act. He proclaims his ferocity more frequently than any other character,[28] but physical encounters are inevitably replaced or prefaced by suspiciously lengthy verbal ones. The author doubles the comedy of these encounters by matching Andrea with a Balthazar who speaks just as fiercely but is, if anything, even more chickenhearted. The first clash of these mighty adversaries deserves full quotation:

BALTHAZAR

I'd make a bridge of Spanish carcasses,
To single thee out of the gasping army.

ANDREA

Woo't thou, prince? why even for that I love thee.

BALTHAZAR

Tut, love me, man, when we have drunk
Hot blood together; wounds will tie
An everlasting settled amity,
And so shall thine.

ANDREA

And thine.

BALTHAZAR

What, give no place?

28. Several of Andrea's ranting speeches (ix.3–11; xi.57–63; and the one cited above), seem to conjure up the ghost of Hotspur, especially in their stress on "honour"; and two scenes—ix, where Andrea parts hastily from Bel-imperia, and xi, where Horatio delivers a soliloquy over and to the body of Andrea, on the battlefield—may echo II.iii and V.iv of *1 Henry IV*. Perhaps the *Hieronimo* author is aiming a few barbs at Hotspur, another favorite target of university and private-theater wits. That Shakespeare's history plays in general are being satirized is also evident at x.100–102, where Balthazar's words ("Why, man, in war there's bleeding amity; / And he this day gives me the deepest wound, / I'll call him brother") echo those of Henry V before Agincourt:

We few, we happy few, we band of brothers;
For he to-day that sheds his blood with me
Shall be my brother.

(IV.iii.60–62)

ANDREA

To whom?

BALTHAZAR

To me.

ANDREA

               To thee? Why should my face
That's placed above my mind, fall under it?

BALTHAZAR

I'll make thee yield.

ANDREA

            Ay, when you get me down;
But I stand even yet, jump crown to crown.

BALTHAZAR

Dar'st thou?

ANDREA

I dare.

BALTHAZAR

I am all vex'd.

ANDREA

                 I care not.

BALTHAZAR

I shall forget the law.

ANDREA

Do, do.

BALTHAZAR

        Shall I?

ANDREA

            Spare not.

BALTHAZAR

But thou wilt yield first.

ANDREA

No.

BALTHAZAR

I hug thee for't,
The valiant'st spirit e'er trod the Spanish court.

(iv.61–75)

In a ludicrous parody, Kydian stichomythia serves as vehicle for a play-by-play description of what is apparently a contest to see which boy can stand taller. One must greet Alexandro's appraisal—"My liege, two nobler spirits never met"—with a large measure of doubt. For both characters, words usually speak louder than actions. Like Andrea's, Balthazar's verbal predilections also spring from traits displayed by his *Spanish Tragedy* counterpart. In Kyd's play, Balthazar was easily the most effete character, a complacent prisoner and an epitome of the forlorn Petrarchan lover. From his lips came all the intricate amorous speeches that gave Jacobean parodists a field day and provoked even his friend Lorenzo to mild protest: "Tush, tush my lord! let go these ambages, / And in plain terms acquaint her with your love" (I.iv.90–91). Balthazar responded to this injunction with four more anaphoral lines in praise of his mistress' perfections. The Balthazar of *Hieronimo*, then, runs true to form. We last see him in a sheepish posture as he surrenders to both Horatio and Lorenzo, an action of questionable integrity which at least Horatio views with scorn: "Oh abject prince! what, dost thou yield to two?" (xi.143)

Kyd's Lorenzo presented a complete contrast to Balthazar. Ever contemptuous of "these ambages," he acted throughout the play with close-mouthed efficiency and unconscionable maleficence. Both characteristics provide the *Hieronimo* author with food for powder. He inflates the maleficence until Lorenzo becomes a grotesque model of the typical public-theater villain, even down to his confessional soliloquy:

> Andrea's gone ambassador;
> Lorenzo is not dreamt on in this age;
> Hard fate,
> When villains sit not in the highest state.
> Ambition's plumes, that flourish'd in our court,
> Severe Authority has dash'd with justice;
> And Policy and Pride walk like two exiles,

> Giving attendance, that were once attended,
> And we rejected that were once high honored.
> I hate Andrea, 'cause he aims at honor,
> When my purest thoughts work in a pitchy vale,
> Which are as different as heaven and hell.
> One peers for day, the other gapes for night,
> That yawning beldam with her jetty skin;
> 'Tis she I hug as mine effeminate bride,
> For such complexions best appease my pride.
>
> . . . .
>
> Oh sweet, sweet policy, I hug thee; good:
> Andrea's Hymen's draught shall be in blood.
>   (i.97–112, 123–24)

That last image may allude to the *Spanish Tragedy* dumb show at the end of Act III, but the speech which precedes it takes a much wider frame of reference. It burlesques the whole spectrum of public-theater villains who aim at Ambition and embrace Policy, a group which includes Marlowe's Barabas, Dekker's Eleazar, and (later) Shakespeare's Iago and Edmund.[29] This Lorenzo plots to kill Andrea, schemes to have the disguised Alcario sleep with an unsuspecting Bel-imperia (Lorenzo's own sister!), arranges the liquidation of his accomplice, and behaves quite despicably on the battlefield:

> [Horatio *has* Prince Balthazar *down;*
> *then enter* Lorenzo *and seizes his*
> *weapons.*]
>
> [HORATIO]
>
> Hand off, Lorenzo, touch not my prisoner.
>
> LORENZO
>
> He's my prisoner; I seiz'd his weapons first.
>
> HORATIO
>
> Oh base renown,
> 'Tis easy to seize those were first laid down.
>
> LORENZO
>
> My lance first threw him from his warlike steed.

29. The author mocks the tradition further by turning the words "villain" and "villainous" into an absurd leitmotif after the discovery of Alcario's murder; the words are used eight times in the space of fifty lines (vii.144–viii.48).

HIERONÍMO

Thy lance, Lorenzo? Now, by my beard, you lie.

(xi.126–132)

The scene presents a sardonic reconstruction of events alluded to in *The Spanish Tragedy* (I.ii.153–65), where Lorenzo's conduct emerged as much less reproachable. There, his claim in fact appeared justified. The *Hieronimo* author darkens Lorenzo's countenance even more by creating a sinister side-kick for him, Lazarotto—

> A melancholy, discontented courtier,
> Whose famish'd jaws look like the chap of death;
> Upon whose eyebrows hangs damnation;
> Whose hands are wash'd in rape, and murders bold.

(i.114–117)

Obviously derived from Kyd's Pedringano—whose fate he shares—this figure parodies another stock public-theater character, the villainous accomplice. "I have mischief / Within my breast, more than my bulk can hold" (iii.6–7), he boasts, echoing the claims of such blackguards as Chettle's Lorrique or Marlowe's Ithamore.[30] Lazarotto even bears the travesty of a typical tag name, which he explicates upon entrance for those who may miss the point:

LORENZO

What's thy name?

LAZAROTTO

My name's an honest name, a courtier's name:
'Tis Lazarotto.

30. Indeed, there are indications that Lazarotto's resemblance to Ithamore and to Shakespeare's Aaron may have extended to their color. When Lorenzo first mentions Lazarotto, he is thinking of "night, / That yawning beldame with her jetty skin; / 'Tis she I hug as mine effeminate bride, / For such complexions best appease my pride"; his next line introduces Lazarotto: "I have a lad in pickle of this stamp" (i.113). He later refers to Lazarotto as "my life's jetty substance" (iii.2) and says that Lazarotto's soul "is blacker than his name" (iii.26). Lazarotto himself tells us, "My soul's a Moor, you know, salvation's white" (iii.61), words redolent of Aaron's in Act III of *Titus Andronicus:* "Aaron will have his soul black like his face" (III.i.206). Finally, when Lazarotto is carried out gagged at viii.56, he duplicates an exit of Aaron's (V.i.151). The resemblance is skin-deep and more.

LORENZO

What, Lazarotto?

LAZAROTTO

Or rather rotting in this lazy age.

(iii.2–5)

Since Lorenzo has already demonstrated intimate knowledge of Lazarotto, it is obvious that the author has Lorenzo ask the question just to
point up the satire. The plots which these two conspirators cook up are
more ludicrous than those of their opponents, Hieronimo and Horatio.
For instance, when Lorenzo asks Lazarotto how the love of Andrea
and Bel-imperia may be frustrated, Lazarotto responds with a scheme
to have Alcario present her with rich jewels, for "gifts and giving /
Will melt the chastest-seeming female living" (iii.47–48). But what if
this plan should fail, asks Lorenzo. Lazarotto's alternate scheme leaves
something to be desired in the way of subtlety or sophistication: "I'll
murder Don Andrea."

Lorenzo's most elaborate plot entails a splendid *reductio* of another
dramatic convention, the disguise. This convention, a staple of popular
romantic drama, usually worked to deepen an audience's involvement in
the action: it let the audience share in the deception of uninformed characters, and thus participate more fully in the experiences of the disguised protagonist. But the *Hieronimo* author, like his private-theater
colleagues,[31] uses disguise in an antimimetic fashion. Lorenzo's disguise
intrigue deliberately strains our credibility, calling parodic attention to
the device as such. He remarks on how Alcario resembles Andrea, and
plots to dress him up in a suit like Andrea's; in this way, says the wily
Lorenzo, Alcario will be able to woo Bel-imperia. Alcario is ecstatic:
"This falls out rare; in this disguise I may / Both wed, bed, and board
her?" (v.19–20). Lorenzo assents, helping Alcario as his *Spanish Tragedy*
counterpart helps Balthazar's courtship, and we are treated to a grand
reunion scene between Bel-imperia and "Andrea." The fact that she

---

31. Cf. the disguises in *The Widow's Tears, May-Day, Epicoene, A Mad World,
My Masters,* and *The Fleire.* Disguise is usually employed parodically on the
private-theater stage until about 1610, when Beaumont and Fletcher begin to use
it for romantic effect in their plays.

cannot tell Alcario from her lover is perhaps a wry commentary on the celerity with which Kyd's heroine shifted her affections from Andrea to Horatio. At any rate, the scene explodes the disguise device through this kind of preposterousness, as the two lovers talk, whisper, and kiss.

We cannot speculate on how far Alcario's disguise might have taken him, for he immediately falls victim to an error in Lorenzo's strategy. The error guys that second idiosyncrasy of Kyd's Lorenzo, his penchant for secrecy. Just as Kyd's villain did not let Balthazar in on his plan to kill Serberine—

> I list not trust the air
> With utterance of our pretense therein,
> For fear the privy whisp'ring of the wind
> Convey our words amongst unfriendly ears,
> That lie too open to advantages.
>
> (III.iv.82–86)

—so this Lorenzo keeps Lazarotto in the dark about the disguise ruse:

> The fewer in a plot of jealousy
> Build a foundation surest, when multitudes
> Makes it confused ere it come to head.
> Be secret, then; trust not the open air,
> For air is breath, and breath-blown words raise care.
>
> (vii.22–26)

But, alas, Lazarotto also falls for the disguise and kills Alcario instead of Andrea, in a flash of anaphoral antithesis: "Now lives Andrea, now Andrea dies" (vii.78). The blunder may discommode Lorenzo, but it gives his author a fine opportunity to parody yet another incident from *The Spanish Tragedy,* the discovery of Horatio's body. First the real Andrea and Rogero enter, and "Rear up the bleeding body to the light." There follows a series of comic entrances and reactions which keep us from feeling anything deeper than hilarity. The author has, of course, never allowed Alcario to become a fully developed character, so that our detachment has combined with the absurd circumstances of his death to elicit a decidedly comic response. Now he creates an uproariously funny sequel through a patterning and reiteration similar to the "tragical mirth" of the Pyramus and Thisbe interlude in *A Midsummer Night's Dream:*

[*Enter* Hieronimo *and* Horatio.]

HIERONIMO

Son Horatio, see Andrea slain!

HORATIO

Andrea slain? Then, weapon, cling my breast.

ANDREA

Live, truest friend, forever loved and blest.

HORATIO

Lives Don Andrea?

ANDREA

           Ay; but slain in thought
To see so strange a likeness forged and wrought.
Lords, cannot you yet descry
Who is the owner of this red, melting body?

ROGERO

My lord,
It is Alcario, Duke Medina's son;
I know him by this mole upon his breast.

LAZAROTTO

Alcario slain? Hast thou beguil'd me, sword?
Arm, hast thou slain thy bountiful, kind lord?
Why then rot off, and drop upon the ground,
Strew all the galleries with gobbets round.

[*Enter* Lorenzo.]

LORENZO

Who names Alcario slain? It is Alcario.
Oh cursed deed:
Couldst thou not see, but make the wrong man bleed?

LAZAROTTO

'Sfoot, 'twas your fault, my lord; you brought no word.

LORENZO

Peace; no words; I'll get thy pardon.
Why, mum then.

[*Enter* Bel-imperia.]

BEL-IMPERIA

Who names Andrea slain? Oh, 'tis Andrea:
Oh, I sound, I die.

(vii.96–118)

The melodramatic words and gestures are pounded by repetition into farce: Horatio's initial response parallels Lazarotto's, and Bel-imperia's repeats her brother's. The effect is heightened by travesties of heroic bombast and of the conventional "mole upon his breast" from countless recognition scenes, as well as by the universal confusion of Alcario with Andrea. And the frantic whispers between Lorenzo and Lazarotto underline the ineptitude of their villainy.

Bel-imperia undergoes two radical changes in the transition from *The Spanish Tragedy* to *Hieronimo*. To begin with, she seems to have taken the pledge. The fiery woman who lusted for Horatio and whom Don Andrea "In secret . . . possess'd" is now, in a complete comic reversal, as meek and virtuous as this Andrea's "chaste self" (ii.55). Her actions here are nothing short of demure, and when Lazarotto asserts that "gifts and giving / Will melt the chastest-seeming female living" (iii.47–48), Lorenzo affirms his certainty that Bel-imperia would meet such tokens with contempt. Nowhere does the play intimate that Andrea has requested or received anything more than a scarf from this Bel-imperia. The second change in her character was noticed by Boas: "the proud, self-reliant heroine of Kyd's play is metamorphozed into a sentimental girl, 'a most weeping creature'" (p. xliii). References to her propensity for emotional display follow her through the play: Andrea uses the epithet quoted by Boas at scene ii, line 3, and asks her at line 61 to "play not this moist prize"; Lazarotto comments, "Why, is she not a woman? she must weep" (iii.65); upon discovering the dead "Andrea" at scene vii, line 118, she falls in a swoon; Horatio, ruminating on Andrea's death, says "Alas, I pity Bel-imperia's eyes" (xi.169). I believe that the *Hieronimo* playwright paints such a lachrymose picture of his heroine for several satiric purposes. First, as with Bel-imperia's chastity, he effects a comic inversion of Kyd's characterization, a travesty which moves us to laughter by being so topsy-turvy. Secondly, his references to the "weeping creature" burlesque the great numbers of shrinking violets who populated romantic drama. "Your tears show you a woman" was a shibboleth on the popular stage, answered to by Dekker's Jane (in *The Shoemakers' Holiday*), Millicent (in *The Merry Devil of Edmonton*), and dozens of other dampened damsels. The *Hieronimo* author mocks the lot by creating a heroine who is tearful with a vengeance, and he provides her with a sentimental platform by staging two separate farewell scenes with Andrea. But the most interesting comic effect he achieves with this Bel-imperia is one which complements the self-conscious gestures of his boy actors. Just as the actors call attention to the fact that they are boys, so the repeated references to "playing the woman" cannot but make us aware that we are indeed watching someone who only "plays" the woman. Especially in a context of other such references, a speech like Andrea's underscores and exploits the gap between actor and role:

> What, playing the woman, Bel-imperia?
> Nay, then you love me not; or, at the least,
> You drown my honors in those flowing waters.
> Believe it, Bel-imperia, 'tis as common
> To weep at parting as to be a woman.
> Love me more valiant; play not this moist prize;
> Be woman in all parts, save in thy eyes.
>
> (ii.56–62)

The manifest impossibility that "Bel-imperia" can carry out that last admonition strikes us delightfully and immediately. As he had done with Alcario's disguise, the playwright holds one of the conventional tricks of his trade up to parody.

The satiric art of *Hieronimo* is, as we have seen, rooted in a comprehensive knowledge of those tricks. Parodies of specific characters and incidents from *The Spanish Tragedy* broaden out to burlesque the many theatrical traditions described above, as well as a large number of conventions which fall outside the scope of this study. One last aspect of the play's satire demands attention here. Like most plays, *The First Part of Hieronimo* possesses a singular range of diction and imagery which all of its characters share, regardless of their idiosyncrasies. This common language flows through the play's diverse characters and incidents like an undercurrent, and gives them a measure of unity. The peculiar vocabulary of *Hieronimo*, as Boas observed with some disdain, "delights in giving prominence to the various parts of the human body" (p. xliv). In particular, references abound to blood, veins, hearts, and variously located wounds. One can choose to attribute this lurid vocabulary to the author's poor taste or neurosis, but the controlled comic art manifested in other areas of the play makes another explanation more likely. The vocabulary, like the characterization and the staging, is a satiric weapon. The author takes aim in this instance at the "blood and guts" plays of the public theaters, the heroic tragedies and histories which loaded every rift with gore. His target here is not primarily *The Spanish Tragedy,* although Kyd's play refers to blood no fewer than thirty times and presents such visual reminders as the bloody napkin, the letter in "Red ink," and the bloody dumb show. But mainly, he derides works like Dekker's *Lust's Dominion* or Shakespeare's early histories, the most sanguinary example of which is probably *Richard III.* That play makes over seventy allusions to gore; the references never stop after they come streaming in with Anne's speech to Richard:

> O, gentlemen, see, see! Dead Henry's wounds
> Open their congeal'd mouths and bleed afresh.
> Blush, blush, thou lump of foul deformity,
> For 'tis thy presence that exhales this blood
> From cold and empty veins where no blood dwells;
> Thy deed inhuman and unnatural
> Provokes this deluge most unnatural.
> O God, which this blood mad'st, revenge his death!
> O earth, which this blood drink'st, revenge his death!
>
> (I.ii.55–63)

Consistent use of such language creates a compelling if unsubtle image of Richard's reign, but lends itself readily to parody. So Andrea and Balthazar speak of "welt'ring in . . . gore," "blood's / A-tiptoe," "crimson streams," "mean blood," "meet in blood," "valiant blood," and "crimson tincture's shine" in the space of fourteen lines (xi.92–106), and so Horatio tells his King:

> Let not my youthful blush impair my valor:
> If ever you have foes, or red field scars,
> I'll empty all my veins to serve your wars:
> I'll bleed for you; and more, what speech affords,
> I'll speak in drops, when I do fail in words.
>
> (i.11–15)

Every other page of *Hieronimo* provides similar examples of this exaggerated style, surely a deliberate device which strengthens the play's parodic thrust.

The nature of its satire makes it certain that *The First Part of Hieronimo* was written sometime between 1599–1600 (when the private theaters reopened) and the quarto's 1605 date. But I believe that the date can be narrowed down even further when we take into account two other pieces of evidence, one internal and one external. We can add at least three years to the earliest date by accepting Arthur Freeman's likely suggestion that the "letter" scene is based on a similar episode in Chapman's *The Gentleman Usher* (1602–1604).[32] The external evidence concerns a reference in *The Malcontent* "Induction," the 1604 date of which would lower the top figure for *Hieronimo*. I believe that the "Induction" makes an allusion to this burlesque play. When Sly wonders why a public theater is about to produce *The Malcontent*, Condell replies: "Why not Malevole in folio with us, as Jeronimo in decimosexto with them?" If we equate "Jeronimo in decimosexto" with *The First Part of Hieronimo*, the statement may be paraphrased in general terms as "Why cannot we adult actors perform our version of a children's play, since they staged their version of an adult play?"[33] And we can arrive at a more particular paraphrase to satisfy the qualms of those who object that Condell's "them" relates to Sly's talk of "another company," and that it therefore implies a specific children's troupe. We know that *The Malcontent* was originally a Queen's Revels play; and Freeman has recently presented a convincing argument that the Chamberlain-King's Men held an interest in *The Spanish Tragedy* and staged it between 1600 and 1604.[34] These details lead to a more specific paraphrase which interpolates "the King's Men" for "us" and "the Queen's Revels" for "them": the Queen's Revels

---

32. *Thomas Kyd: Facts and Problems*, p. 176.

33. The view that "Jeronimo in decimosexto" is *Hieronimo* has been held by many scholars who viewed *Hieronimo* as a corruption of a serious play. But, in comments which I read after arriving at the same view independently, Philip Edwards voices his belief that the play mentioned in the "Induction" is *Hieronimo*, and that it was "almost certainly intended as a burlesque" (Appendix A of his Revels Plays edition of *The Spanish Tragedy* [London, 1959], p. 138; see also Appendix F).

34. *Thomas Kyd: Facts and Problems*, pp. 121–125.

had adapted a King's Men play, *The Spanish Tragedy,* and now the adult company was retaliating. I suggest, then, that *The First Part of Hieronimo* was performed by the Queen's Revels between 1602 and 1604; and this fact makes it all the more likely that the *Hieronimo* author would borrow from *The Gentleman Usher,* another Queen's Revels play. Another view of Freeman's reinforces my theory. After Condell's speech in the "Induction," Sly asks "What are your additions?," and he is told that they are not extensive. Freeman writes: "If 'your' is emphasized, the suggestion might be that the Children had again altered *Jeronimo* when they appropriated it; whereas the King's Men's additions to Marston are 'not greatly needefull, only as your sallet to your greate feast, to entertaine a little time.'"[35] As this paper has shown, the Children *did* alter *Jeronimo* radically—into a full-blown burlesque. Finally, Condell's wish to "entertain a little more time" reminds us that children's plays were shorter than adult plays. I suggest that *Hieronimo*'s brevity arises from its private-theater origins rather than from the nature of its text. When Condell refers to "Jeronimo in decimosexto," he is talking about the diminutive *Hieronimo* which exists today, originally a private-theater play with a correspondingly diminutive Hieronimo—in decimosexto.

35. *Ibid.,* p. 130.

Othello *and the Conventions of Romantic Comedy*

SUSAN SNYDER

T HE MOTIVES are sexual love and jealousy; intrigue and deception propel the plot; the outcome is engineered by a clever manipulator; the impact is personal, "domestic," rather than political and cosmic. These features strike us as appropriate to Shakespeare's comedies. Yet they also characterize one of his greatest tragedies. *Othello* is based, not on the chronicles and lives of the great that supply plots for most of the other Shakespearean tragedies, but on a *novella* in Giraldi's *Hecatommithi*. Shakespeare often turned to tales of this sort for the plots and situations of his comedies; in fact, Giraldi's own collection, the certain source of *Othello,* is a probable source for *Measure for Measure* and a possible one for *Twelfth Night.*[1] Yet *Othello* is overwhelmingly tragic in movement and effect. Are the close ties to comedy at all significant,

1. Kenneth Muir, *Shakespeare's Sources* (London, 1957), pp. 70, 101–102. Italianate tragedies of domestic passion and intrigue were common enough on the contemporary stage, but *Othello* is Shakespeare's first real venture into the field. His earlier work distinguishes sharply between tragedies based on historic personages and affairs of state and comedies based on private love troubles. The exception, his early love tragedy *Romeo and Juliet,* really strengthens my point that *novelle* suggested comedic treatment to Shakespeare, as the characters and devices of comedy are prominent in the play and the tragedy is shaped by their disappearance or revealed irrelevance [see my article *"Romeo and Juliet:* Comedy into Tragedy," *Essays in Criticism,* XX (1970), 391–402].

then? I shall argue that they are, that the tragedy is generated and heightened *through* the relation to comedy rather than in spite of it, and that *Othello* develops a tragic view of love by moving from the assumptions of romantic comedy to the darker vision already articulated in some of Shakespeare's lyric poetry.

To see how this is so, we need to look at comedy, and especially at that romantic mode that was dominant in Shakespeare's comic writing in the decade or more preceding *Othello*. What are pertinent here are not the explicit themes of these plays but their common underlying assumptions about love, the values and beliefs that go largely unquestioned and unanalyzed in the dialogue but can be deduced from comic forms and conventions.

Shakespearean comedy invariably presents as all or part of its initial situation individual characters in a single and unsatisfied state and directs them through plot complications toward appropriate pairings-off at the end. Plays like *The Merchant of Venice, As You Like It, Twelfth Night,* even *The Taming of the Shrew,* find their generating tension in barriers between characters, and they stress the uneasiness of isolation even when those barriers are self-imposed. Singleness is no more satisfying to Olivia in her bored mourning or Kate in her temper tantrums than to the more approachable Rosalind and Portia. The plays' unquestioning drive toward mass marriage suggests that young individuals are to be seen as incomplete identities, the hemispheres of Aristophanes' myth in the *Symposium* which find rest and completion only in union with their opposite halves. The marriage-endings operate as symbols for full participation in life. Marriageable young people who deny or hesitate on the brink are all pushed in. The pushing may be a painful process, involving various kinds of corrective humiliation: Kate endures hunger and embarrassment, Olivia and Phebe fall in love with disguised girls, Beatrice and Benedick hear home truths about themselves in their eavesdropping, Bertram is publicly disgraced, Navarre and his men prove that "the tongues of mocking wenches are as keen / As is the razor's edge invisible."[2]

2. *Love's Labour's Lost,* V.ii.256–257. On corrective satire in the "closed world comedy," see Sherman Hawkins, "The Two Worlds of Shakespearean Comedy," *Shakespeare Studies,* III (1967), 68–73.

One basic premise of Shakespeare's comedies, then, is the value of pairing and participation. Unanimous approval extends from supernatural Oberon to bumpkin Costard; Jaques is the only significant dissenter, and even he is made to bless the Arden marriages (one of which he actively promoted) before bowing out of society to brood in his hermitage.[3] Indeed, Jaques' permanent residence in the forest has a certain irony, for his real adversary in this debate is nature itself. The naturalness of mating is explicit in some comedies (*Love's Labour's Lost,* for example), implicit in all. Those that promote release and resolution of conflicts by moving the action to an out-of-bounds locale—described for us spatially by Northrop Frye's "green world" and temporally by C. L. Barber's "holiday"[4]—give structural reinforcement to this sense of nature as love's ally. For all of the artificial and magical elements in the forests of *The Two Gentleman of Verona, A Midsummer Night's Dream,* and *As You Like It,* nature in those places is less trammeled and perverted than in the polite, treacherous court of Milan, Theseus' lawbound Athens, or the dominions where Duke Frederick sets the ethical standard by crimes against his kindred. Turned out or self-exiled from civilization, the lovers are righted and united in the woods.

Love is natural, then, as well as right. Comedy answers to our wishes in this respect, not our fears. But comedy also affirms that love is irrational and arbitrary. Here the fear is dealt with not by ignoring but by disarming it. Bottom's comment that reason and love keep little company[5] holds true generally in these comedies. Oberon's potent flower is an emblem, not only for the unreasonable passions of Titania, Lysander, and Demetrius, but for those that instantly enslave Orlando to Rosalind (but not Celia), Oliver to Celia (but not Rosalind), Navarre and his friends to the Princess and *her* friends (with balletic tidiness); and, less fortunately, Phebe to Rosalind, Proteus to Silvia, Olivia to Viola. If some of these shifts seem slightly less arbitrary than those of, say, Ariosto's characters as they veer from one course to another with each sip from the fountains of love and hate, it is only that Shakespeare has provided

---

3. *As You Like It,* III.iii.

4. Frye, "The Argument of Comedy," *English Institute Essays 1948* (New York, 1948); Barber, *Shakespeare's Festive Comedy* (Princeton, N.J., 1959).

5. *A Midsummer Night's Dream,* III.i.131–132.

for his *final* couplings an acceptable degree of compatibility in sex, rank, and temperament. But there is no suggestion that this compatibility was reasonably appraised by the lovers or that it influenced their decisions at all.

This insistence that something as vital as the love-choice is totally beyond rational control might be a disturbing note in comedy, but it is not. Bottom is untroubled by his pronouncement, and by the fairy queen's amazing dotage that provokes it. Lovers generally abandon what reason they have without a struggle, and this course appears to be the approved one: when they attempt to rationalize their new emotions, as Lysander does when the misapplied love-juice compels him to love Helena, the result fools no one.

LYSANDER

Not Hermia but Helena I love:
Who will not change a raven for a dove?
The will of man is by his reason sway'd,
And reason says you are the worthier maid.
Things growing are not ripe until their season;
So I, being young, till now ripe not to reason;
And touching now the point of human skill,
Reason becomes the marshal to my will,
And leads me to your eyes . . .

HELENA

Wherefore was I to this keen mockery born?

(II.ii.113–123)[6]

What provides the security in which we dismiss Lysander's attempts at reason with laughter and adopt instead the spirit of Bottom's "gleek"? In *Midsummer Night's Dream* the most obvious answer is Oberon: love's unreason cannot lead to destruction with this powerful and benevolent figure in charge. The other comedies we have been considering lack an Oberon, but they share what may be called an Oberon-principle. That is, the people whose extra wit and knowledge put them one up on the others are men and (more usually) women of good will.

---

6. Characters of more depth, like Helena in *All's Well That Ends Well* and Viola in *Twelfth Night*, recognize that they love against all reason, but still irrational emotion prevails over self-awareness. They go right on loving.

Rosalind deceives for Phebe's good, Helena for Bertram's, Petruchio for Kate's, Portia for Antonio's and Bassanio's. And beyond the partial control of such characters is a benevolent universe that seconds the drive of nature to unite Jack with Jill, that allows happy coincidences, adjustments, and second chances. This operative benevolence is clear in *Twelfth Night,* where no character manipulates the happy ending; rather, the comic "natural law" of Illyria dictates that shipwrecks will not be fatal and that a chance meeting will save the situation just before it crosses into irrevocability with the deaths of Antonio and Viola. The same natural law of comedy prevents Silvia's rape and Aegeon's execution by timely encounters, insures that Claudio's cruelty doesn't quite kill Hero, gives time for Dogberry and Verges to bumble their way into awareness and uncover Don John's villainy.

The convention of ending comedies with marriage promised (*Love's Labour's Lost, Two Gentlemen, Much Ado About Nothing, Twelfth Night*), or marriage celebrated (*Midsummer Night's Dream, As You Like It*), or marriage ratified emotionally or socially (*Taming of the Shrew, Merchant of Venice, All's Well That Ends Well, Twelfth Night*) has a further corollary. Comedies in this dominant pattern[7] by implication locate the important stresses and decisions of love in the courtship period. Their silence about postmarital shifts of direction suggests that there will be none, that once Jack has Jill nought can go ill—or, if couples like Touchstone and Audrey seem headed for less than perfect harmony, at least that the "story" is over.

To sum up: Shakespeare's comic forms and conventions assume (1) the value of engagement with a mate and with society at large, and (2) the cooperation of forces beyond man, natural and otherwise, in achieving this mating and forestalling the consequences of human irrationality and malice, as well as plain bad luck. To call these *assumptions* does not, of course, mean that Shakespeare or his audience accepted them without question as universally true. Rather, the playwright's use of the comic formulas and the playgoers' familiarity with them directed which aspects of their diverse perception of experience should be brought forward— wish as well as belief—and which should be held in abeyance. Comedy

---

7. Only *Merry Wives of Windsor* and *The Comedy of Errors* to some extent depart from it to find plot material in post-marital strain as well as courtship.

does not depend for its success on telling the whole truth, any more than tragedy does.

The tragic truth of *Othello* develops out of a closer look at these very assumptions about love, nature, reason. Just as such a scrutiny logically comes *after* the first unquestioning acceptance, so Othello's story is deliberately presented as post-comic. Courtship and ratified marriage, the staple of comic plots, appear in *Othello* as a preliminary to tragedy. The play's action up until the reunion of Othello and Desdemona in Act II, scene i, is a perfect comic structure in miniature. The wooing that Othello and Desdemona describe in the council scene (I.iii) has succeeded in spite of barriers of age, color, and condition of life; the machinations of villain and frustrated rival have come to nothing; the blocking father is overruled by the good Duke; and nature has cooperated in the general movement with a storm that disperses the last external threat, the Turks, while preserving the favored lovers. Othello's reunion speech to Desdemona in Cyprus underlines this sense of a movement accomplished, a still point of happiness like the final scene of a comedy:

> If it were now to die,
> 'Twere now to be most happy; for I fear
> My soul hath her content so absolute
> That not another comfort like to this
> Succeeds in unknown fate.
>
> (II.i.187–191)

But at the same time that Othello celebrates his peak of joy so markedly, his invocations of death, fear, and unknown fate make us apprehensive about the post-comic future. This impression is reinforced indirectly by Desdemona's mode of agreement ("The heavens forbid / But that our loves and comforts should increase . . .") and directly by Iago's threat ("O, you are well tun'd now! / But I'll set down the pegs that make this music . . ."). In these few lines Shakespeare has prepared us for tragedy, in part by announcing the end of comedy. The happy ending is completed, but Othello and Desdemona are left to go on from there.

If I am right to see Othello's tragedy as developing from a questioning of comic assumptions, then this initial comic movement ought to contain the seeds of tragedy. And it does, in various ways. Othello's account of their shy, storytelling-and-listening courtship, however moving and beautiful, is in retrospect slightly disturbing. "She lov'd me for the dangers I had pass'd; / And I lov'd her that she did pity them" (I.iii.167–168). Is it enough? Some critics upon this hint have proclaimed the Moor totally self-centered, incapable of real love. This is surely too severe. Nevertheless, in his summary their love has a proxy quality. "The dangers I had pass'd" have served as a counter between them, a substitute for direct engagement, or at best a preliminary to something not yet achieved. Twice before, Shakespeare had used comedy to explore the inadequacies of romantic courtship, cursorily in *Taming of the Shrew* and more thoroughly in *Much Ado*. In the latter play, Claudio and Hero move through the paces of conventional wooing, depending on rumors and go-betweens, with no direct exploration of each other's natures. Thus, Hero can be traduced and Claudio can believe it, lacking the knowledge of the heart that should counteract the false certainty of the eyes. *Much Ado* is a comedy, so the presiding deities give time for Dogberry's muddled detective work and provide in the Friar a benevolent counter-manipulator against Don John. The love of Othello and Desdemona has the same vulnerability, but no time is given; and, instead of Friar Francis, Iago is in charge.

Iago is the most obvious potential force for tragedy in the early part of the play. We see him thwarted in his first plot against Othello, but already, at the end of Act I, planning the next. In this speech both overt statement and imagery suggest the thrust beyond the comic, the germination out of the first failure of a deeper evil:

> I ha't—it is engender'd. Hell and night
> Must bring this monstrous birth to the world's light.
>
> (I.iii.397–398)

To a large extent Iago embodies in himself the play's questioning of comic assumptions. He is the most intelligent character, and reason—or the appearance of reason—is his chief means of controlling others. The *power* of the rational view, so easily dismissed with laughter or overruled by emotion in the comedies, is grimly realized in Iago's accurate estimates of character ("The Moor is of a free and open nature . . . And will as tenderly be led by th' nose . . ."), his telling arguments from experience ("I know our country disposition well: / In Venice they do let God see the pranks / They dare not show their husbands. . . . She did deceive her father, marrying you . . .") his plausible hypotheses

("That Cassio loves her, I do well believe it; / That she loves him, 'tis apt and of great credit . . ."), his final triumph in converting Othello to the philosophy of "ocular proof."[8] Against him the love of Othello and Desdemona is vulnerable, rooted as it is not in rational evaluation or empirical knowledge, but in instinctive sympathy. The same scene (I.iii) that underlines the indirectness of their courtship indicates the peculiar strength of their love that is also a weakness:

DESDEMONA

I saw Othello's visage in his mind . . .

(l. 252)

OTHELLO

My life upon her faith!

(l. 294)

There is a core of power in this instinctive mutual recognition that survives Iago's rational poison and in a sense defeats it, but this victory comes only in death. In his posing of Iago against Othello / Desdemona, Shakespeare fully explores the conventional dichotomy between reason and love and discovers its deeply tragic implications.[9]

If reason's opposition to love is traditional, nature in *Othello* appears to change sides. Love's ally is now love's enemy, partly because the angle of vision has changed: nature as instinctual rightness gives way to nature as intellectual concept, susceptible like all concepts to distortion and misapplication. Brabantio, Iago, and finally Othello himself see the love between Othello and Desdemona as unnatural—"nature erring from itself" (III.iii.231). But there is more to it than this. In key scenes of *Othello* a tension develops between two senses of "nature," the general and the particular. It is to general nature that Brabantio appeals in the council scene, the common experience and prejudice by which like calls to like. Attraction between the young white Venetian girl and the aging black

8. I.iii.393–395; III.iii.205–210; II.i.280–281; III.iii.364.

9. The irrationality of love in *Othello* has called forth some perceptive comment from critics, e.g., Winifred Nowottny, "Justice and Love in *Othello*," *UTQ*, XXI (1952), 330–344, and R. B. Heilman, *Magic in the Web* (Lexington, Ky., 1956), especially the discussion of "wit" versus "witchcraft," pp. 219–229. Terence Hawkes explores the same opposition in "Iago's Use of Reason," *SP*, LVIII (1961), 160–169, using for Heilman's wit / witchcraft the opposition of *ratio inferior / ratio superior*.

foreigner, since it violates this observed law of nature, could only have been "wrought" by unnatural means:

> She is abus'd, stol'n from me, and corrupted,
> By spells and medicines bought of mountebanks;
> For nature so preposterously to err,
> Being not deficient, blind, or lame of sense,
> Sans witchcraft could not.
>
> (I.iii.60–64)

The other sense of "nature" is particular and personal. For example, when Iago says in his soliloquy at the end of this scene that the Moor is of "a free and open nature," he uses the term to define individual essence: the inscape of Othello.

Brabantio tries to bring in this nature to support the other. Desdemona is essentially timid, thus by nature (her own) she cannot love the fearsome Moor.

> A maiden never bold,
> Of spirit so still and quiet that her motion
> Blush'd at herself; and she—in spite of nature,
> Of years, of country, credit, every thing—
> To fall in love with what she fear'd to look on!
> It is a judgment maim'd and most imperfect
> That will confess perfection so could err
> Against all rules of nature . . .
>
> (I.iii.94–101)

But this nature is the very ground of Desdemona's love. In her answer to the Venetian Senate and her father, she relates how, penetrating through the blackness and strangeness, she saw Othello's visage in his mind and subdued her heart to that essence, his "very quality" (I.iii, 250–252).[10]

For Desdemona, then, nature as individual essence is not the enemy of love. But Iago has the last word in this scene, and his conclusion is ominous: Othello's very generosity and openness will make him take the appearance of honesty for the fact. That is, Othello will act instinctively according to the laws of his own nature, rather than according to reasoned evaluation (which would perceive that most liars pretend to

10. The First Quarto has "utmost pleasure" for "very quality."

be telling the truth). This internal law of nature, then, implies the same vulnerability we have seen in the instinctive, nonrational quality of Othello's and Desdemona's love.

Brabantio's general nature is implicitly reductive in that it derives rules for individuals from the behavior of the herd. Iago's is explicitly reductive. The view he expounds to Roderigo has no regard for human values and ethical norms. Natural law for Iago, as for Edmund in *Lear,* is Hobbesian—a matter of animal appetites promoted by cleverness, with the strongest and shrewdest winning out.[11] Desdemona, he assures Roderigo, will tire of Othello because appetite demands further stimuli:

Her eye must be fed; and what delight shall she have to look on the devil? When the blood is made dull with the act of sport, there should be—again to inflame it, and to give satiety a fresh appetite—loveliness in favour, sympathy in years, manners, and beauties—all which the Moor is defective in. Now for want of these requir'd conveniences, her delicate tenderness will find itself abus'd, begin to heave the gorge, disrelish and abhor the Moor; very nature will instruct her in it, and compel her to some second choice.
                                                               (II.i.222–231)

Compel her—here is yet another "law," generalized from the ways of man's animal nature. The context is wholly physical, as the persistent images of eating and disgorging emphasize. Iago has begun the discussion by prodding the hesitant lover Roderigo with a bit of folk wisdom: "they say base men being in love have then a nobility in their natures more than is native to them" (ll. 213–214). But he does not pretend to believe it himself. Love is rather "a lust of the blood and a permission of the will"; Roderigo, in love or not, is a snipe; our natures are "blood and baseness" (I.iii.333–334; 379; 329).

In Shakespeare's portrayal of Iago we can see a version of the clash I have been describing. In spite of his reductive general view, he can recognize the essential goodness of Othello ("free and open nature," "constant, loving, noble nature . . .") as well as Desdemona's generosity and Cassio's daily beauty (I.iii.393; II.i.283; II.iii.330–331; V.i.19–20). Critics have complained of the inconsistency; and if *Othello* were naturalistic drama they would be right to do so. But Iago is not just an envious spoiler; he is the symbolic enemy of love itself. The play's

11. See J. F. Danby, *Shakespeare's Doctrine of Nature* (London, 1949), pp. 31–43.

conception demands that the weapons of both "natures," like those of reason, be put in his hands.

In his great self-summation at the play's end, Othello says he was "wrought" from his true nature, and so he was. His own nature, noble and trusting, gave him an instinctive perception of Desdemona's, a perception which breaks forth at the sight of her even while Iago is poisoning his mind: "If she be false, O, then heaven mocks itself! / I'll not believe it" (III.iii.282–283). But Iago is able to undermine this trust with false rationality, the insistence that Desdemona's honor, which is "an essence that's not seen," be made susceptible of ocular proof.[12] He succeeds, where Brabantio failed, in using both conceptions of nature against Othello. The Moor's own generosity of nature, Iago suggests, makes him an easy dupe: "I would not have your free and noble nature / Out of self-bounty be abus'd; look to't" (III.iii.203–204). Taught to look instead of trust, Othello soon sees Desdemona's choice of him as an aberration, nature erring from itself, and Iago quickly advances the general nature, the law of "all things," to reinforce the idea:

> Ay, there's the point: as—to be bold with you—
> Not to affect many proposed matches
> Of her own clime, complexion, and degree,
> Whereto we see in all things nature tends—
> Foh! one may smell in such a will most rank,
> Foul disproportion, thoughts unnatural.
>
> (III.iii.232–237)

And so Othello violates his own peculiar essence and yields to Iago's law of the many. Desdemona soon recognizes uneasily that he is altered ("My lord is not my lord") and, in an ironic reflection of Othello's state, seeks the reason in a generalization: "Men's natures wrangle with inferior things, / Though great ones are their object" (III.iv.125; 145–146). Later the Venetian visitors gaze horrified at the change in that nature that passion could not shake, while Othello strikes his wife and then exits mumbling of goats and monkeys. He has internalized Iago's reductive view of man as animal. In the next scene (IV.ii) he will see Desdemona in terms of toads mating and maggots quickening in rotten meat.

---

12. G. R. Elliott notes that under Iago's influence Othello submerges the individual nature of Desdemona in an impersonal, general conception of nature: *Flaming Minister* (Durham, N.C., 1953), p. 122.

In the comedies love was a strength, but in *Othello* it is vulnerable to attacks of reason, arguments from nature. More than that, vulnerability is its very essence. Before falling in love with Desdemona, Othello was self-sufficient, master of himself and the battlefield. After he believes her to be false, his occupation is gone. Why? Love has created a dependency, a yielding of the separate, sufficient self to incorporation with another. What comedy treated as a new completeness becomes in *Othello* the heart of tragedy. Tragic vulnerability is there, even in the play's comic phase. Othello's images for his love-commitment are those of narrowing and confining:

> But that I love the gentle Desdemona,
> I would not my unhoused free condition
> Put into circumscription and confine
> For the seas' worth . . .
>
> (I.ii.25–28)

To love totally is to give up the freedom of self for the perils of union and the expansive great world for a personal and contingent one. Othello's comparison in the last scene is significant in this connection:

> Nay, had she been true,
> If heaven would make me such another world
> Of one entire and perfect chrysolite,
> I'd not have sold her for it.
>
> (V.ii.146–149)[13]

"My life upon her faith!" is literally true. Desdemona has become Othello's world.[14]

It is in this light, I think, that we can best understand why Othello responds to Iago's insinuations by renouncing his profession. The great lines on military life notably invoke not chaos and carnage, but *order*.

---

13. The idea of Desdemona as a world also animates "I had rather be a toad, / And live upon the vapour of a dungeon, / Than keep a corner in the thing I love / For others' uses" (III.iii.274–277), and "Methinks it should be now [at Desdemona's death] a huge eclipse" (V.ii.102); it is implicit in his characterization of her as a place "where I have garner'd up my heart, / Where either I must live or bear no life" (IV.ii.58–59).

14. Theodore Spencer relates some of these speeches through the similar notion that Othello has *given* his world to Desdemona: *Shakespeare and the Nature of Man,* 2d ed. (New York, 1961), pp. 129–130, 135.

War is individual passion subordinated to a larger plan: martial harmony, formal pageantry, imitation of divine judgment.

> O, now for ever
> Farewell the tranquil mind! farewell content!
> Farewell the plumed troops, and the big wars
> That makes ambition virtue! O, farewell!
> Farewell the neighing steed and the shrill trump,
> The spirit-stirring drum, th' ear-piercing fife,
> The royal banner, and all quality,
> Pride, pomp, and circumstance, of glorious war!
> And O ye mortal engines whose rude throats
> Th' immortal Jove's dread clamours counterfeit,
> Farewell! Othello's occupation's gone.
>
> (III.iii.351–361)

Stylistically, the formal catalogues and ritual repetitions strengthen this selective picture of war as majestic order. Earlier in this scene, Othello has said that when he stops loving Desdemona chaos will come again, and now it has happened. With his own world dissolving in chaos, his ordering generalship is gone.

Othello's disintegration of self is the dark side of comedy's insistence on interdependence, on completing oneself with another. But Shakespeare goes deeper in his exploration of comic assumptions by showing that the desired merging of self and other is, in any case, impossible. The more or less schematized couplings of the comedies combined necessary opposition (male / female) with a series of sympathies in age, background, temperament. Wit calls to wit in Beatrice and Benedick, Berowne and Rosaline; royalty to royalty in Navarre and the Princess of France; rowdiness to rowdiness in Petruchio and Kate. It is enough in comedy to suggest compatibility by outward signs and to look no further than the formal union. But in *Othello* Shakespeare has taken pains in several ways to emphasize the separateness of his lovers.

In the original *novella* Giraldi's Moor is handsome, apparently fairly young, and a long-time Venetian resident. Apart from sex, his only real difference from Desdemona is one of color, and Giraldi does not dwell on it much. But Shakespeare dwells on it a great deal; black-white oppositions continually weave themselves into the verbal fabric of *Othello*. Indeed, the dark skin of Giraldi's hero, which the author capitalizes on so little, may have been one of the story's main attractions for Shakespeare. Certainly he alters other details of the story to reinforce this paradigmatic separation into black and white, to increase Othello's alienness and widen the gulf between his experience and Desdemona's. Shakespeare's Moor is a stranger to Venice, to civil life in general: his entire life, except for the brief period in which he courted Desdemona, has been spent in camp and battlefield (I.iii.83–87). Even Othello's speech constantly and subtly reminds us of his apartness. If not rude, as he claims to the council, it is certainly different. His idiom invokes anthropophagi and Pontic seas, roots itself in the exotic rather than in the details of everyday social life familiar to others but not to him. He knows as little of Venetian ways as Desdemona knows of "antres vast and deserts idle," and he is given no time to learn. While Giraldi's Moor and his bride live for some time in Venice after their marriage, Othello and Desdemona are immediately swept off to Cyprus. When Iago generalizes about his country's habits ("In Venice they do let God see the pranks / They dare not show their husbands . . ."), Othello can only answer helplessly, "Dost thou say so?" (III.iii.206–209). Shakespeare has deprived him of any common ground with Desdemona from which he can fight back—not only to facilitate Iago's deception, but to heighten the tragic paradox of human love, individuals dependent on each other but unalterably separate and mysterious to one another in their separateness. To sharpen the contrast, Othello is made middle-aged, thick-lipped—everything Desdemona is not. The image of black man and white girl in conjunction, so repellent to earlier critics that they had to invent a tawny or *café-au-lait* Moor, is basic to the play's conception of disjunction in love, giving visual focus to the other oppositions of war and peace, age and youth, man and woman. This disjunction serves the tragic action: it assists Iago's initial deception, and it provides most of the tension in the period between the deception and the murder, as Desdemona inopportunely pleads for Cassio and Othello can communicate his fears only indirectly, through insults and degradations. But beyond this plot function, it is a tragic vision of love itself.

What I am suggesting is that the action of *Othello* moves us not only as a chain of events involving particular people as initiators and victims, but as an acting out of the tragic implications in any love relationship. Iago is a human being who generates the catastrophe out of his own needs and hatreds, but he is also the catalyst who activates destructive forces not of his own creation, forces present in the love itself.[15] His image of "monstrous birth" quoted above has special significance in this regard: coming at the end of a resolved marriage scene, it suggests that the monster is a product of the marriage. He says, "it is engender'd," not "I have engendered it," because he is not parent but midwife. "Hell and night," embodied in this demidevil who works in the dark, will bring the monster forth, but it is the fruit of love itself.

Because *Othello* is a play, and a great one, tragic action and tragic situation are fully fused in it, and it would be pointless to try to separate them. But a look at some of Shakespeare's nondramatic work may help clarify the paradoxical sense of love as both life and destruction that informs the events of the play. The sonnets present a range of attitudes toward love, from joyous assurance to disgust and despair, but they return again and again to certain types of tension between lover and beloved. An apparently positive statement like Sonnet 57 ("Being your slave") belies its own assent to the relationship by the double-edged quality of phrases like "I have no precious time at all to spend" and "Nor dare I chide the world-without-end hour," and the bitter wordplay in the couplet:

> So true a fool is love that in your will,
> Though you do anything, he thinks no ill.

"So true a fool" suggests not only the loyally loving innocent, but also "so absolutely a dupe." "Fool" recalls and completes the sonnet's identification of beloved as monarch and lover as slave; he is not just any kind of servant but the king's fool, a hanger-on who is valued only for occasional diversion. The total effect is of a speaker pulled in contrary directions by need of his friend and esteem of himself.

In Sonnet 35, "No more be griev'd," images and syntax make us feel the high price that must be paid for commitment in love.

---

15. In reaching this conclusion I have been influenced by Kenneth Burke's idea of the "agent / act ratio"; see especially his *"Othello:* An Essay to Illustrate a Method," *HudR,* IV (1951), 165–203, in which he shows how the characters of Othello, Desdemona, and Iago are determined by their roles in the play's central tension, which they actualize. My view of that tension, however, differs from Burke's emphasis on love as exclusive ownership.

> No more be griev'd at that which thou hast done:
> Roses have thorns, and silver fountains mud;
> Clouds and eclipses stain both moon and sun,
> And loathsome canker lives in sweetest bud.
> All men make faults, and even I in this,
> Authorizing thy trespass with compare,
> Myself corrupting, salving thy amiss,
> Excusing thy sins more than thy sins are;
> For to thy sensual fault I bring in sense—
> Thy adverse party is thy advocate—
> And 'gainst myself a lawful plea commence;
> Such civil war is in my love and hate
>   That I an accessary needs must be
>   To that sweet thief which sourly robs from me.

If we see the poem as striving to repair the damaged relationship by creating a new equality between lover and beloved, it does indeed achieve this, but only at the cost of the speaker's own integrity. He manages to absolve the friend of fault by natural comparisons, nature having no moral dimension to justify blame, and then implicates himself in fault for making those very comparisons. The last part of the sonnet strains against the first quatrain, and in that strain lies its real impact. Can we accept the absolution given in lines 1–4 if the mode of absolution turns out to be sinful? The images reinforce this sense of disjunction, those of the first quatrain drawn exclusively from the natural world and those of the remainder from the civilized world of moral man, especially the law courts. "Civil war," finally overt in line 12, is implicit earlier in the like-sounding antitheses that shape lines 7–10 into a series of tensions. The couplet, its message of inner division supported by the difficult twisting of the last line, completes the violation of self that love has required.

The same kind of violation, expressed with less anguish and more wry acceptance, is the theme of Sonnet 138:

> When my love swears that she is made of truth,
> I do believe her, though I know she lies . . .

Here is a comic answer to the problem of integrity compromised by dependence on another, as *Othello* is a tragic answer. In its mutual accommodation reached through lies and pretenses, Sonnet 138 also underlines the other side of the paradox, the necessary separateness of lovers. Even the more idealistic sonnets never proclaim the possibility of complete union; and the most idealistic of all presents quite an opposite picture, of love persisting on its own in spite of the beloved's infidelity:

> Love is not love
> Which alters when it alteration finds,
> Or bends with the remover to remove.
> . . . .
> Love alters not with his brief hours and weeks,
> But bears it out even to the edge of doom.
>
> (Sonnet 116)

It is selfless but ultimately single, more like God's love for man than any human relationship. Edward Hubler sees in Sonnet 116 Shakespeare's affirmation of mutuality as the essence of love,[16] but it seems to me just the contrary, a recognition that the love which depends on being requited is neither lasting nor true. It must necessarily bend with the remover, meet defection with defection.

Enduring mutuality does not seem to be a possibility in the sonnets. When Shakespeare does address himself to the merging of separate identities, the result is the rarefied allegory of "The Phoenix and Turtle," which makes the impossibility even clearer. Phoenix and turtle dove are a perfect union, but they are dead. Most of the poem is a dirge sung at their funeral, and it ends in complete stasis—triplets with a single rhyme sound asserting that these lovers left no progeny, that what they represented is gone forever.

> Leaving no posterity—
> 'Twas not their infirmity,
> It was married chastity.
>
> Truth may seem, but cannot be;
> Beauty brag, but 'tis not she:
> Truth and beauty buried be.
>
> (ll. 59–64)

What do we make of this? It could be argued that "The Phoenix and Turtle" approaches "pure poetry" in being all vehicle with no tenor; certainly it is hard to relate these dead birds and their metaphysical-paradoxical union to the affairs of mortal men and women. Do phoenix and turtle die because annihilation is implicit in perfect union, or because

16. *The Sense of Shakespeare's Sonnets* (Princeton, N.J., 1952), pp. 92–93.

their obliteration of distance, number, and individuality offends against natural law, or because such perfection is possible only outside of time? In any case, the poem makes it clear that the ideal will never again be realized on earth.

The dead-end quality of "The Phoenix and Turtle" illuminates tragic love in *Othello* in one way, just as the sonnets' tensions and compromises do in another. In the opening lines of 36, the sonnets, indeed, provide the most succinct statement of the paradox I have been examining in *Othello*:

> Let me confess that we two must be twain,
> Although our undivided loves are one . . .

In the comedies Shakespeare viewed the coming together of incomplete opposites from a certain intellectual distance. In *Othello* he struck a vein of tragedy by exploring the contradiction within such a conception: destruction of self-sufficiency combined with continued isolation in the self. This was, it seems, his general way in *Othello*. Starting from a romantic story in which love goes wrong, he was sufficiently reminded of his own comic patterns and assumptions to manipulate them consciously in the play, creating the tragic mood (which is lacking in Giraldi's brisk tale of intrigue) by looking more deeply into the ambiguities and vulnerabilities of romantic love.

I have been emphasizing the internal flaws of Othello's and Desdemona's love, but it should not be overlooked that the play nevertheless celebrates that love fully. Maynard Mack's comment on *King Lear* may serve us here as well:

Cordelia, we may choose to say, accomplished nothing, yet we know it is better to have been Cordelia than to have been her sisters.[17]

So with *Othello*. At the end the lovers are dead and their destroyer is still alive, but we know that it is better to have been Othello and Desdemona than to be Iago.

After I had reached my own conclusions on *Othello*, I came upon a similar emphasis in John Middleton Murry's *Shakespeare*. For him, *Othello* is the great tragedy of human love, expressing "the pain and anguish and despair which true lovers must inevitably inflict upon one

17. *King Lear in our Time* (Berkeley and Los Angeles, 1965), p. 117.

another, because they are one, and because they are not one."[18] Iago is central to the tragedy, not merely as an intriguer but as the embodiment of love's inevitable flaw.[19] This reinforcement of my reading of the play was welcome, especially since Murry's starting point was quite different from mine. He began with the handkerchief, and the paradoxical fact that Desdemona forgets to be concerned for it because she is concerned about Othello's sudden illness. That is, she loses the love-token because she loves.

To call *Othello* a tragic statement about love in general is not to see it as the vehicle of "Shakespeare's philosophy of love." It is one artistic whole, and it expresses one kind of perception, which is demonstrably different not only from that of the romantic comedies but also from those of *Troilus and Cressida, Antony and Cleopatra,* the late romances. No one of these cancels out the others; they are all part of Shakespeare's truth. *Othello* is not an allegory, but a very human drama. Nevertheless, its exploration of romantic love and marriage does give *Othello* a universal dimension, the wider reverberations that many critics have felt to be lacking in the play. We have perhaps spent too much time asking the traditional questions about this play: is Othello culpable in succumbing to Iago's suggestions? and what makes Iago do what he does? These are important questions, but it is also important to see beyond the individual events of *Othello,* beyond the defeat of a more or less noble dupe by an obscurely motivated villain, to the tragic inadequacies and contradictions of all human love.

18. *Shakespeare* (London, 1936), pp. 316–317.
19. *Ibid.,* p. 319.

Visual and Aural Signs in the Performed English Renaissance Play

BROWNELL SALOMON

A N IMPORTANT TREND in modern Renaissance drama criticism has been to allow presentational elements like costume, gesture, and properties a status in "practical," explicative criticism equal to that enjoyed by rhetorical elements like imagery and metaphor, which have been prime matter for analysis since the advent of the New Criticism. In the wake of an influential 1949 essay by the late Alan S. Downer,[1] which made use of such terms as the "language" of props, setting and action, "imagery in action" and "costume as symbol," there emerged in style studies a fresh awareness that the domain of drama criticism is the play not merely as verbal matrix, but as *dromenon*—something to be performed.[2] Pro-

---

1. "The Life of Our Design: The Function of Imagery in the Poetic Drama" has been reprinted in two popular anthologies of Shakespearean criticism, most recently in *Modern Shakespearean Criticism,* ed. Alvin B. Kernan (New York, 1970), pp. 30–44.

2. See, for example, R. A. Foakes, "Suggestions for a New Approach to Shakespeare's Imagery," *ShS,* V (1952), 81–92; T. W. Craik, *The Tudor Interlude: Stage, Costume, and Acting* (1958; rpt. Leicester, 1967), esp. Chaps. 3, "Dress," and 4, "Changes of Costume"; Maurice Charney, *Shakespeare's Roman Plays: The Function of Imagery in the Drama* (Cambridge, Mass., 1961), who uses the word image "in two distinct senses, one verbal and the other nonverbal," and coins the term "presentational imagery" (p. 7); Charney's *Style in "Hamlet"* (Princeton,

fessor Downer and others can be praised for helping to bridge that traditional gap between theatrical and literary criticism through the application of a modern, total concept of style: one directed toward a thematic understanding of the whole work. Yet one notes that these critics rely upon terminology derived from *literary* stylistics, often straining the terminology to embrace nonverbal elements. The unique requirements of the drama, however, might be better served by a thoroughly interdisciplinary approach to the two diverse but still complementary modes —discursive and presentational—by which meaning is communicated in the theater. An interdisciplinary method would provide the best theoretical base from which a critic's attention could properly range beyond words spoken aloud by actors, to include as integral to the playwright's aesthetic blueprint the many explicit and latent stage directions in the text. The present essay attempts to show the ways in which semiology, the general science of signs, provides interpretive criticism of the drama with an instrument for organizing verbal and nonverbal elements systematically so that they might be analyzed in line with any thematic strategy. The advantage of the semiological technique is that, in providing a unifying way to approach the complex epistemology of a performed play, it first accepts the play as a gestalt, a composite of interrelated "signs"; then, each of the component sign systems (language, costume, music, hand props, etc.) is allowed to be the focus of orderly analysis.

Semiology, as a modern discipline of communications, had its origin in Ferdinand de Saussure's posthumously compiled lectures on linguistics, the *Cours de Linguistique Générale* (1916); but before and after World War II, Continental theorists like Jan Mukařovský and Roland Barthes began to apply the theory of sign to literature and the arts. Nowadays, the possibilities which an intelligent use of semiology holds out to students of literature are being recognized by Anglo-American critics as

---

N.J., 1969), where style is interpreted "in its widest sense, which includes *all the means of expression* used by an author to accomplish his purposes; in this broad meaning it would designate the *imaginative embodiment of a theme* in an individual and distinctive manner" (p. xvii; italics mine); and J. L. Styan, *Shakespeare's Stagecraft* (Cambridge, 1967), much of whose discussion of symbolic hand properties, gestures, costumes, stage movement, and vocal tone (cf. pp. 30–36, 58–68, 141–192) complements my own.

well.[3] Even so, the fact remains that until now developing uses for semiology in the arts has been a European endeavor. Indeed, the pioneer article bringing semiotic technique to the theater is by Tadeusz Kowzan, a Pole who now resides in Paris.[4] Kowzan asserts that "Everything is sign in a theatrical presentation," and in semiological terms this is obviously true. But the matter is not so easily concluded for the interpretive critic, who, as he makes the science of sign serve the art of criticism, must select discriminatingly from a congeries of phenomena in a theatrical performance on the basis of *relevancy* to his own critical strategy. On this basis, all of the verbal, visual, and aural data occurring in a performed play could be ranked as to function on an ascending scale, evolving from the most concrete insignificancy up to essentializing abstraction, from the merest naturalism up to ritual. It seems desirable, then, that a semiological method offer easily recognizable categories whereby critically relevant signs can be distinguished from those that are not. Fortunately, there already exists for the theory of sign a threefold classification of semiotic "messages" that is readily adaptable as a means of organizing theatrical data hierarchically according to function and relevancy. This is the triad of signals, signs, and symbols (respectively, "pure instinctive action, reflex action, and symbolically-conditioned action") which was set forth in Alfred N. Whitehead's 1927 lecture, *Symbolism: Its Meaning and Effect* (New York, 1959), and later supported by Ernst Cassirer and Arthur F. Bentley.[5] I will shortly provide working definitions of these terms as they are applicable in drama criticism.

But at the outset one must recognize that when sign classifications have been applied to literary criticism, definitions have tended to blur because of a lack of uniform usage. In his classic study of the subject, William York Tindall noted that "The words symbol and sign are commonly interchangeable, yet at times some of us mean one thing by sign and another by symbol. That is a cause of trouble and this is

3. See Graham Hough, *Style and Stylistics* (London, 1969), p. 109; René Wellek, *Discriminations: Further Concepts of Criticism* (New Haven, Conn., 1970), p. 295.

4. Tadeusz Kowzan, "The Sign in the Theater: An Introduction to the Semiology of the Art of the Spectacle," *Diogenes*, no. 61 (1968), 52–80.

5. Lawrence K. Frank, "The World as a Communications Network," in *Sign, Image, Symbol,* ed. Gyorgy Kepes (New York, 1966), p. 3.

another: sign, taken to mean exact reference, may include symbol, and symbol, taken to mean a suggestive device, may include sign." [6] Warily, recognizing the "trouble" attending sign and symbol, I will introduce the third term, signal, as a special designation for signs in the theater that are not thematically relevant. Though signal normally refers to the lowest order of stimuli, following Pavlovian usage, this term need not always be so limitedly defined. Indeed, there are instances when signal is interchangeable with sign, much as sign is interchangeable with symbol. Signal can be fulfilled of its potential for higher levels of import —can be transformed to sign—because of an a priori disposition of the human mind to impose form on sense data, to perceive sensory experiences unconsciously as receptacles of meaning. [7] It is in this meaning-laden sense, then, that the term signal is adopted in this paper.

In spite of the difficulty in arriving at precise definitions for symbol, sign, and signal as terms for drama criticism, their usefulness as guides to critical function and significancy justifies their wide acceptance even in the form of provisional definitions. One simply bears in mind that, as these terms are applied to categories of theatric phenomena, the categories are not to be thought of as being mutually exclusive. The three orders comprise, in fact, an evolutionary pyramid in which signal is subsumed in sign, and both signal and sign are subsumed in the most complex order, symbol. Differences among them are ones of degree rather than kind, for it will be apparent that all three may involve figurative meanings such as are conveyed through metaphors, tropes, allegorical situations, and the like. Symbol and sign, however, designate the only pertinent semiological data in English Renaissance plays, and will be the central focus of the pages that follow; signal is the lowest category, a negative one with regard to relevancy, and it is applied to any theatric percept which, in *critical* terms at least, is inconsequential.

Here, then, are working definitions of sign categories which may be useful to drama criticism:

6. *The Literary Symbol* (New York, 1955), pp. 5–6.

7. Susanne K. Langer, *Philosophy in a New Key,* 3d ed. (1942; rpt. Cambridge, Mass., 1960), pp. 89–90. Cf. Charles Morris, *Signification and Significance* (Cambridge, Mass., 1964), p. 64: ". . . it would be possible to develop a semiotic which included . . . 'signals' as signs."

SYMBOL: *a theatrical sign that functions in the capacity of an aesthetic symbol by connoting, suggesting, or standing for its referent by reason of an imputed relationship, association, or convention; a communicable unit that serves as the physical vehicle for a conception evoked supralogically by it.*

SIGN: *an aural, visual, verbal, or (though rarely) olfactory datum that is explicitly demanded by the playwright's text (or that would arise inevitably therefrom during a "faithful" theatrical performance), which denotes or represents a preassigned (by convention) expressive or ideational content; contextualized in a play, it assumes interpretive relevance to the whole work.*

SIGNAL: *a sensory-perceptual / verbal datum, which, though experienced from a theatrical performance, is not pertinent to interpretive criticism; ideational or emotive content of sorts there may be, but it is gratuitous to critical exegesis of the play (e.g., imagery with incidental thematic value; actors' involuntary, natural gestures; physical realia [props, costumes, etc.] unparticularized by the dramatist, which merely complement a given setting).*

By way of example, a prominent hand property in Chekhov's *The Cherry Orchard*—a pocket watch that is habitually glanced at—will demonstrate the foregoing categories and suggest how varying levels of meaning may inhere in the same detail. The boorish merchant Lopahin consults his watch some half-dozen times in that play, and recurrent use only strengthens the prop's operation as *sign:* a conventional mannerism that denotes Lopahin's Philistine efficiency at the same time that it brings the indecisiveness of Lyubov Ranevsky and her circle into sharp relief. But Lopahin's conspicuous watch also functions as *symbol:* a graphic reminder that reality impinges upon Lyubov's world, and that "time is running out." In its indifferent use by another character (by Dunyasha in the play's opening minutes, for example), a watch is without metaphoric effect and may be designated *signal*. Perhaps the most extreme example of interpenetrating levels of meaning in Renaissance drama is afforded by Middleton's *A Game at Chess*. The satirical energy of that play can, in a real sense, be said to depend upon the continuous tension between signal (the milieu of courtly ceremony), sign (chess combat as the mode of action), and symbol (the moral and political allegory).

It is, however, when the three categories are called upon to interpret specific dramatic functions of sense data in particular plays that they will be of greatest practical use to criticism. If, for example, one were setting out to make a complete semiological analysis of Middleton's *A Chaste Maid in Cheapside,* one might elect to approach the play spatially, in line with certain major elements of its thematic structure (e.g., gold in its commercial aspect, the human bodily processes, or the paradoxical Lenten fasting from meat) in order to deal with each motif in some unifying, coherent way. Or, another possible strategy might be to treat the play's semiological data chronologically, in the same order that a theatrical performance would unfold them to an audience. Accordingly, among the first data to be presented in *A Chaste Maid* is the decor, which the opening stage direction stipulates in *"Enter* Maudline *and* Moll, *a shop being discovered"* (I.i.). Middleton's decision to have his setting—Yellowhammer's goldsmith shop in the heart of London's Cheapside ward—not merely alluded to, but given continuous visual reinforcement throughout the first scene, invites inquiry as to its dramatic implications. The existence of a goldsmith's gilt-painted placard or heraldic device above the shop can be inferred from historical evidence; Yellowhammer's balance scales are explicitly called for (l. 93). How variously, then, in terms of signal, sign, and symbol, might the significance of these collective, scenographic details be interpreted? To the commentator who can find no particular critical importance in them, other than as incidental evidence perhaps of Middleton the social realist documenting Jacobean London in "photographic" detail, such data should be designated signal, as defined above. T. S. Eliot's reading of Middleton's comedies in *Elizabethan Essays* (London, 1934) comes to mind. But to the commentator who weighs the mercantile associations of the decor in relation to the dramatic situation which Maudline Yellowhammer and her daughter play before it early in the scene, the setting clearly reflects thematically upon Moll's predicament. The shop is a sign —a theatrical datum functioning metaphorically—that points up the fact that Moll's parents, especially her badgering mother, view her marriageability as but a saleable, retail commodity that could bring in

"Two thousand pound . . . in goldsmith's ware" (ll. 22–23). Another dramatic idea being developed at the same time in the scene is the sexual suggestiveness of Maudline, in both her language ("quick," "he miss'd me not a night," "piece of flesh," etc.) and in the mincing, insinuative gestures (ll. 48–52) which she believes are a model of seductiveness for her daughter. The resulting interplay of commercialism and vulgar sexuality contrasts strongly with the values of Moll, who represents an incongruous vitality and innocence in Cheapside and who must weep (l. 5) out of suppressed frustration. Contributing as they do to the play's over-all effect, these particular semiological facts work together, as symbol, to express meaning on the intensional, connotative level: namely, that the world of the play has for a decadent norm the reduction of human relations to crassly physical dimensions, or to barter transactions. Shortly afterward, Middleton caps this twofold idea emblematically with the arrival (l. 93 s.d.) of Moll's antitype, Sir Walter Whorehound's red-haired Welsh doxy.

At the most palpable level, then, a play's unity of style, form, and content is to be found in the aggregate of its sign data. A datum may have autonomous sign value apart from its dramatic context (as, for example, the act of weeping can be denotative of sadness or pain); or its function in a particular play may be determined by any of several aspects of formalist criticism.[8] Insights derivable from the data are limited only by the critic's powers of creative synthesis and the knowledges (biographical, ideological, historical, psychological, literary, etc.) he brings to his task. Any performed play, because it is so integral and controlled a context, can be expected to abound in purposeful signals, signs, and symbols. The last two categories, though, are especially appropriate

---

8. E.g., juxtaposition; sequence; recurrency; cumulation, either in a spatial or temporal frame of reference; shifting contexts that alter a vehicle-tenor relationship; synchronous signs of different orders (language and gesture, say) complementing one another positively or negatively; multiple denotations or connotations (plurisignation); signs creating parallelism or analogy between plot and subplot, or a *liaison des scènes*. For the last-named facets of structure see William R. Elton, *"King Lear" and the Gods* (San Marino, Calif., 1966), Chap. 11, "Irony as Structure"; David P. Young, *Something of Great Constancy* (New Haven, Conn., 1966), pp. 97–106, on "mirroring scenes"; Richard Levin, *The Multiple Plot in English Renaissance Drama* (Chicago, 1971), esp. pp. 1–20.

discernments for plays written for a Renaissance auditory, for whom the theater, civic pageantry, and the masque were expectedly emblematic, and whose world view was predicated on metaphor and symbolism.

I

From a discussion of how sign theory can be useful to drama criticism, we turn now to a consideration of the histrionic sign systems themselves. Signal, sign, and symbol, it has been shown, are the evaluative concepts that discriminate sense data according to their function in a performed play; sign systems, on the other hand, constitute the diverse physical forms or modes in which sense data occur in a play. When used in conjunction with one another, the concepts and sign systems afford a method of subjecting any individual play to an intensive analysis governed by the critic's own perspective. For the present, though, it suffices just to outline the various sign systems. My discussion is plainly indebted to the earlier-mentioned essay of Tadeusz Kowzan, not only for many comprehensive definitions but for minor refinements as well. However, in adopting Kowzan's sign classifications, in the interest of greater simplicity and utility for early English drama, I reduce their number from thirteen to eleven by absorbing *facial mime* into *gesture* and *hairstyle* into *make-up*. It is a compliment to Kowzan's theory that it can so readily become the basis of a more specialized purpose: to review in semiological terms, alluding to the widest possible range of examples, the manifold ways that thematic meaning is communicated in Renaissance plays.

LANGUAGE. Until recently the words of a play were assumed to be its principal reality, and the ways in which drama differs from other literary forms were virtually excluded from consideration. Language is so much more important than any other sign category, and is so broadly the subject of critical scrutiny, that a demonstration of its significance need hardly be extensive. Linguistic signs perform the identical semantic and expressive functions for drama as for written literature. Northrop Frye's restatement of the Aristotelian term for poetic diction (*lexis*) in the glossary of his *Anatomy of Criticism* (Princeton, N.J., 1957) serves well to define this category: "The verbal 'texture' or rhetorical aspect of a work of literature, including the usual meanings of the terms 'diction' and 'imagery.' " Elizabethan drama has benefited from the modern demand that literary texts be closely read, and book-length studies of verbal imagery in particular have been typically of high quality. Examples that come to mind are Robert B. Heilman's *This Great Stage* (Lexington, Ky., 1948) and *Magic in the Web* (Lexington, Ky., 1956), on *King Lear* and *Othello,* respectively; G. Wilson Knight's *The Crown of Life* (London, 1947) and Donald A. Stauffer's *Shakespeare's World of Images* (New York, 1949), both notable for close, thematic readings of Shakespeare's late romances; Edward B. Partridge's *The Broken Compass* (New York, 1958), on Jonson's use of comically indecorous metaphor; and the above-mentioned studies by Maurice Charney.

In addition to its purely semantic dimension, however, language can perform other semiological functions at the phonological, syntactic, or prosodic level (Kowzan, p. 62). In Shakespeare's *Henry V,* for example, there is phonological sign value in Pistol's habit of making alliterations like "vaunted veins" and "mickle might." One effect of their stilted, pseudoarchaic quality is to represent Pistol as a parody of the heroic ideal which the main plot embodies in King Henry. Also common in Renaissance drama is the symbolic use of language that involves syntactic (in prose) and prosodic (in verse) devices such as formally ordered dialogue, balanced or parallel clauses, or verse-patterning figures like stichomythia, anaphora, and epiphora. Striking examples are the incantatory laments of Queen Margaret and the Duchess of York in *Richard III* (IV.iv), and, earlier in that play, the Queen's litany of execration against Richard:

> Thou slander of thy heavy mother's womb,
> Thou loathed issue of thy father's loins,
> Thou rag of honour, thou detested—
>
> (I.iii.231–233)[9]

9. On "patterned speech" see M. C. Bradbrook, *Themes & Conventions of Elizabethan Tragedy* (1935; rpt. Cambridge, 1960), pp. 97–109; and Angus Fletcher, *Allegory: The Theory of a Symbolic Mode* (Ithaca, N.Y., 1964), pp. 161–172, who also discusses the ritual form of cursing, pp. 205–208.

All Shakespearean references in *Renaissance Drama* are to the Alexander edition. Regents Renaissance editions are used for the citations from Chapman's *All Fools,* ed. Frank Manley, and *Bussy D'Ambois,* ed. Robert J. Lordi; Ford's *The Broken Heart,* ed. Donald K. Anderson, Jr., and *'Tis Pity She's A Whore,* ed. N. W. Baw-

In both instances a monotonous, archetypal rhythm is achieved through word order, and the effect is formal and allegorical, not simply one of aesthetic heightening: for the ceremonial style befits a purpose to "ascend the sky" (l. 287), to elicit that divine aid which, in the last scene, will actually be deemed the efficient cause of Richard's downfall.

VOCAL TONE. Words spoken in the theater may have their literal meanings qualified by the playwright's indications for pronunciation.[10] Vocal tone may therefore be as important an index of a dramatic character's attitude, and of the standards by which he is to be judged, as the language he utters. Tone, as a sign system, corresponds to what is embraced by melopoeia—all aspects of language connected with, or analogous to, music: intonation (including pitch, inflection, and quality of vocal sound), rhythm, pause, speed, and intensity. As Kowzan suggests (p. 63), unique accents (e.g., country, aristocratic, regional, foreign) will also be considered a function of vocal tone. In Marston's *The Dutch Courtesan,* for example, the exotic accent of the perfidious Franceschina ("Dere sall noting tought good for me, but dat is mischievous for others," IV.iii.42–43) is, throughout, an ever-present cachet of her social and moral alienation in London, where she is known to be "as prostituted and

---

cutt; Jonson's *Catiline,* eds. W. F. Bolton and Jane F. Gardner; Lyly's *Gallathea,* ed. Anne Begor Lancashire; Marston's *The Dutch Courtesan* and *The Malcontent,* ed. M. L. Wine; Middleton's *Michaelmas Term,* ed. Richard Levin; Tourneur's *The Revenger's Tragedy,* ed. Lawrence J. Ross; and Webster's *The Devil's Law-Case,* ed. Frances A. Shirley. Revels Plays editions are used to cite from Middleton's *A Chaste Maid in Cheapside,* ed. R. B. Parker; Middleton and Rowley's *The Changeling,* ed. N. W. Bawcutt; Tourneur's *The Atheist's Tragedy,* ed. Irving Ribner; and Webster's *The Duchess of Malfi* and *The White Devil,* ed. John Russell Brown. New Mermaid editions are used in citations from Kyd's *The Spanish Tragedy,* ed. J. R. Mulryne; and Middleton's *Women Beware Women,* ed. Roma Gill. Yale Ben Jonson editions are used to cite from *Bartholomew Fair,* ed. Eugene M. Waith; *Volpone,* ed. Alvin B. Kernan; and *The Complete Masques,* ed. Stephen Orgel. Marlovian references are to *The Complete Plays of Christopher Marlowe,* ed. Irving Ribner (New York, 1963). Citations from Dekker's *The Shoemaker's Holiday* are from the edition of J. B. Steane (Cambridge, 1965); for *Old Fortunatus* the reference is to *The Dramatic Works of Thomas Dekker,* ed. Fredson Bowers (Cambridge, 1953–1961), Vol. I.

10. See related discussions by Cleanth Brooks and Robert P. Warren, *Modern Rhetoric,* Shorter 3d ed. (New York, 1972), pp. 332–349; and Thomas F. Van Laan, *The Idiom of Drama* (Ithaca, N.Y., 1970), pp. 149–155, on "sound patterns."

adulterate, as some translated manuscript" (ll. 7–8). In *Bartholomew Fair,* by having three major regional British dialects (Scottish, Somersetshire, and Irish) represented by three "vaporous" characters who come together at one time (IV.iv), Jonson pointedly develops his theme of the Fair as a microcosm of English appetite and quarrelsomeness. Among the melopoeic elements, intonation offers probably the widest semical possibilities. For his *Volpone* Jonson made notable use of it in characterizing the old roundback "crow," Corbaccio, whose croaking speech verges on animal mimicry; and, as this occurs within the pervasive beast-fable context, it becomes a symbolization of human depravity.

Modulations in vocal intensity have an ethical significance of their own in Marston's *The Malcontent.* Surrounded by every sort of immorality in a usurper's court, Malevole, who is the rightful duke in disguise, personifies disvalued justice and virtue as he is forced to speak *sotto voce* to his confidant ("Peace, speak low. . . . How is't? Speak low . . . trees have ears," I.iv.2; III.iii.2–3), to dissemble in order to survive ("Malevole *shifteth his speech,*" I.iv.43 s.d.). We are aware that the Elizabethan conventions of the aside or the stage whisper, which require changes in tone as mentioned above, are ways of making a remark at the expense of a third party who supposedly cannot hear. An interesting usage of this device, and one which serves as a self-expressive tour de force of deception in a play where hypocrisy is a controlling motif, occurs in that episode in Webster's *The White Devil* (I.ii.123–144) where Flamineo speaks fulsome compliments aloud for Camillo's overhearing, but constantly undercuts them in mid-sentence with insults directed aside to Vittoria. If it is easily inferable that a speech is meant to be delivered at a rapid pace, that fact itself may be seen as a semiological effect. For example, when the Notary reads aloud Cornelio's bill of divorcement against Gazetta in Chapman's *All Fools* (IV.i.305–330), no less than a full minute is needed to recite that mouthful of legal jargon, even at top speed. In purely denotative terms—that is, on the meaning level of sign —the technical diction and the monotonous, singsong cadence of the speech provide but another instance of anti-lawyer satire in the play (cf. II.i.300–346). Seen symbolically, however, as expressive equivalents of Cornelio's married love, which Cornelio has already tainted by his suspicion and would now by passionless legalisms wholly destroy, the speech and its tonality have added relevance.

GESTURE. To be brought to life in performance, all plays require actors to effect bodily movements or attitudes. Every purposeful shrug, wave, or mime indicated by the text may be a kinesthetic sign laden with meaning. Perceptive Renaissance audiences must have noted an agreement between linguistic and bodily means of communication, between rhetoric and action, for so-called *"Rhetoricall* daunsing" or *"Histrionicall Rhetorike"* was but as easy extension of classical rhetorical theory.[11] Where movement joins with metaphor to create a signifying "dance" (i.e., a kinetic expression of an idea not fully statable in words alone), modern criticism can find much of importance. It may take the form of meaningful patterns, like those of "Stabbing; rising; falling; leading; following; gathering; dispersing; shaking hands, weeping, and other 'shows of love,'" which have been discerned in *Julius Caesar*.[12] Or perhaps a coherent gestural idea may dominate an entire scene, affecting our interpretation of all that went before or comes after. Gestures associated with melancholia in all its forms, including insanity, are an example of such a pattern. In Webster's *The White Devil,* one recalls Bracciano's horrible suffering from a poison-induced madness. Inasmuch as a stage direction assigns special emphasis to gestures (*"These speeches are several kinds of distraction and in the action should appear so,"* V.iii.82 s.d.), in their performance we become aware that Bracciano's convulsions are graphic metaphors that augment many verbal allusions to madness and poison to magnify the theme of courtly decadence. In two other Jacobean tragedies the appearance of several madmen performs an essential symbolic function: the dancing, singing, and lunatic gesticulations are actional images which give form to terror and evil infecting the playworld. The antic, gibbering madmen sent by Duke Ferdinand as mental torture for the imprisoned Duchess have the identical semantic effect in Webster's *The Duchess of Malfi* (IV.ii.60–114). Similarly, in Middleton and Rowley's *The Changeling* (III.iii) the inmates of Alibius' asylum who imitate the appearance, sounds, and gestures of animals depict emblematically the crucial unity of madness and uncontrolled sexuality

11. Cornelius Agrippa, *Of the Vanitie and uncertaintie of Artes and Sciences,* trans. James Sanford (1569; rpt. London, 1575), pp. 32–33.

12. Robert Hapgood, "Speak Hands for Me: Gesture as Language in *Julius Caesar,"* DramS, V (1966), 162.

in the play. Frequently, a gesture may be a complex dramatic image, as when Lady Macbeth seems to wash the blood from her hands in mime during her sleepwalking scene (*Macbeth,* V.i). Associations of personal torment, the indelibility of guilt, and the consequences of evil are evoked at that dramatic moment. Sometimes a character's entire body can be said to have indexical value, as when the limping gaits of Richard III, Don John (*Much Ado About Nothing,* III.iii.113–116), and Caliban (*The Tempest,* I.ii.283–284; V.i.268) become means of figuring forth ethical deformities; conversely, Rafe Damport's limp in Dekker's *The Shoemaker's Holiday* involves pathos as it recalls battlefield sacrifices made to acquit social duty and the honor of fellow shoemakers ("Hector of Troy was an hackney to him, Hercules and Termagant scoundrels," I.i.171–172).

Certain gestures have meanings familiar to an initiated audience. More codifiable than everyday, conventional gestures (as a handshake is a universal sign of amity), these gestures are hyperconventional signs, such as the ones used in religious ritual or in the stylized drama of Japan. The meaning of any one gesture derives from ideas associated with an entire mimetic category. There are many examples in Renaissance drama. When Othello and Iago kneel to swear execration and revenge against Cassio (*Othello,* III.iii), theirs is a sacramental gesture intended to ritualize heavenly approval for Othello's plan ("In the due reverence of a sacred vow . . . ," l. 465). In *Shakespeare's Stagecraft,* J. L. Styan correctly states that the irony of this gesture depends upon its religious symbolism (p. 63). Similarly, in Marlowe's *Doctor Faustus* a satanic parody of the Mass is given visual force when Faustus, intoning a Latin invocation to the infernal trinity, makes the sign of the cross (*"signumque crucis quod nunc facio,"* I.iii.20–21). This gesture reinforces other semantic ironies, such as "necromantic books are heavenly" and "pray devoutly to the prince of hell" (I.i.51; I.iii.54), to demonstrate Faustus' religious heterodoxy. In the piazza scene of *Volpone* (II.iii), where a disguised Volpone woos Corvino's wife, a unique mode of satire results from the fact that the theatrical situation and its appropriate gestures derive from Italian *commedia dell'arte.* In the course of this episode, Volpone, Nano, Celia, and Corvino "become" the *commedia's* stock characters, Flamineo, Zan Fritada, Franciscina, and Pantalone.

MOVEMENT. Both categories of kinesthetic signs, an actor's bodily

gestures and his movements on stage, complement one another and are
sometimes inseparable. For our purposes movement is confined to two
provinces of semiological importance: first, the significance of an actor's
bodily positions in relation to those of other actors on stage, or to the
surrounding scenic space; and secondly, the sign value of movement qua
movement by one or more actors. The first province concerns the spatial
organization of actors in the playing area into patterns that are not only
naturalistic, but also meaningfully artificial, schematic, or diagrammatic.
Of particular importance are English scenic techniques involving dumb
shows, allegorical tableaux, or emblematic staging, whose influences can
be seen in the traditions of popular pageantry, *tableaux vivants,* and allegorical processions,[13] and in the close Renaissance tie between graphic
and poetic arts, especially evident in the iconography of contemporary
emblem books.[14] In *Richard III,* for example, the villainous Richard and
the Earl of Richmond, who as Henry VII is shortly to be England's
savior, personify ethical opposites which are simultaneously contrasted
by means of nonnaturalistic staging. At Bosworth Field, before the battle,
where both men lie asleep in tents placed at opposite sides of the stage,
positioning serves to externalize the antithetic nature of good and evil.
In addition, both men are visited by the ghosts of Richard's eleven victims, who alternately wish prosperity to the one and death to the other
("God and good angels fight on Richmond's side; / And Richard falls in
height of all his pride," V.iii.175-176). Positioning an actor at an upper
level of the stage can be an ideogrammatic statement of his proximity to
"higher" powers, or a reminder that he represents supernatural values.
Prospero's overseeing from aloft the temptation of Antonio and Sebastian
with a magic banquet has this connotation in *The Tempest* ("*Solemn
and strange music; and* Prospero *on the top, invisible,*" III.iii.17 s.d.).
Jupiter's theophany in *Cymbeline* (V.iv) and the ascent to heaven of the
Good Angel's throne in Marlowe's *Doctor Faustus* (V.ii) are other instances where there is semantic content in positioning, or in a spatial

13. See Alice S. Venezky, *Pageantry on the Shakespearean Stage* (New York,
1951); Dieter Mehl, *The Elizabethan Dumb Show* (Cambridge, Mass., 1966);
David M. Bergerson, *English Civic Pageantry, 1558–1642* (Columbia, S.C., 1971).

14. See Dieter Mehl, "Emblems in English Renaissance Drama," *RenD,* N.S. II
(1969), 39–57; Stephen Orgel, "The Poetics of Spectacle," *NLH,* II (1971), 367–389;
and the several essays devoted to the subject in *RORD,* XIII–XIV (1970–1971).

relationship. In Ford's *'Tis Pity She's a Whore,* there is symbolic fitness in Annabella's standing above the stage when she repents of her incestuous affair with her brother Giovanni. Friar Bonaventura, standing below, overhears and confirms her reconciliation with "higher" morality, saying, "Lady, Heaven hath heard you" (V.i.37).

Movement qua movement has sign value in *Richard II,* when the King's literal descent from the walls of Flint Castle to the "base court" below adumbrates a fall from power ("Down, down I come, like glist'ring Phaëthon," III.iii.178). Similarly, in Marlowe's *1 Tamburlaine,* IV.ii, the play's central action is momentarily epitomized *en tableau,* when Tamburlaine uses the captive Emperor Bajazeth as a footstool to ascend his throne. Entries and exits can also have signification. Marston's *The Malcontent* employs these structural devices for thematic purposes, in the form of what Maynard Mack has called the emblematic entrance and exit.[15] The virtuous courtier, Celso, is juxtaposed with characters who provide the strongest ethical contrast with him. His entrance at Act I, scene iv, almost immediately after the departure of the weak, vacillating Duke Pietro, lends emphasis to the fact that he is the moral antitype of the Duke. Similarly, the necessity of Celso's hasty exit before the arriving footsteps of the devilish Mendoza in Act III, scene iii, is emblematic of the upside-down inferiority of virtue in Pietro's court. Ensemble movements by groups of actors can also have an expressiveness that transcends mere spectacle. Political or social cohesion, for instance, may be depicted either processionally, as in the opulent coronation march in Shakespeare's *Henry VIII* (IV.i); or balletically, as in the graceful movements of shepherds and shepherdesses in *The Winter's Tale* (IV.iv), or in the celebratory dances at or near the conclusions of *Much Ado About Nothing* and Marston's *The Malcontent.*

MAKE-UP. Facial and bodily details of a dramatic character that are stipulated by the playwright, and which must be achieved by make-up effects, provide a wide range of semiological data. Black skin coloring, for example, was a noticeable and conventional use of a special cosmetic in Renaissance drama. Its customary theatrical referent was wantonness and sensuality, as with Cleopatra, whose "tawny front" was "with

---

15. "The Jacobean Shakespeare," in *Jacobean Theatre,* ed. John R. Brown and Bernard Harris (New York, 1960), pp. 28–30.

Phoebus' amorous pinches black" (*Antony and Cleopatra*, I.i.6; I.v.28). Another tradition of the drama, one that harkened back to the various mystery-play versions of the Fall of Lucifer and the Harrowing of Hell, called for devils to be acted in blackface. The adverse connotation of diabolism, reinforced by the popular Platonic notion that fair skin was an attribute of virtue, helped to raise swarthiness to the level of symbolic metaphor. In *The White Devil*, for example, "The devil, hell, and their accompanying colour of black are woven into the language of the play as if Webster were repeatedly reminding his audience that behind the fair exteriors of his characters hell constantly lurked. To make symbol flesh, he intermingled black faces with his white characters on the stage." [16] Comparably sinister associations of blackness are present in Aaron, the villainous Moor in *Titus Andronicus* ("Let fools do good, and fair men call for grace: / Aaron will have his soul black like his face," III.i.205–206), and in the Prince of Morocco in *The Merchant of Venice*. The tawny Prince is clearly Shylock's surrogate in terms of the "dark" and "unenlightened" nature of his perceptions, and the nuance of diabolism ("the complexion of a devil," I.ii.117) is added by his electing the casket of gold, the metal having the least spiritual value.

Unusual forms of bodily make-up can have thematic importance. Shakespeare's stagecraft, for example, deliberately requires vast quantities of blood to cover both Brutus during the assassination scene in *Julius Caesar*, and Coriolanus during his singlehanded combat with the Volscian army in Act I of *Coriolanus*. Each of these horrifying, brutal, and yes, messy spectacles is a powerfully visual commentary upon the ambivalent nature of the respective protagonists; yet, incredulous critics and producers have been loath to accord them full value.[17] Hair that hangs down lankly about the ears is, at least for such female characters as Cassandra (*Troilus and Cressida*, II.ii.100 s.d.) and Queen Elizabeth (*Richard III*, II.ii.33 s.d.), a theatrical sign denoting madness. Prosthetic

16. Eldred Jones, *Othello's Countrymen: The African in English Renaissance Drama* (London, 1965), p. 78; cf. B. J. Layman, "The Equilibrium of Opposites in *The White Devil*," *PMLA*, LXXIV (1959), 339: "Zanche the Moor—a lesser devil whose hue, real and symbolic, provides us with a means of judging Vittoria's . . ." (quoted by Jones, p. 79).

17. Leo Kirschbaum, "Shakespeare's Stage Blood and Its Critical Significance," *PMLA*, LXIV (1949), 517–529.

pieces may also be signific. One thinks of the "long nails" of the sub-human Caliban in *The Tempest* (II.ii.158), or Barabas' bottle nose in Marlowe's *The Jew of Malta* (III.iii.9), which is expressive of both the wearer's Jewishness and his moral resemblance to Satan, who, as Craik has suggested in *The Tudor Interlude* (p. 51), has traditionally had this characteristic. The facial mask is perhaps best classified an element of make-up rather than costume. The device functions at various levels of meaning in plays of the period, though in Tourneur's *The Revenger's Tragedy* disguises and masks are richly ironic plurisigns for corruption and self-delusion. Bertram's facial "patch of velvet" in *All's Well that Ends Well* (IV.v) is a properly ambiguous sort of mask for one who is honorable in war and dishonorable in love: for Bertram it is the badge of honor ordinarily used to conceal war wounds ("a noble scar is a good liv'ry of honour," ll. 90–91); but as the Clown remarks apropos, the patch might well be a disreputable mask that hides syphilis surgery on a "carbonado'd face" (l. 92).

COSTUME. Someone rightly emphasized the importance of costumes by terming them "scenery worn by actors," though the signs of costume are complements to make-up as well as *mise-en-scène*. There are innumerable details connected with theatrical dress—color, texture, footwear, head-gear, armor, overgarments, trimming and accessories, etc.—which are capable of expressing a dramatic idea. However, two major aspects of vestimentary signs will command our attention here: the significance of color, and the implications of certain costume changes or disguises.[18] A most familiar example of instrumental coloring is the black suit, sugges-tive of melancholy and alienation, such as the "customary suits of solemn black" worn by Hamlet (*Hamlet,* I.ii.78), or the "old garb of melancholy" which is Bosola's apparel in Webster's *The Duchess of Malfi* (I.i.278). The color yellow, often linked to ideas of envy, jealousy, or spleen through its association with jaundice (*OED,* s.v. yellow 2, jaundiced 3),

18. For additional examples of symbolic costume see Hal H. Smith, "Some Prin-ciples of Elizabethan Stage Costume," *JWCI,* XXV (1962), 240–257; Styan, *Shakespeare's Stagecraft,* pp. 34–36; on Renaissance color symbolism in costume see M. C. Linthicum, *Costume in the Drama of Shakespeare and his Contemporaries* (1936; rpt. New York, 1963), pp. 13–52; D. C. Allen, "Symbolic Color in the Literature of the English Renaissance," *PQ, XV* (1936), 81–92; Craik, *The Tudor Interlude, vide* Index, s.v. "Colour-Symbolism."

is the ensign for cowardice and false chivalry in Parolles, "That jack-an-apes with scarfs" who wears "villainous saffron" in *All's Well that Ends Well* (III.v.82; IV.v.3). Yellow may even have been used in make-up form to distinguish the quack Doctor Pinch's "saffron face" in *The Comedy of Errors* (IV.iv.58), or the swarthiness of "yellow Iachimo," the treacherous Italian in *Cymbeline* (II.v.14).

Costume changes have fulfilled symbolic needs in English drama since the morality play and the Tudor interlude. As Craik has said of the early plays in *The Tudor Interlude*, ". . . since so many of the moral interludes are concerned with changes of heart (either falls to wickedness or conversions to virtue) it is appropriate that changes of dress should signify them" (p. 73). Marlowe realizes the thematic effectiveness of this device in *1 Tamburlaine*. Only moments after his first appearance and in full view of the audience, Tamburlaine casts aside the humility represented by his shepherd's clothes and asserts his new desire for power, represented by the armor underneath ("Lie here, ye weeds that I disdain to wear!," I.ii.4). In Chapman's *Bussy D'Ambois,* our first view of Bussy establishes his straitened circumstances (*"Enter* Bussy D'Ambois *poor,"* I.i s.d.), though to him there is virtue in humility ("Who is not poor is monstrous," l. 3). The tragedy of Bussy's rise in ambition and pride is hauntingly visualized when later (V.iii s.d.) he surrounds himself with the identical trappings of wealth as his decadent sponsor, Monsieur (I.i.33 s.d.). Irony is a major factor in some costume shifts, such as the ceremonial exchange of clerical vestments for a soldier's habit by the evil Cardinal, who as a fornicator is already a travesty to the religious office he holds (*The Duchess of Malfi,* III.iv.6 s.d.); or the comic decorum of the obtuse Sir Politic Wouldbe's being discovered hiding in a tortoise shell in Jonson's *Volpone* (V.iv). A final example combines both symbolic colors and a costume change. For the allegorical Induction of Middleton's *Michaelmas Term,* the title character emerges to remove a "whitish cloak" which he claims signifies his honest way of life before coming to London ("Lay by my conscience, . . . that weed is for the country," Ind. 1–2). He then puts on a "civil" gown of black, a color intended to "match our evil; / Who first made civil black, he pleas'd the devil" (ll. 3–4).

HAND PROPERTIES. Unanchored physical objects, light enough for a person to carry on stage for manual use there, define hand properties for semiological purposes. Elements usually thought of as part of the decor, or clothing accessories like jewelry or handkerchiefs which are normally considered articles of costume, become hand properties when they assume this independent function (cf. Kowzan, p. 68). Articles of clothing quite readily become props that are virtual symbolic extensions of their owners. In Kyd's *The Spanish Tragedy,* for example, Horatio's "bloody handkercher" is continually produced or referred to by his father, Hieronimo, as the literal sign of Horatio's murder and the blood vengeance that it demands ("This was a token 'twixt thy soul and me / That of thy death revenged I should be," III.xiii.88–89; cf. II.v.51–52; III.vi.16; IV.iv.122–129). A more complex significance attaches to the handkerchief of Desdemona's which has "magic in the web of it" (*Othello,* III.iv.69). Its associations with Othello's imputed powers of witchcraft contrast with, at the same time that they interact with, its function as the symbolization of love.[19] Chess playing, with appropriate *double-entendres,* is a sign correspondent to a heated verbal dispute in Chapman's *Bussy D'Ambois* (I.ii), and to sexual intrigue in Middleton's *Women Beware Women* (II.ii). Certain hand properties have a metaphoric value matching that used in Renaissance iconography. Commentators have, for example, recognized the emblematic function of a human skull as *memento mori* in *Hamlet* (V.i), Tourneur's *The Revenger's Tragedy* (III.v) and *The Atheist's Tragedy* (IV.iii), and Webster's *The White Devil* (V.iv).[20] Another important dramatic emblem is the bleeding heart of Giovanni's sister-lover, Annabella, that Giovanni climactically brings in on the point of a dagger in Ford's *'Tis Pity She's A Whore* (V.vi). The heart supports concurrently two opposite but equally persuasive symbolisms throughout the play, resulting in an ambivalence that goes to the essence of Giovanni's and Annabella's relationship. Their love has both negative and positive valences which intermix in the literal, sensational reality of the dripping heart. In negative terms the heart connotes the dangerous fervor of their love ("Rip up my bosom, . . . behold / A heart . . . ," I.ii.206–207), its tragic vulnerability now expressed in Giovanni's

19. Robert B. Heilman, *Magic in the Web* (Lexington, Ky., 1956), p. 212.
20. Cf. Bridget Gellert, "The Iconography of Melancholy in the Graveyard Scene of *Hamlet*," *SP,* LXVII (1970), 57–66; Mehl, "Emblems," pp. 52–53; John Russell Brown, ed., *The White Devil* (London, 1960), p. 167 n.

derangement, and especially its flout of moral law, for which the lovers' condign deaths will atone. Positively, however, the heart stands for the benign indivisibility of their union ("O the glory / Of two united hearts like hers and mine!," V.iii.11–12; cf. I.i.34; II.i.32, 39–40), which by the heart's "reeking blood . . . triumphs over death" (V.vi.9–10). There is, then, an apotheosis of forbidden love which recalls the *Liebestod* of the analogous Tristan-Isolde myth. The symbolic potential of the heart, one of the most popular emblems in Renaissance religious and amatory poetry,[21] has been ably realized by Ford.

THE DECOR. The plays of Shakespeare and his contemporaries, though written for performance on a nonillusionistic, platform stage that afforded great flexibility and fluidity of movement, nevertheless demanded an assortment of scenic furnishings, devices, and decoration for use as signs and symbols.[22] A collaboration of architecture and its related arts, painting and sculpture, also produced the façade of the Elizabethan theater, which, with its curtains and hangings, "was itself a symbol of castle, throne, triumphal arch, altar, tomb, and several other shows long familiar in art and pageantry."[23] Ideas associated with locality or setting have an important bearing upon theme and structure in many plays, especially those of Shakespeare: witness the purposeful contrast between the profane world of Shylock's Venice and the idyllic world of Portia's Belmont in *The Merchant of Venice;* or the movement from Venice to Cyprus in *Othello,* which can be seen as an archetypal descent from an orderly society to a private sphere domineered by one man's anarchic passions.[24] Of course, setting can be indicated as well by sign systems

21. See Rosemary Freeman, *English Emblem Books* (London, 1948), pp. 148–149, 164–167. The heart-oblation motif is recurrent, and heart / blood imagery almost obsessive, in Ford's own religious poem, *Christ's Bloody Sweat* (1613). An emblematic anticipation (and possibly a germinal idea for Ford's *'Tis Pity*) of an agonized man sword-impaling a heart is the title page of John Haywarde's popular *The Sanctuarie of a Troubled Soule* (ed. 1616), rpt. in Samuel C. Chew, *The Pilgrimage of Life* (New Haven, Conn., 1962), Fig. 156.

22. See Glynne Wickham, *Early English Stages,* Vol. II, pt. 1 (London, 1963), pp. 206 ff.

23. George F. Kernodle, *From Art to Theatre: Form and Convention in the Renaissance* (Chicago, 1944), p. 130.

24. See Clifford Leech, "The Function of Locality in the Plays of Shakespeare and His Contemporaries," in *The Elizabethan Theatre,* ed. David Galloway

other than the *mise-en-scène,* such as costume or lighting, or allusively in the dialogue. An example of the latter use is the casual mention that a chapel—because of its connotation of numinous influence—is the setting for Leontes' and Hermione's "miraculous" reconciliation in *The Winter's Tale* (V.iii.86). Presumably an altar, with or without tapers (cf. *Pericles,* V.iii; Ford's *The Broken Heart,* V.iii), is the natural scenic unit for expressing the idea scenographically.

Large properties, furnishings, or scenic devices, which can be moved on stage during the performance or fixed in place for the duration of a scene, are frequent semiological data. Trees, for example, had been in use as scenic emblems in the mystery plays. One well-known Elizabethan example is the garden in *Richard II,* which becomes an elaborate political metaphor for England, seen as a *hortus conclusus* ("our sea-walled garden, the whole land, / Is full of weeds," III.iv.43–44). In Lyly's *Gallathea* an oak tree that has been dedicated to Neptune serves as an abiding token of the god's implacable power which looms over the play (". . . this tree, this fatal tree," IV.i.8). Withered but sweet apples from the tree of Virtue, and "rare red-cheeked" apples from the tree of Vice create an emblematic parable in Dekker's *Old Fortunatus* (IV.i). Interestingly enough, in Act IV of each of the two parts of *Tamburlaine,* Marlowe employs a different, larger-than-man-size, mobile property to symbolize Tamburlaine's domination over his enemies: the cage that houses Emperor Bajazeth, and the chariot that Tamburlaine draws by two reined kings. The caves of Timon in *Timon of Athens* and of Belarius in *Cymbeline* function as scenographic metaphors for the alienated condition of their inhabitants—much as a hovel on a desolate, unlocalized heath in *King Lear* (III.iv) represents the human situation in a *paysage moralisé.*

LIGHTING. Torches, lanterns, and tapers are frequently called for in plays of the period. Most of these lighting effects, including light needed for simple visibility, are quite conventional and belong to the semiological category I have designated as signal. Some examples are lights used to

---

(Toronto, 1969), pp. 103–116; Alvin B. Kernan, " 'Othello': An Introduction," in his *Modern Shakespearean Criticism,* pp. 353–357, on "symbolic geography"; cf. R. B. Parker, "Themes and Staging of *Bartholomew Fair," UTQ,* XXXIX (1970), 293–309, on the play's "symbolic loci" (pig booth / appetite; stocks / law; puppet show / art).

create the theatrical pretense of darkness or shadows (cf. *Romeo and Juliet,* V.iii), or to indicate a time lapse between scenes or the time of day (cf. *Julius Caesar,* IV.iii).[25] But dramatists were also alert to the capabilities of lighting effects as signs or symbols. The presence of lighted candles, as for example in *Much Ado About Nothing* (V.iii) or Ford's *'Tis Pity She's A Whore* (III.vi), can evoke a hallowed or penitential atmosphere, even when the setting itself is not a particularly religious one. Occasional lighting effects such as lightning or blazing meteors are invariably signifiers of preternatural forces, and one, fire, the means by which Dido immolates herself in Marlowe's *Dido Queen of Carthage* (V.i), is effectually the symbol of Dido's all-consuming passion. A burning candle or torch, regarded as a lighting effect rather than a hand property, can have a qualitatively different metaphoric power. There is the vivid instance in *Othello,* where Othello extinguishes the flame that is equated with Desdemona's life ("Put out the light, and then put out the light," V.ii.7). A comparable usage occurs in Chapman's *Bussy D'Ambois,* where Montsurry demonstrates to his faithless wife the extinction of their love: "And as this taper, though it upwards look, / Downwards must needs consume, so let our love" (V.iv.208–209). Both of these examples correspond to the employment of torches and tapers in Renaissance emblem books, where they are often images of life and death.[26] A torchlight and a lantern, carried respectively by Gloucester in *King Lear* ("Now, Edmund, where's the villain?," II.i.37; cf. III.iv.108) and Bosola in Webster's *The Duchess of Malfi* (II.iii s.d.), emblematize the quest of both men for palpable evidence of another's guilt. Visual irony is potent in each case, however, for though their lights dispel the physical darkness, both men act upon their perceptions with a false "insight" that causes them tragically to misinterpret or misuse their findings.

Volumetric control of lighting by electronic dimmers is a common enough technique in modern theaters. But consider the resourcefulness

25. Lee Mitchell, "Shakespeare's Lighting Effects," *SM,* XV (1948), 72–84, who provides many examples of conventional and symbolic usages.

26. Mehl, "Emblems," p. 52. In both plays, moreover, the effects are no isolated, painterly symbolism, but elements in a comprehensive opposition of darkness and light; see Heilman, *Magic in the Web,* pp. 64–73, and Peter Bement, "The Imagery of Darkness and of Light in Chapman's *Bussy D'Ambois,*" *SP,* LXIV (1967), 187–198.

of Ben Jonson, when he utilized intensifying and diminishing illumination without benefit of complicated equipment. For *Catiline,* Jonson made a theatrical sign of Plutarch's suggestion that natural portents accompanied Catiline's conspiracy, by calling for the stage to be thrown into an ominous darkness ("Darkness grows more and more!," I.i.314). The effect would have been well within the capacity of Jonson's playhouse, the artificially lit Blackfriars. For his masques, always more conspicuously symbolic productions, Jonson freely used light as pure metaphor. In *The Golden Age Restored* the descent to earth of the goddess of justice, Astraea, moves Pallas to make all "doubtful darkness yield" to wisdom's enlightenment (*"The scene of light discovered,"* l. 135 s.d.). In *Hymenaei* the ushering in of the emblematic figure, Truth, involves a similarly metaphoric use of light: *"When on a sudden . . . a striking light seemed to fill the hall, and out of it an angel or messenger of glory appearing"* (ll. 791–793 s.d.).

Music. Signification in musical signs can range from the merest "signalling" function to the level of complex dramatic ideas. For example, the use of trumpets on the Elizabethan stage—for flourishes, sennets, tuckets, alarms, etc.—is in most cases entirely conventional. "Directly or indirectly there is always a connection between the sound of trumpets and the idea of royalty. When trumpets 'sound,' intransitively, without sounding a particular signal, the likelihood is that the dramatist wants to stress the direct link with royalty." [27] But often, music can expand information transmitted by other signs. One recalls the masquelike episode in Webster's *The Duchess of Malfi,* in which a "wild consort" of madmen arrives to work the imprisoned Duchess into despair. A lunatic's howling song, accompanied by *"a dismal kind of music"* (IV.ii.61 s.d.), together with the wild dancing and bawdy dialogue of the other madmen, are combinative signs depicting the lewd, paradoxical play-world where reason is madness and folly is sanity (ll. 5–7). In *King Lear* (IV.vii) the soft music accompanying the reconciliation of the exhausted king with Cordelia is, in naturalistic terms, a customary remedy for madness. But it is also metaphor, an equivalent in tone of psychological

27. J. S. Manifold, *The Music in English Drama* (London, 1956), p. 35, citing numerous Marlovian and Shakespearean examples: e.g., *1 Tamburlaine,* I.i.132, 188; *2 Tamburlaine,* I.i, I.ii; *Richard II,* I.iii *passim.*

and ethical modulations which have been internalized in Lear. As the storm (II.iv-III.iv) had been a noisy analogue of Lear's "untun'd and jarring senses," so these musical harmonies are the auditive sign of their restoration.[28]

Instrumental music performs a different semiological role on the occasions when it is in itself the vehicle for philosophical ideas, though in a manner unlike that of the Wagnerian leitmotiv. A well-known example occurs in *The Merchant of Venice,* where Lorenzo contemplates with Jessica the "harmony" of the universe: "There's not the smallest orb which thou behold'st / But in his motion like an angel sings" (V.i.60-61). The myth of heavenly music, to which Lorenzo alludes, was part of the elaborate rationale of Renaissance music (*musica speculativa*) which held also that man's instrumental music imitated the ideal order of the cosmos.[29] Significantly, the actual music which Lorenzo calls upon Belmont's musicians to play as an accompaniment to his disquisition on musical symbolism (V.i.70-88) becomes per se the aural mode of that symbolism. Musical sound has semantic value in all of Shakespeare's late romances,[30] but especially in *The Tempest.* A frequently stressed theme in that play—that supernatural powers actively guide the lives of men through a benign providence (cf. I.ii.159; III.iii.53-61)—is made concrete by the theophany of Ceres and Juno at the betrothal masque (IV.i). The visible presence of the goddesses, attended by vocal and instrumental music and the graceful dance movements of their nymphs, all create "a most majestic vision, and / Harmonious charmingly" (ll. 118-119). The immanence of heavenly harmony on Prospero's island is of course the episode's central transumptive effect, and it is produced largely through Neo-Platonic associations which the context allows the theatrical music to convey.

SOUND EFFECTS. Sound effects comprise the eleventh and final sign system for discussion. Under its rubric one includes all inarticulate, non-

28. See the related commentary of Thelma N. Greenfield, "Nonvocal Music: Added Dimension in Five Shakespeare Plays," *Pacific Coast Studies in Shakespeare,* ed. W. F. McNeir and T. N. Greenfield (Eugene, Oreg., 1966), pp. 106-121.

29. John Hollander, *The Untuning of the Sky: Ideas of Music in English Poetry, 1500-1700* (Princeton, N.J., 1961), pp. 20-31, 150-153.

30. Catherine M. Dunn, "The Function of Music in Shakespeare's Romances," *SQ,* XX (1969), 391-405, summarizes modern criticism.

musical sound illusions to be executed either on- or off-stage during a performance. The acoustic dimension in Elizabethan drama has long been recognized for its variety, uniqueness, and importance.[31] The illustrative examples given here, however, will avoid retracing well-trodden ground by giving prominence once more to what is thematically relevant (here, the sound effect as aural sign or symbol), and not to contemporary attempts at stage realism, such as imitated birdsong or the baying of hounds (the aural signal). Animal sounds in *Macbeth,* for example, not only produce an aesthetic weirdness of atmosphere, but they suggest as well the supernatural influences which are mysteriously at work. Specific instances are the calls of the witches' familiars, a cat and a toad, in the play's opening moments, and Lady Macbeth's hearing "the owl scream and the crickets cry" (II.ii.15) while Duncan is murdered. In *Macbeth's* larger thematic context these sounds also figure in what G. Wilson Knight describes as a recurrent animal disorder-symbolism that gives body to all-pervading evil in the play, and which includes mentionings of such fierce, ugly, or ill-omened animals as wolves, maggot-pies, and rooks.[32]

Bell sound is a representative and versatile aural sign. The strident clangor of the alarm bell announcing Duncan's murder in *Macbeth* (II.iii.78) is a "hideous trumpet," a correlative in sound of the horrible trauma which Macbeth's bloody deed represents. A similar sonic metaphor is the "dreadful bell" in *Othello* that loudly accompanies the drunken brawl of Cassio and Montano for a duration of seventeen lines of dialogue (II.iii.152–168), and which betokens incipient social and personal chaos in Cyprus. Webster uses the knell of a hand-bell to supply an auditive foreboding of death in two of his plays: in *The Duchess of*

31. Some useful studies are W. J. Lawrence, *Pre-Restoration Stage Studies* (Cambridge, Mass., 1927), pp. 199–220; and *Those Nut-Cracking Elizabethans* (London, 1935), pp. 84–96, on the use of bells; James W. Brock, *A Study of the Use of Sound Effects in the Elizabethan Drama* (diss., Northwestern University, 1950); Frances Ann Shirley, *Shakespeare's Use of Off-Stage Sounds* (Lincoln, Nebr., 1963).

32. *The Wheel of Fire,* 4th ed. (London, 1949), pp. 145–146; cf. stage thunder, extensive in *Macbeth* and *King Lear,* which has supernatural or cosmic significance and never attends purely personal conflicts, as Knight reminds us (*Shakespearian Production* [Evanston, Ill., 1964], pp. 54–58); so, e.g., in *Doctor Faustus* (I.iii; V. i–ii) and *The Revenger's Tragedy* (IV.ii; V.iii).

Malfi (IV.ii.165 ff.), when Bosola employs one to bring the Duchess "By degrees to mortification"; and in *The Devil's Law-Case,* when Leonora hears two bellmen sound the fatal result of her lover's duel: "What a dismal noise yon bell makes! / Sure some great person's dead" (II.iii.83–84). But in a totally contrasting context, the merry ringing sound of the "pancake bell" in Dekker's *The Shoemaker's Holiday* becomes, in effect, an aural sign of the boisterous good feeling among the shoemakers, the quintessence of the play's holiday spirit ("Oh brave, oh sweet bell! Oh, delicate pancakes! Open the doors, my hearts . . . ," V.ii.193–194).

II

In summary, we have noted that modern students of English Renaissance drama are more than ever aware that their subject is a highly developed, experiential art form, one in which nonverbal elements are often quite as significant as verbal ones. Perhaps, too, the value of theatrical semiology will be as widely acknowledged; for it is a useful technique in designating the important actualities of a performed play—the data which function as style, form, and content in the fullest sense—for interpretation in a systematic manner. Thematically relevant details can be organized so that they will more effectively demonstrate how or to what extent theater poets have realized dramatic meaning in phenomenal terms, in a total, histrionic frame. My last example is a fortunate crystallization of all that has gone before, as well as striking proof of Ben Jonson's comprehensive stagecraft. In a few lines describing the performance of *The Masque of Queens* (1609), Jonson manages to specify at least one datum of every one of the eleven sign systems outlined in this essay:

> . . . *the scene which first presented itself was an ugly hell, which flaming beneath, smoked unto the top of the roof. And in respect all evils are, morally, said to come from hell, . . . these witches, with a kind of hollow and infernal music, came forth from thence . . . all differently attired: some with rats on their head, some on their shoulders; . . . all with spindles, timbrels, rattles or other venefical instruments, making a confused noise, with strange gestures. The device of their attire was Master [Inigo] Jones his, with the invention and architecture of the whole scene and machine. Only I prescribed them their properties of vipers, snakes, bones, herbs, roots*

and other ensigns of their magic. . . . These eleven witches beginning to dance (which is an usual ceremony at their convents, . . . where sometimes also they are vizarded and masked) on the sudden one of them . . . interrupted the rest with this speech. . . .

(ll. 21–39 s.d.)

On the Ancestry
of the Gracioso

EDWIN J. WEBBER

L OPE DE VEGA evidently claimed, in 1620, that he had introduced the dramatic personage of the Gracioso for the first time in a play that he had written about twenty-five years before. It has not yet been possible to accommodate Lope's claim easily, either to his own dramatic production of that period, or to what is known of dramatic conventions preceding the New Comedy. When the antecedents of the Gracioso have been sought in the earlier history of Spanish drama, an occurrence of the term *gracioso,* in a comedy of Torres Naharro (bef. 1524), usually has been thought to refer to an already existing prototype of that comic character, if not to that character himself. However, it has never been explained in what way this early, and apparently isolated, designation fitted into an assumed tradition that spanned nearly a century. An examination of a part of the broad spectrum of meaning that the word *gracioso* possessed, particularly the area in which it came in contact with connotations of *truhán,* offers a new perspective of the problem. Although the ancestry of the Gracioso, viewed from this angle, can be traced back into the Middle Ages, it will suffice here to begin his history in the pre-Renaissance, in the reign of Juan II.

Among the secular moderators and legislators of practical morality in the early Renaissance in Spain, Aristotle, Cicero, and Seneca were the prestigious authorities. Divulged in Latin, or in the vernacular, or in adaptation, they provided instructive comments on humor and joking and, in particular, on the part that jesting played in conversation among people of quality and sensibility. The paraphrases, especially, permit this influence to be appraised, revealing—as they must—the language, the corresponding concepts, and often the practice of the modern interpreter.

Of the three, Aristotle provided the most formally worded, and possibly the most quoted, definition of jesting. There are those, he says in the *Ethics,* who will go to any length to raise a laugh, even if this involves indecency or offense. These people resemble buffoons: *albardanes* in the version of his fifteenth-century translator, rendering the Latin *scurre.*[1] On the other hand, there are those who never joke, or permit others to do so. These are rude and boorish: *torpes e rústicos.* But the one who jokes with moderation may be called graciously amusing or witty, that is to say: *gracioso,* translating *comis.* It is not that the buffoon might not appear to be elegantly witty, for there is much to laugh at, and we are all too ready to enjoy the jokes and witticisms of the *albardanes;* it is that the truly witty man, the one who observes moderation in jesting, is characterized by courtesy and urbanity, as is appropriate to one who is temperate and well-bred. *Cortesía* is the key word here, the Latin *urbanitas.*

Since the man who is deficient in a sense of humor is automatically excluded from any discussion of the art of witty conversation, only the two other types may be considered in this respect: the one who is *gracioso* and the *albardán* (also called *truhán* and later *chocarrero*). These are the two classes that Cicero contrasts, when he speaks of the two *maneras de burlar.* One of the kinds of joking, he says, is unworthy of the gentleman, namely, the one that is *ssoberuia, maliciossa e ssuzia.* The other manner is *fermossa, cortés, ingeniossa e doñossa.*[2] Seneca knows this classification, too, and he approves the introduction of *burlas graciosas* into conversation, provided it is done discreetly. One should not indulge in any *burla deshonesta,* in the style of the *truhanes.* But if the occasion calls for it, one should use *graciosas e honestas burlas,* remembering that these *donayres* ("witticisms") should not be biting:

1. Aristotle, *Ethicas,* B.M. MS. Add. 21,120, fol. 95.
2. Cicero, *De oficios,* B.N.M. MS. 10,246, fol. 33ʳ.

sin diente.[3] The glosser of the fifteenth-century manuscript here not only recalls what Aristotle and Cicero had said concerning *graciosidad,* but also relates an instance taken from Valerius Maximus and concludes with another definition, drawn from Macrobius. In the course of this discussion he reveals that the term has for him a meaning somewhat narrower than *comitas.* Alluding to Aristotle's comments on the quality in *juegos e burlas* called *eutrapelia* in Greek, he adds: "in the vernacular we can call it *graciosidat.*" And later: "the speaking in jest (*burla*) that we call *graciosidat* may be divided into two styles; one is *ledoria,* which in the vernacular we may call *alvardanía;* the other is *estomata,* which is called *graciosidat.*" Another manuscript specifies here: "*honesta graciosidad.*"[4] In spite of the asymmetry of this definition, it makes clear that an important connotation of *graciosidad* is "jesting." What is especially significant, however, is that evidently the term could encompass all jesting, not merely the polite. In cases of doubt, one infers, *honesta* could be supplied. In fact, *gracioso* appears to be synonymous with *donoso,* and the two are becoming increasingly colored with this meaning. Both stand in the same relationship with *albardán,* obviously, when the glosser of Artistotle explains that the latter "derides, vilifies, and hurts; but the *donoso* speaks his pleasing *donaires* without offending or harming anyone."[5]

Another view of this relationship was offered by an anonymous lexicographer. The word *donoso* expresses an idea, he says, which has often been called *sabroso,* because of the *sabor,* the taste of the sweet and pleasing words. The one who is *donoso* utters *donayres.* The *donayre* is a manner of speaking sweet and merry words—naturally at the proper time and in the properly discreet manner, without injury to anyone. If the words were intended to dishonor or insult someone, of course, they would be the words of a *truhán* or *aluardán* rather than of a gentleman. Turning from his copy of Aristotle or Seneca, the commentator offers one further observation. The word *donoso,* he adds, is used in Castile

---

3. Seneca, *Obras traducidas por Alonso de Santa María,* B.N.M. MS. 6962, fol. 155ᵛ.

4. Seneca, *Varias obras,* B.N.M. MS. 6765, fol. 163.

5. Aristotle, *Ethicas,* fol. 96.

and in Portugal. "In other lands they say *gracioso,* and even in Castile they have recently taken to saying it." [6]

Whether the impression of newness was well-founded, or whether the writer had just taken note of an existing phenomenon, he revealed a curious observer's awareness of the special area of meaning that *gracioso* and *donoso* shared by the end of the fifteenth century. This might appear to be contradicted by Nebrija, the most formidable grammarian of the Renaissance. Recording what people said, however, was not his method. In his zeal to correct the Latinity of his time, as well as to codify both it and the vernacular in grammars, style manuals, and dictionaries, Nebrija preferred rather to reduce and regularize. Accordingly, *gracioso* [*en hablar*] and *donoso* are neatly distinguished: the first is "lepide"; the second, "facetus, festivus, comis." [7] Nebrija's contemporary and rival classicist, Alfonso de Palencia, in turn, appeared to be more closely attuned to the trend of the period. In his dictionary, *facetus* spans "donoso, alegre, gracioso"; *lepidus* also joins "dulce fabla e suaue eloquencia" with "cortesano fablar e donoso razonamiento en las burlas." [8]

From such learned and quasi-learned discussions these concepts passed into literature and—to judge from copious evidence—into the halls of the nobles, the parlors of the gentry, and into the personal worlds of all who cherished the ideal as well as its negotiability in society. It would be difficult to exaggerate the importance that was attached to all that was connoted by *gracioso* and *graciosidad* as a quality of character revealed by the individual's appearance, actions, and words. As for *graciosidad* in speech, in particular, one may observe its full range of meaning exemplified repeatedly: from the somewhat unspecific "charming, pleasing, ingratiating, entertaining," to the narrower aspect of "amusing, jocular and witty."

Pérez de Guzmán, for example, related how the lively intelligence of Juan II enabled him to size up the men about him, noting which "fablaua mejor e más atentado e más *gracioso";* and how it pleased him to listen to "omes auisados e *graciosos,"* and to hear merry words, well

6. *Vocabulario castellano,* R.A.H. MS. N.73, fol. 15.
7. *Vocabulario español-latino* (Salamanca, 1495?), s.v.v.
8. *Universal vocabulario* (Seville, 1490), s.v.v.

aimed, the kind that he himself knew well how to speak.[9] Ruy López Dávalos was very jolly and *gracioso;* and Diego Hurtado de Mendoza was not only very *gracioso* in his manner of speaking, but so bold and daring in speech that King Enrique criticized his brashness and lack of restraint.[10] Not the least attractive quality of a certain count, according to Fernando del Pulgar, was that he was an "ome palanciano" and always spoke "cosas breues e *graciosas.*"[11] As for the other extreme, Pulgar mildly protested that he had been reproached for being an *aluardán,* because he sometimes wrote "cosas jocosas."[12] Miguel Lucas de Iranzo spent Christmas Eve of 1461 gaming, during which *"graciosos y donosos* motes" flew about.[13]

Fifteen rules concerning propriety in speech were so many blossoms in a "Nosegay of Virtues" typical of an earlier period, but set down at this time (1470). These represented an aspect of *moderança* or *mesura,* from which *cortesía* originated. Among the gifts of courtesy was to "fablar *graciosas* palabras."[14] In the royal court, Hernando de Ludueña offered loyal lovers an extended treatment of the art of jesting in his versified manual of courtesy, the *Dotrinal de gentileza.* The gentleman who won favor, who was not only *discreto* but *donoso,* was the one who was *gracioso,* skilled in repartee. He needed to be particularly discerning, as well as deft, in the art of *motejar:* coining the clever insult or barbed witticism.[15] In a less elaborate spate of advice, the gallant is again counseled to be a "donoso motejador."[16] Only the *grosseros* pervert the

---

9. F. Pérez de Guzmán, *Generaciones y semblanzas,* ed. J. Domínguez Bordona (Madrid, 1954), p. 118.

10. *Ibid.,* pp. 31, 44.

11. *Claros varones de Castilla,* ed. J. Domínguez Bordona (Madrid, 1954), "Conde de Alva de Liste," p. 84.

12. *Letras,* ed. J. Domínguez Bordona (Madrid, 1929), p. 95.

13. *Hechos del Condestable Miguel Lucas de Iranzo,* ed. J. de Mata Carriazo (Madrid, 1940), p. 39.

14. J. Fernández de Ixar, *Cancionero,* ed. J. M. Azaceta (Madrid, 1956), II, 744–745.

15. R. Foulché-Delbosc, *Cancionero castellano del siglo XV* (Madrid, 1912–1915), II, 718–734.

16. Hernando del Castillo, *Cancionero general* (Valencia, 1511), ed. A. Rodríguez Moñino (Madrid, 1958), fol. 51.

use of "el honesto motejar," said Ugo de Urries, devoting a rhymed treatise to these inept people, incapable of engaging in *"gracioso fablar."* [17] The ideal was far-reaching, Juan del Encina would jokingly have his audience believe. The shepherd Mingo demanded to know of a courtly squire whether he was aware of the fact that country folk, too, have the tongue to utter *motes.* [18]

An earlier poet had likened his amorous perturbation to the merriment that the *gracioso* physician tries to arouse in his patient, seeking to divert him instead of dealing with the cause of his pain. [19] At the turn of the century, this therapeutic method found its most talented practitioner in the court physician, Francisco de Villalobos, whose sense of humor was to become legendary: "el mayor burlador de Castilla." Indeed, he cultivated the reputation of wit with both tongue and pen. Another doctor once took exception to a funny story that Villalobos had told to the king; being a doctor and a teacher and concerned with loftier matters, he said, he could only disapprove of such jokes, fit only for *chocarreros* to tell. At a glance from the king, Villalobos answered: "Would Your Grace please teach me how to be a fool, since you are an authority, and I will stop being a *gracioso,* in order not to annoy Your Grace." [20] The line between amateur wit and professional jester must often have been faint. "My brother-in-arms and *donoso* physician of His Majesty," Villalobos was called by Francesillo de Zúñiga, ostensible chronicler and, in fact, jester, of Carlos V. [21]

It is self-evident, nevertheless, that the *truhán* was no less a real and substantial element in that same society: the jester, whose whole professional existence was predicated on his ability to amuse others. It was no doubt inevitable—given the vulnerability of connotations to changing conditions—that if the *gracioso* gentleman and the *truhán* were using nearly identical means to achieve nearly identical aims, an identification of their art would emerge. This had already been represented as a literal

17. *Le Chansonnier espagnol d'Herberay des Essarts,* ed. C. Aubrun (Bordeaux, 1951), pp. 65, 66.

18. *Teatro completo,* ed. M. Cañete and F. Barbieri (Madrid, 1893), p. 94.

19. *Le Chansonnier,* "Otro dezir gracioso," p. 77.

20. *Los problemas de Villalobos,* BAE, XXXVI (Madrid, 1871), p. 445.

21. *Crónica,* BAE, XXXVI (Madrid, 1871), p. 53.

fact by the Senecan scholar who subsumed the styles of these two under the single term of *graciosidad*.

That the *gracioso* ("jester") existed as an entity early in the sixteenth century, that he had a fully achieved identity as a personality with this title—and was not exclusively a mask donned by various individuals—appears to be demonstrated by the routine (and for that reason convincing) account of Sancho Cota. Recording the names of a number of dignitaries and officials who left Spain for Flanders, he listed one "Juan de Pedraza *el gracioso*."[22] Unless this was a semi-private joke, akin to the remark of Zúñiga concerning Villalobos, it implied that Pedraza was an acknowledged jester or well-known comedian. Pedraza's ostensible profession would seem to be identical to that of a certain Cervantes who went to the New World as a soldier. He was known variously as a *truhán*, as "Cervantes el Loco," or "Cervantes el Chocarrero," and his *gracias* were popular among his fellows until he was killed by the Indians.[23] In other words, the traditional jester, having nearly outlived his ancient names of *juglar* and *albardán*, and commonly called *truhán* or *chocarrero*, was now sporting the designation applied to his fashionable counterpart.

The fact that these two entertainers were evidently independent comedians sets them apart from the majority of those whose existence has been recorded. The memory of most jesters depended upon the prominence of their patrons. On the arrival of the Duque de Alba at Tormes on December 13, 1524, for example, seventeen *albardanes* greeted him festively—with very poor jokes, according to the disdainful report of Don Francesillo de Zúñiga.[24]

The identification of the two types of practitioners created also the possibility—a further source of humorous effect—of viewing the injudicious *gracioso* as a *truhán*, of the *truhán* parodying the pretentious *gracioso*, or of the would-be humorist of any category being classified as one or the other. The servant Faceto, practicing his master's wooing tactics on the maid, Dileta, found his *motejar* and his *chocarrerías* (as

22. *Memorias*, ed. H. Keniston (Cambridge, 1964), p. 42.

23. Bernal Díaz, *Historia verdadera de la conquista de la Nueva España*, BAE, XXVI (Madrid, 1862), pp. 16, 105, 113, 305.

24. *Crónica*, p. 30.

she called them) to be fruitless. To a neat poetic conceit she responds: "¡O *gratioso!* / Nunca te vi tan donoso, / ni en tus hablas tan galán." [25] This comprised a veritable definition of the name *Faceto,* one observes, but a *facetus* already being parodied on the stage. In a discussion of *palabras deshonestas* ("indecent words"), which neither seriously nor jokingly are to be tolerated in a woman's presence, Francesch Eximenis observed that no Christian should be a "jutglar, ne gran burler, ne truffador." [26] His Spanish translator turned these terms, quite predictably, into "chocarreros, burladores e moffadores," adding: "which they now call *graciosos.*" [27] As for women who presumed to be "decidoras, *graciosas* y mofadoras," Guevara observed that what in men is called *gracia,* in women is called *chocarrería* ("scurrility"). [28]

The reputation of the entertainer had always been low. One official view is set forth matter-of-factly, directing that great care should be exercised in administering the sacrament to *truhanes,* "who rarely exercised their profession without sinning." [29] A contrary opinion was voiced by Venegas, who argued that not only was the entertainment of the *truhán* not prejudicial to the Prince, but that poetry could even exercise the office of *truhana juglar* for Sacred Theology, Princess of all Knowledge. [30] In the same spirit, the allegorical character, Eutrapelus, the *truhán* (that is, "a debased *graciosidad*"), reported that the wise King Solomon conceived that even *truhanes* such as he could become spiritually pure. [31]

As has been seen, from the dawn of the Renaissance in Spain, there had existed in polite circles a clearly defined concept, supported by classical authority, of the social grace of charmingly amusing and witty conversation, a grace that had to be cultivated with the greatest care, lest it fall into a tasteless scurrility. This was an accomplishment that could be ex-

25. B. de Torres Naharro, *Propalladia,* ed. J. Gillet (Bryn Mawr, Pa., 1946), Vol. II, p. 501, ll. 410–412.

26. *Libre de les dones* (Barcelona, 1495), fols. 185ᵛ–186ʳ.

27. *El carro de las donas* (Valladolid, 1542), sig. H.

28. *Epístolas familiares,* BAE, XIII (Madrid, 1872), p. 161.

29. Fray Hernando de Talavera, *Breve forma de confesar,* NBAE, XVI, (Madrid, 1911), p. 12.

30. León Baptista Alberto, *El Momo* (Madrid, 1553), "Exposición," sig. bᵛ.

31. In *Comoedia Solomonia* (bef. 1572). See J. García Soriano, *El teatro universitario y humanístico en España* (Toledo, 1945), p. 294.

pected of every gentleman, the virtuoso skill of the amateur; to practice it professionally or in the professional manner, like the *albardán* or *truhán*, would be a gross breach of courtesy. It is also plain that if the broad connotation of "charming graciousness" had earlier seemed to represent the primary sense of *graciosidad*, this had given way to the evident belief that "wittiness" lay at its heart.

As the pace of the Renaissance quickened, other manuals of courtesy came to elaborate and to consecrate the conception of *gracia, graciosidad,* as "wit, wittiness." The most prestigious of these was *El cortesano* (1534), Boscán's version of Castiglione's treatise. Among the qualities of the "perfect courtier" figured prominently a knowledge of the "diversas maneras de hablar graciosamente y de decir donaires." [32] "Please tell us," says the Prefect, "what a man needs to have, principally, in order to be *gracioso;* and how those *motes* and *gracias,* which you mentioned a while ago, should be used; and, finally, explain the technique to use with various kinds of *burlas* and *donaires* for getting laughs and giving entertainment with propriety; because I think that all this is very pertinent and necessary for the Courtier." [33] Extremely important for those who set themselves up as *graciosos* ("toman por oficio ser graciosos") is the scrupulous care they must exercise in their joking, for they are particularly liable to let themselves be carried away, to the detriment of their reputations. [34] "In telling stories or in mimicking, we must try with all our might to avoid resembling *truhanes* or *chocarreros";* that is, *buffoni e parassiti* in the original. [35]

It remained for Luis Milán to define *cortesía* exclusively in terms of excellence in genteel conversation. Unlike the rounded portrait presented by his model, Castiglione, Milán offered the aspiring courtier only "methods and advice on speaking tersely, but spontaneously, and without being overly laconic; together with model dialogues for learning how to

---

32. B. Castellón, *Los cuatro libros del Cortesano,* ed. A. Fabié (Madrid, 1873), "Epístola de Garcilasso," p. 14. See Margherita Morreale, *Castiglione y Boscán: El ideal cortesano en el renacimiento español* (Madrid, 1959), II, 159–163, 203–227.

33. *El cortesano,* p. 206.

34. *Ibid.,* p. 196.

35. *Ibid.,* p. 229; B. Castiglione, *El libro del cortegiano,* ed. V. Cian (Florence, 1947), p. 225.

joke (*burlar*) in the courtly fashion."[36] As one might expect, all principles were reexamined, expounded, and elaborated; instances abounded; fine points were further subtilized. For example, a courtier's jest should not offend his victim. If he is unable to jest without offense—assuming that he does not want to cause offense—he should refrain from the practice. Annoying jokes can scarcely be tolerated from a *truhán*, who, being a fool by profession, does not raise the question of honor; much less can they be endured from a gallant, in whom offense is not *cortesanía*, but *descortesía;* etc.[37] In the course of his book, Milán concluded, he had treated all styles of speaking: from the lofty, for the serious affairs of life; through the middling, with which he represents the jocose conversations of dignified courtiers; to the lowly, for the amusing chatter of *donosos* and *truhanes*.[38]

If Milán concerned himself with the rhetoric of courtesy, Doctor Juan Huarte offered supplementary scientific opinion on an important aspect of the art. Huarte was pondering the nature of the differences in intellectual endowment which enabled one man to master a field of knowledge and made another totally incapable of doing the same. He observed that the imagination of the *graciosos* and other sharp-witted jesters and gibers was quite different from, and antithetical to, their capacity in cognition and memory. Their sharpness, their cleverness in anything they undertook, their readiness in speech, and the aptness of their responses, all made them particularly suited to *servir en palacio*.[39]

From the halls of the nobles, the art of polite conversation moved into the parlors of all the citizenry in Gracián Dantisco's *Galateo español* (1582). This manual aspired principally to give advice on conducting ordinary conversations in such a way as to gain the favor and friendship of all. Gracián repeated the familiar ideas concerning jesting and the care to be employed in its practice. He quoted "un cortesano" on spicing conversation with biting witticisms and offered the story in which Villalobos was called *gracioso* and *chocarrero* (in his version) as a perfect example of a witty retort. "The truth is," he observed, "in order to endure

---

36. Luis Milán, *El cortesano* [1561] (Madrid, 1874), p. 5.
37. *Ibid.*, p. 266.
38. *Ibid.*, p. 471.
39. *Examen de ingenios* [1575], BAE, LXV (Madrid, 1873), p. 449.

this difficult life, we seek relaxation and diversion; and the *motes* and *burlas* are common sources of amusement and recreation." [40]

This philosophy and this spirit infused several dialogues composed, according to their author, with no other aim than to offer a variety of pleasant and witty conversations held by five "people of good taste." [41] A noteworthy feature of that group was the participation of the *truhán* Castañeda, who was charged with a large share of the wittier remarks; and he performed to perfection the role of the classical parasite, long identified with the *truhán*. "Truhán por comer: parasitus," wrote Nebrija a century earlier. [42]

If the *Galateo español* was less pretentious and less heavily ballasted with distinguished model courtiers, it was no less highly regarded by its well-wishers. The young Lope de Vega hailed its appearance, calling it "la curiosa Princesa Cortesía" ("the rare Princess Courtesy"), a guide for those who sought the "perfect grace of the polished courtier." Its author was called, among other things, *Cortesano* and *Gracioso*. [43]

The lesson taught by the foregoing moderators of taste was that being *gracioso,* in the sense of cultivating an urbane, witty, discreet mode of conversing, represented one of the loftiest virtues of the Renaissance courtier; and that attempting to be *gracioso* by perverting this style was one of the most reprehensible of faults. It was possible to transgress not only by lack of moderation in jesting, but also by engaging in the art of entertaining for self-interest and especially for gain. So, if a man deemed himself *gracioso,* he was often, for one reason or another, also *chocarrero* and *truhanesco*. Indeed, the moralizers of the century would hold that the great halls and the courts of Spain were filled with them. "Oh, Kings and Princes!" exclaimed Policronio, "how blind you are, who . . . give more ready welcome to *chocarreros* than to wise men!" [44] "These ill-fated people!" exclaimed the Gallo, "their name is *truanes*

---

40. Gracián Dantisco, *Galateo español,* ed. M. Morreale (Madrid, 1968), pp. 105, 147–148, 149.

41. G. Lucas Hidalgo, *Diálogos de apacible entretenimiento* [1606], BAE, XXXVI (Madrid, 1871), p. 279.

42. *Vocabulario español-latino,* s.v.

43. *Galateo,* p. 102.

44. Juan de Pineda, *Diálogos familiares de la agricultura cristiana* [1589], BAE, CLXI (Madrid, 1963), p. 62.

chucarreros and they glory in their name!" This introduced an extravagant picture of the sordid and licentious life at court, in which the art of wit served only for personal gain: flattering those who were present and abusing those who were absent.[45] One was given to understand, too, that devils played ball in hell with the souls of the flatterers of princes and lords, and those of *truhanes* and *chocarreros*.[46]

One of the factors that made the proliferation of servitors possible was implied by Castiglione in his prologue, namely, that the purpose of his book was to produce a courtier of such excellence that any Prince worthy of being served by him could call himself a great lord, no matter how small his estate.[47] That is to say, the sole destiny of the courtier was to serve. While this could include the nobleman who must conduct himself affably and discreetly in the presence of his king, it most appropriately designated the servant, the advisor, and, hence, the confidant and the boon companion. Within this context can be discerned the existence of a certain kind of servant or companion, attached to a gentleman or nobleman, whose primary office was to amuse, to divert and, inevitably, to flatter. While Sempronio identified the type in the *Celestina* (II.i), the deftest portrait—in reverse—was sketched by the Squire of the *Lazarillo de Tormes*, who lamented that he had been unable to find the gentleman for whom he could become a most proper *privado* ("confidant"), though he was as skillful as the next man in serving and pleasing such a master. He could lie to him, amuse him wonderfully, laugh at his jokes and antics, poor as they might be; and he had many other ideal qualities such as he observed were common in the courts of the day.[48] In the candid mirror of the *Lazarillo*, the converse of the "perfect courtier" saw himself reflected. Possessing the shadow of the qualities and talents of the *galán gracioso*, he was the very image of the reviled *truhán* who was held up so often as a monitory example. That is to say, he was the image of that ancient type of *truhán*: the boon companion, compounded of servant, confidant, sycophant, buffoon, and minstrel.

45. Cristóbal de Villalón (?), *Diálogo que trata de las transformaciones de Pitágoras*, NBAE, VII (Madrid, 1907), p. 106.

46. "Christophoro Gnosopho," *El crotalón*, NBAE, VII (Madrid, 1907), p. 214.

47. Castellón, *El cortesano*, p. 29.

48. *La vida de Lazarillo de Tormes*, ed. J. Cejador (Madrid, 1914), pp. 215–217.

The traditional *truhán* displayed many talents; or, rather, the many kinds of entertainers who were known as *truhanes* displayed their individual skills, or combinations of skills, with a common goal in mind: to amuse, to divert, to gain and hold the good will of their audience by the exercise of their wit and art, and with this to discharge their professional commitment. "Por ser mi oficio de gracias" ("Because my province is that of *gracias*"), said Alvaro de Luna's fictional *truhán,* "Fortune sends me from your table, since today she begins to *des-graciar* your house." [49] The province of the *truhán* ranged from the clown and professional fool—natural and pretended—to the most accomplished singer, dancer, jester, and raconteur; always the aim was to win the viewer and listener with his art. It should cause no surprise, if the courtier was reminded occasionally that his *graciosidad* bore a noticeable resemblance to the art of the *truhán.*

The contrast between *gracioso* and *truhán* was a source of witty or ironic effect that was repeatedly drawn upon. "When the Prince is a poet, we all write verses, . . . when he takes a fancy to *truhanes,* we are all tricked out as *graciosos,*" said the counselor, referring to the courtiers. [50] When Mercury was called *donoso* by Alcumena, his immediate thought was that he was now ready to serve as *truhán o de alcahuete.* [51] Casandra, disguised as a shepherd, is picked up and brought to court as a *graciosísimo* page. Charmed by the comical figure, the rustic speech, and the expert guitar playing and singing of the "page," Prince Enrique offers her the ritual gift of one of his fine suits. She accepts it, she said, not as a gift to a needy person, but for being a *truhán.* "I am giving it to you for being a *gracioso,*" answered the Prince. [52] There are various kinds of *graciosos,* explained Guzmán de Alfarache (bef. 1598). Some are *discretos,* who utter wise sayings and like to be private counselors to their masters and assume positions of great importance in their households. Other *graciosos* are the simple-minded type who, inspired by God, are able to come out with witty remarks. There is yet another class of

49. A. Durán, *Romancero general,* II, BAE, XVI (Madrid, 1861), p. 56.

50. F. Furio Ceriol, *El concejo y consejeros del príncipe,* BAE, XXXVI (Madrid, 1871), p. 337.

51. Juan de Timoneda, *Obras* (Madrid, 1911), I, 27.

52. *Comedia yntitulada del Tirano Rrey Corbanto,* ed. I. Laas (Iowa City, 1931), p. 79.

graciosos who are only good for dancing, playing, singing, gossiping, etc. Those are the ones who get the jewels, the rich clothes, the fistfuls of money. Of himself, referring to his entry into the service of the French ambassador, he said: "My duties were a little vague . . . the plain fact of the matter is that I was his *gracioso,* although others called me *truhán chocarrero."* [53] "Tell me, modern *truhán* and ancient dolt," fumed Don Quixote, scolding Sancho Panza for teasing the duenna. After tossing about such epithets as "grosero villano" and "mentecato gracioso," he concluded with the warning: "The one who stumbles in playing the chatterbox and the *gracioso,* at the first slip falls, and he ends up a *truhán des-graciado."* [54]

At the turn of the century, at the height of the Golden Age, the *gracioso* was, it seems, an ambiguous figure, a split personality. He was an ideal figure, the model of wit; at the same time, he was a real figure, a member of society. As an ideal figure, his mask could be donned by any who felt inspired, and his existence was no less real for being assumed. But the *gracioso* lived haunted always by his baser self, as well. In the minds of many people, obviously, the *gracioso* and the *truhán* were veritably one.

When Lope de Vega allegorized Gracián Dantisco's courtesy book as "Princesa Cortesía," he likewise bestowed a string of names—mixing figurative with real—upon the author who had introduced the Princess: "Gustoso, General, Gracioso, Grato, / Gracián, Galán, Gallardo, Galateo," all synonymous, of course, with that "Cortesano" (= Gracián), who, he implied, epitomized the ideal. Obviously, also, transposing his thoughts into the key of allegorical and figurative expression was one of the devices of Lope's rhetoric. Some years later, in 1620, when Lope was putting together for publication some of his earlier plays, he recalled that *La Francesilla* (ca. 1595–1596) "was the first [comedy] in which the *figura del donaire* was introduced, which since that time has given rise to so many others in present-day [comedies]." [55]

Lope's assertion has prompted much discussion, but all critics agree, evidently, that he was referring to the Gracioso, that conventional, if

---

53. *La novel picaresca,* ed. A. Valbuena y Prat (Madrid, 1962), pp. 372, 393–395.
54. M. de Cervantes, *Obras completas* (Madrid, 1943), p. 1361.
55. *Obras,* R.A.E. (Nueva), V (Madrid, 1918), p. 665.

protean, comic figure so popular in the *comedia nueva*.[56] On the other hand, when investigators examined *La Francesilla* to observe the primordial specimen of the dramatic Gracioso, no little confusion was engendered by the discovery that the character of Tristán seemed very little different from Pinelo, in *El favor agradecido* (1593), Galindo, in *Los comendadores de Córdoba* (1596), and several other comic figures in plays written at about the same time or earlier. In short, having assumed that the reference was exact, that the connotation was certain, it was found that there were inexplicable irregularities. Critics have dealt generously with Lope, nevertheless. It has been remarked that his memory for exact information had failed him on other occasions: for example, he had utterly lost count, apparently by several hundred, of the number of plays that he had written. One might, too, interpret his statement broadly, as meaning that he began toward the end of the century, when *La Francesilla* was written, to use the Gracioso on a systematic basis.[57] The most careful attempt to rationalize the disparity relied upon a definition of the Gracioso that screened out most of the early contenders. This, together with problems of chronology, permitted the writer to conclude that Lope was conceivably correct.[58]

These attempts to resolve the dilemma illustrate a misconception of the basic problem in Lope's phrase, which is a semantic one. Being based, as these discussions were essentially, upon the plays typical of the seventeenth century, the denotation of an expression presumed to stand for "the

---

56. Previous studies on the dramatic Gracioso were reviewed by Juana de José Prades, *Teoría sobre los personajes de la Comedia Nueva, en cinco dramaturgos* (Madrid, 1963). An essential earlier study not mentioned is E. B. Place, "Does Lope de Vega's Gracioso Stem in Part from Harlequin?," *Hispania*, XVII (1934), 257–270. Related are N. D. Shergold, "Ganassa and the 'Commedia dell'arte' in Sixteenth-Century Spain," *MLR*, LI (1956), 359–368; and J. Falconieri, "Historia de la 'Commedia dell'arte' en España," *RL*, XI (1957), 3–37; XII (1958), 69–90. Subsequent to Prades' study were C. Aubrun, *La comedia española* (Madrid, 1968), pp. 208–217; and O. Arróniz, *La influencia italiana en el nacimiento de la comedia española* (Madrid, 1969), pp. 285–290.

57. Menéndez Pelayo's opinion was reaffirmed by A. Castro and H. Rennert, *Vida de Lope de Vega*, ed. F. Lázaro Carreter (Madrid, 1968), p. 343 n.; and by C. Ley, *El gracioso en el teatro de la Península* (Madrid, 1954), p. 16.

58. J. H. Arjona, "La introducción del gracioso en el teatro de Lope de Vega," *HR*, VII (1939), 1–21.

Gracioso" was automatically assigned, in this context, to the familiar dramatic character. Moreover, it was assigned to him exclusively. But when one is speaking of Lope de Vega and his conception of the figure in those earlier years, caution is in order. While the designation "Gracioso" appears to occur in abundance, it is a curious fact that Lope himself has not used it in listing any cast of characters in the autograph plays available at this writing. References to this comic character in the stage directions of Lope's plays seem to resolve themselves mainly into such expressions as "a lo gracioso" and "graciosamente," or to its attributive use: "escudero gracioso, lacayo gracioso, soldado gracioso," and in identical contexts, "calzas graciosas" ("funny breeches") (that is, "breeches of the type worn by comedians for comical effect"). These designations could be interpreted either as "in a comical manner and comically dressed, possibly with stylized costumes," or "in the manner and the garb of the Gracioso, that well-known dramatic character." Lope has not favored the historian of the drama with descriptions of what were obviously commonplaces of staging. But the question of the identity, or the definition, of the dramatic Gracioso and his structural significance in the design of the New Comedy, comprise a separate problem, one that can only be alluded to in the present discussion. The first problem is to determine what idea Lope was trying to convey, which may help to understand how this progenitor of well over two hundred Graciosos and Graciosas conceived of this character.

The assumed reference of the *figura del donaire* may be excessively narrow. The assumption that Lope incorporates an allusion to the popular comic character is probably justified, but it may be questioned that *figura* denotes that concrete entity in the sense of "character." The noun *donaire,* of course, does not count among its concrete denotations "the comic character commonly called 'Gracioso.'" Some scholars, not all, have implicitly acknowledged the figurative use of *donaire* ("wit, witticism"), before assigning this paraphrasis to the "Gracioso." Those who would interpret *figura* as "character, personage in a play," will also grant that it may mean "figure of speech, image, personification, or allegorical representation of something or someone." Since Lope was clearly employing a figurative mode of expression, it would be judicious to paraphrase his declaration as: "the first comedy in which Wit personified, or the Mask of Wit, was introduced." The resemblance to the phrasing of the welcome he extended to the "Princesa Cortesía" will not go unnoticed. Lope's phrase can be considered, therefore, to refer primarily to the *gracioso,* the preceding century's favored figure of wit and, secondarily, to the Gracioso, the succeeding century's favorite comic character. While it is true that Lope's gallants might be charming, polished, and witty—that is to say, approximations of the ideal courtier as depicted in the manuals—it is doubtful that with *donaire* he was epitomizing their character. Lope's gallants, after all, did not routinely provide the comic element in the plays. It was the alter ego of the figure of wit, the professional *gracioso* or *truhán* as jester, and the *gracioso* as ironic or parodic figure—wearing the mask of the jester—who served as the routine vehicle of the *donaire.*

By whatever path he achieved his condition and call him what they would, his identity remained the same. "What do you expect?" protested the pretended shepherd, Sancho, brought to the court and dressed in finery. "They throw these mixed-up things on me, pinning feathers all over me, and first they call me 'Captain,' then they call me 'Caballero'—in reverse." "By my faith," answered Matico, "that's baptizing you as *truhán."* [59] When rustic Fabio was persuaded to go to the court, he resigned himself to donning the habit of the gallant, with his *capa de charlatán* and his lying, flattering, ill-humored courtly pleasantries. Shortly after arriving, he emerged, decked out as an *escudero gracioso* and examining himself: "Breeches these are called, I am told. / Strange and wondrous fabrication!" [60]

The traditional conception of the jester as court buffoon and strolling minstrel was used repeatedly by Lope as a dramatic recourse. Estela, wishing to enter the court unrecognized, weighed the choice between the guise of a page and that of a fool. She chose the latter, for as a court fool she could enter the court freely and make her way straight to the king. With this double-edged device—woman disguised as man and wit

---

59. *Los donaires de Matico* [bef. 1596], *Obras,* R.A.E. (Nueva), IV (Madrid, 1917), p. 703.

60. *La firmeza en la desdicha* [1610–1612], *Obras,* V, 627–628, 632. For an example of the distinctive garb of the Gracioso, see N. D. Shergold, *A History of the Spanish Stage* (Oxford, 1967), p. 294 and fig. 2.

disguised as fool—a multiplicity of complications ensued, all colored by the "truths" that fools traditionally utter.[61]

Laura chose the costume of the *truhán*. Although she startled Leonarda by appearing before her unexpectedly in the palace, she had only to announce: "I am the minister of Pleasure, otherwise known as *truhán*." Leonarda remarked how *galán* the newcomer was, wanting to know only if he could sing and play. Laura, acting the very model of her office, as well as its monitor, "provincial de truhanes," observed that they should all know how to sing, to prevent them from being insufferable bores.[62]

Lope was obviously relying upon a dramatic convention (with costume?) familiar to his audience, when in an opening scene, and with no preamble, Brito explained to his master how he was able to speak to Doña Blanca: "Whenever I want, / con la capa del donaire / I am able to move freely about the palace." [63] It is significant that the word *donaire* appears to be used in a sense identical to that of Lope's remark of some ten years before. Here a play on the sense of *capa* ("cape, guise") has yielded a compound image: "in the guise of [the minister of] wit," that is to say, "with [protected by] the cape of the jester." This strengthens the impression that in Lope's lexicon *gracioso* and *truhán* were to a certain degree synonymous.

It has been pointed out that Lope was not generous with unambiguous references to Graciosos. In fact, only one possible example can be cited here—observed in reading perhaps two hundred plays—and, characteristically, this one still could be construed in a general rather than a specific sense.

When members of an acting troupe were being interrogated, by order of Emperor Diocletian, Albino was asked what roles he played. "I?" he said, "I play the *graciosos,* / the unhappy ones, not the happy ones, / if you wreak your fury here." [64] Whether the word *graciosos* would seem to denote "the personages called Graciosos," or whether it seemed to refer

---

61. *Los torneos de Aragón* [1597], *Obras,* R.A.E. (Nueva), X (Madrid, 1930), pp. 11, 16-18, 33, and *passim.*

62. *La inocente Laura* [prob. 1604-1608], BAE, LII (Madrid, 1860), pp. 490-491.

63. *El guante de Doña Blanca* [prob. 1630-1635], BAE, XLI (Madrid, 1873), p. 17.

64. *Lo fingido verdadero* [ca. 1608], *Obras escogidas,* ed. F. C. Sainz de Robles, III (Madrid, 1955), p. 197.

to "comic characters" in general, it still remains an important clue to Lope's thinking about this dramatic role, but in a curious way, as it turns out.

The rest of Albino's speech, "desdichados, no dichosos," etc., while compatible with the evident sentiment he was expressing, seemed to be singularly uninspired. It not only appeared to lack the neatness and pointedness of phrasing that one expects from Lope, but the character of the Gracioso—and he evidently was that—was left with an insipidity to utter when all the rules of *graciosidad,* as well as of comedy, required that he respond with a sally that would leave the audience laughing. However, when the apparent source of Albino's remark is examined, the anomaly disappears. In the treatise of Donatus on comedy and tragedy, the *parasiti* are said to wear a certain kind of robe. Those who are *happy* wear white robes; the *unhappy* wear soiled robes (*obsoletus* ["dirty, stained"]). Two things are revealed by this. First, the word *graciosos* was a rendering of *parasiti,* a correspondence more often identified by the term *truhán.* The second realization is that the reputation for wit that the Gracioso possessed was preserved, although the joke might not be to the taste of all, and assuming that it was intelligible to Lope's audience. It is true that Albino's words were an exact—if partial—quotation, but this would not suffice for comic effect. What, after all, did the "soiled robes of the unhappy" mean? In light of Albino's fear that the Emperor's fury might fall upon him, one can only recall the plight of Sancho Panza when, only a couple of years before Lope wrote this play, Don Quixote's squire underwent a comparable upsetting experience.

As has been said, from his explicit statements it is difficult to determine to what extent Lope had formalized his conception of the Gracioso. It is obvious, of course, that one or another of his characters may be pointed to as exemplifying the role. The lackey was undoubtedly the most prominent. But, in a certain sense, the lackey's part was not a role; the lackey *filled* a role. He filled the role which was structurally a constituent of not merely a given plot, but any plot of this theater. The fact that the role was not filled exclusively by the lackey—but also by a shepherd, a farmer, a soldier, or even a Moor—has prevented the construction of neat schemata. The role was endowed with certain properties, largely traditional in derivation, but flexible enough to assimilate whatever the unfolding art form received: by chance from an author—a Lope; by

chance from a novel artistic conception—the Italian comedians (?); by
chance from an inspired actor—a Nicolás de los Ríos (?). Ultimately,
in the very allusive art of Lope, the role was endowed with his view of
the world. It had its correspondence in the actual world of men—the
gracioso—but perhaps to an even greater extent in the world of the
mind—*la graciosidad.*

The *figura del donaire* had existed as far back as men can remember,
his mask passing from jester to jester. Lope may not have composed this
witty Golden Age credo of Bitonto, the *gracioso,* but he could have;
and he would have been speaking of all *graciosos:* "Que si me muero, se
acaba / toda la graciosidad" ("For if I die, all Wit dies with me").[65]

65. *El buen vecino, Obras,* R.A.E. (Nueva), IV (Madrid, 1917), p. 12. Attribution
to Lope is questionable.

Italian Renaissance Comedy and Its Critics: A Survey of Recent Studies

Review Article

BEATRICE CORRIGAN

A S ONE OF THE MOST POPULAR GENRES during the sixteenth century which saw its birth, comedy combined in typically Renaissance fashion the authority of classical theories and models, the native Italian tradition of *novella* and romance, and a keen observation of contemporary life. Working within the rigid framework of five acts, three unities, and traditional plot outlines, the dramatists treated this iron form as though it were as light as a soap bubble, and projected on it a thousand capricious multicolored designs. They peopled their stage with a myriad of fantastic characters, some of whom acquired a protean immortality, and set them in mad pursuit of unachievable goals of wealth and amorous conquest, bringing them back at last from the labyrinths of folly to the sane familiar paths of civil life.

Widely read, as shown by the numerous editions through which many of them passed, they were the delight of at least three generations, but were eclipsed early in the next century by the novel enchantments of the musical dramas, which rapidly developed into opera. Their fortunes were strangely affected by changing political and social currents. Midway through the eighteenth century they were rediscovered, reprinted, sometimes adapted for new stage techniques, but again they were eclipsed, this time by Romantic poetic tragedy. Not until late in the last century were they once more the subject of interest, and then only as an aspect of Renaissance literature, dismissed by De Sanctis as a negative aspect of sixteenth-century culture, and subjected to the methods of German philological scholarship by professors who deplored their lack of moral seriousness and had little esteem for the theater as a living art.

In England little critical attention was paid to Italian comedy, though the British Museum catalogue and John L. Lievsay's *The Englishman's Italian Books, 1550–1700*[1] prove that plays were popular reading: their format, generally duodecimo, made them admirable traveling companions, and they were an excellent guide to lively conversation. Joseph Cooper Walker published a book on Italian tragedy in 1799, but it was perhaps John Addington Symonds who, in 1881, with his own peculiar brand of horrified fascination, first dealt with comedy in the *Italian Literature* volumes of his *Renaissance in Italy* series. The English-speaking world was, however, attracted rather to the *commedia dell'arte,* and continued until fairly recently to neglect the written plays. But during the last ten or fifteen years much serious study has been devoted to Renaissance comedy, both in Italy and in the United States, by scholars who have been attracted to the subject for different reasons.

In North America the remarkable development of interest in Elizabethan and Jacobean drama has stimulated a study of comparative literature, of sources, affinities, influences, and theories. Indeed, it was Marvin Herrick's work on *Comic Theory in the Sixteenth Century* which led him to publish in 1960 his *Italian Comedy in the Renaissance,* a book and a date which provide the starting point for the present survey. He explains in his preface that this is the book he would have welcomed himself when, thirty-five years earlier, he began to teach. Little had been available in English then, and little had been published since on "the golden age of Italian comedy." Indeed, his is probably the first monograph in English to be devoted to the subject. Written primarily for readers with no knowledge of Italian, it names and summarizes some 230 plays (not all of them comedies) in the course of 227 pages, and so provides a valuable collection of brief plot analyses. Herrick had little room for critical appraisals, but he produced a most useful handbook, which has become one of the standard references on the subject.

---

1. Works mentioned in the text are listed more fully in the appended bibliography.

It was supplemented in 1969 by Douglas Radcliff-Umstead's *The Birth of Modern Comedy in Renaissance Italy,* which, as the title indicates, deals chiefly with the first half of the century. It discusses, as Herrick does not, critical theory of the period, but it is particularly useful for the plot analyses it contains. These are traced at some length in the text, and an additional summary of twenty-one plots, including those of plays by Ariosto, Aretino, and Machiavelli, is provided in an appendix. The book is also valuable because it makes available for English readers the fruits of Italian scholarship. The author is widely read in Italian criticism, and he has brought together material on the plays and their authors published by leading Italian scholars over a long period. He also supplies the only extensive account in English of Latin humanist plays written by Italians: their plots, too, are summarized in an appendix. Two important accounts of Italian theater in the fifteenth century which he does not mention are Vito Pandolfi's *Teatro goliardico dell'Umanesimo* and Antonio Staüble's *La Commedia umanistica del Quattrocento.* The former presents ten Latin antecedents of Renaissance comedy with Italian translations; the latter analyzes forty-nine comedies, discusses their structure, characters, and settings, and contains a bibliography of texts and criticism.

The plots of eleven comedies are included in Appendix A of David Orr's *Italian Renaissance Drama in England before 1625,* but with some inevitable overlapping with other works, as Louise George Clubb had already given an account of all Della Porta's plays, and Douglas Radcliff-Umstead had discussed Ariosto's *I Suppositi.*

Only the scantiest of biographical information can be included in such surveys, and with the exception of such writers as Ariosto, Machiavelli, and Aretino, famous for their nondramatic works rather than for their plays, many Renaissance writers for the theater remain shadowy figures. Two excellent studies have appeared to supply this deficiency in recent years, each the first full-length monograph in English on its subject. The first, in 1965, was Louise Clubb's *Giambattista Della Porta: Dramatist,* a distinguished and authoritative work which illuminates a whole intellectual movement in late sixteenth-century Naples, where the Spanish viceroys who loved the theater were often at variance with the Tridentine authorities who condemned it. Dr. Clubb draws an admirable portrait of one of the most remarkable men of his age, a student of physiognomy, natural science, and magic, a friend of Galileo and Tasso. The recent interest in the history of science has given Della Porta new importance, and his plays are now acknowledged as some of the most vigorous and original of the late Renaissance. A monograph on *L'Attività teatrale di G. B. Della Porta* by R. Sirri Rubes was published in 1968.

The second biography in English, Robert J. Rodini's *Antonfrancesco Grazzini: Poet, Dramatist, and Novelliere, 1503–1584* is also a skillful treatment of a polygraph who portrayed in his comedies as well as in his *novelle* the everyday life of his native Florence in the earlier part of the century. That city is better known to most readers than Della Porta's Naples; a less familiar and later period in its history is described by Andrew C. Minor and Bonner Mitchell in *A Renaissance Entertainment,* which translates a contemporary account of the festivities for the marriage of Cosimo I de' Medici and Eleonora da Toledo in 1539. During the prolonged series of rejoicings a comedy was performed—Antonio Landi's *Il Commodo*—and this, too, is included, in its first translation into English.

A still later and more elaborate period of the court dramas of Florence is described and lavishly illustrated in A. M. Nagler's *Theatre Festivals of the Medici, 1539–1637.* The opening of the Uffizi theater in 1586 saw the performance of Giovanni Bardi's *L'Amico fido,* and in 1589 Girolamo Bargagli's *La Pellegrina* was performed. These, however, were exceptions, for despite the architectural magnificence with which the designer might crowd his set, often in skillful imitation of an actual cityscape, the unity of place and the bourgeois rank decreed for the characters had already damaged the popularity of comedy with both noble audience and producer, who preferred mythological plays, *intermezzi,* and ballets, dazzling with exotic costumes and cunningly devised machines.

Ferrara, a city much less familiar to English readers, but the cradle of vernacular comedy, was quite as passionately devoted to the theater as either Florence or Naples. It is the background for Anthony Gisolfi's "Ariosto's Delightful Prologue to *La Cassaria,*" published in *Theater Annual,* which describes the circumstances in which this first of all *commedie erudite* was performed, and includes a lively verse translation of Ariosto's witty address to the audience. The role of both Ferrara and Rome in encouraging the staging of comedy was recently examined in *Renaissance Drama* by Bonner Mitchell in an article, "Circumstance and

Setting in the Earliest Italian Productions of Comedy." It is evident from his quotations that the comparatively humble social station of the characters was not always allowed to exclude opulence of costume.

A complete description taken from contemporary documents, to which Bonner Mitchell refers, of a contemporary theater in Rome is published in Fabrizio Cruciani's *Il Teatro del Campidoglio e le feste romane del 1513*. Elaborate architectural design and decoration were lavished on the building erected to celebrate the admission to Roman citizenship of Leo X's brother and nephew. The comedy performed was not by an Italian author but by Plautus, and its staging and costuming were magnificent. The staging of another comedy, Belisario Bulgarini's *Gli Scambi,* in 1574 in Siena, is described by Florindo Cerreta in *Italica*.

Many articles have been written on the relations between Italian and English comedy, but, as this interest was keen from the 1920's on, the major part of them fall outside the time boundary of this survey. David Orr's monograph, mentioned above, deals with English plays which owe a demonstrable debt to Italian sources. He devotes a chapter to comedy, but his treatment is superficial, as is his discussion of possible ways in which Italian models became known in England. He makes one valuable suggestion which it is to be hoped will be pursued, perhaps by a group of graduate students: that is the desirability of individual plot-character-motif indexes for Plautus and Terence, Italian drama, and English drama, similar to Stith Thompson's *Motif-index of Folk Literature*. Dr. Orr's bibliography is surprisingly incomplete, and he seems unaware of Louise Clubb's articles on Anglo-Italian relations in drama, as well as of her Della Porta study, though her "Italian Comedy and the *Comedy of Errors"* was published in 1968. Robert C. Melzi's "From Lelia to Viola," which appeared in 1966, is also not referred to, though it traces the development of the boy-girl heroine of *Gl'Ingannati* through Secchi's *L'Interesse* and Della Porta's *Cintia* into the Viola of *Twelfth Night,* and shows that the gentle character of this "first modern female of the Italian Renaissance" made steady progress in humanity and charm. Robert J. Williams' comparison of *La Mandragola* and Middleton's *A Chaste Maid in Cheapside* did not appear until 1970, and Louise Clubb's "The Tragicomic Bear," on Italian analogues with *The Winter's Tale,* belongs to 1972. Her paper on the *commedia grave,* the pastoral, and their associations with Shakespeare, will eventually appear in the *Atti* of the 1972 conference at Montepulciano of the Centro degli Studi Humanistici.

Research in Italian drama has been facilitated during the period under survey by the publication of catalogues of three major collections in North America. Beatrice Corrigan's *Catalogue of Italian Plays, 1500– 1700, in the Library of the University of Toronto* appeared in 1961, and has been followed by two supplements published in *Renaissance News* in 1963 and 1966. *Renaissance Quarterly* will soon print a third supplement. The Toronto Library now contains over 630 items. In 1966 Marvin Herrick's *Italian Plays, 1500–1700, in the University of Illinois Library* listed more than 550 plays, many of them comedies, rustic comedies, and farces. Louise Clubb's *Italian Plays in the Folger Library,* with an important preface, lists nearly 900 items. It was published by Olschki in 1968, and is well illustrated with reproduced title pages, portraits, and plates of scenery from the original editions. Dr. Clubb's interest in pictorial sources later resulted in an article, "Pictures for the Reader: A Series of Illustrations to Comedy." Forty plays in the University of Iowa Library have also been listed by Florindo Cerreta. Yet Marvin Herrick was right in saying that what is needed is a joint index of Italian plays in North American libraries, which would save time and expense both for scholars and for interlibrary loan departments.

Few scholars outside Italy have edited plays, but a model for future editors of Renaissance texts is Florindo Cerreta's critical edition of Alessandro Piccolomini's *L'Alessandro,* which appeared in 1966 and which is based on a study of all existing manuscripts and early editions. It contains variants, linguistic commentaries, and an introduction on the origin and fortunes of the play. Particularly useful is an analysis of sixteenth-century punctuation. This was followed in 1971 by a similar edition of Scipione Bargagli's *La Pellegrina.* Professor Cerreta's work on Sienese comedy has also resulted in four articles, one refuting a suggested attribution of *Gl'Ingannati* to Lodovico Castelvetro, two on early editions of the same play, and the fourth describing the Sienese holograph manuscript of *La Pellegrina* which he used for his edition.

Dennis E. Rhodes in "The Printer of Ariosto's Early Plays," published in England in 1963, has by expert typographical examination demonstrated that both *La Cassaria* and *I Suppositi* were pirated and printed in 1510 or 1511, possibly as early as 1509, by Bernardo Zucchetta of Florence.

This identification was later challenged by Roberto Ridolfi. The dating of the *Mandragola* was discussed by Sergio Bertelli in *Renaissance Quarterly*.

Addressing successive meetings of the MLA conference "Research Opportunities in Renaissance Drama," (*q.v.*) Marvin Herrick, Daniel Boughner, John Lievsay, and Beatrice Corrigan spoke of the many unexamined aspects of Italian comedy; Leicester Bradner and Louis A. Schuster discussed Neo-Latin comedy. Very little work on subjects suggested by those papers has yet been undertaken, and particularly evident still is the need for translations. Machiavelli's *La Mandragola* and *La Clizia* are available in English, but very little else has been translated. Eric Bentley included in *The Genius of the Italian Theater*, published in 1964, three Renaissance comedies: Bernardo Dovizi da Bibbiena's *La Calandria;* the anonymous *Gl'Ingannati* (an abridged translation by Thomas Love Peacock); and Giordano Bruno's *Il Candelaio*. J. R. Hale's *The Literary Works of Machiavelli* includes translations of *La Mandragola* and *La Clizia*.

La Mandragola has been a popular play for student performances, one of which, at Merton College, Oxford, inspired Dr. Hale's translation. In 1972 it was twice performed in California with the original music, recently discovered by Dr. H. Colin Slim of the Department of Music at the Irvine campus. It was an American, too, Professor Theodore A. Sumberg, who in 1961 in the *Journal of Politics* interpreted the play as a political allegory of young political wisdom taking power by a conspiracy, its union eventually blessed by the Church. This reading was more fully developed by Alessandro Parronchi in "La Prima Rappresentazione della *Mandragola*"; he identifies in Messer Nicia the impotent gonfalonier, Piero Soderini, in Lucrezia Florence herself, and in Callimaco the vigorous young Medici captain, Lorenzo, slightly blemished by his sojourn in France. This interpretation has been angrily dismissed by traditionalists, but it is well within the conventions of Renaissance allegory and indeed has some contemporary confirmation. In 1969, writing in *Italica,* Franco Fido suggested an even wider political significance for the play, as did Ezio Raimondi in 1972, extending his interpretation to *La Clizia* as well. Particularly original is Raimondi's analysis of Machiavelli's debt to Plautus for structural and stylistic elements.

Another play which has been popular with the critics and on the stage is

Giordano Bruno's *Il Candelaio*. It has recently been the subject of a highly original article by Alan P. Barr.

In Italy the very nationalism that damaged the cause of Renaissance comedy in the nineteenth century has enhanced it in the twentieth. The prejudice against the sixteenth century as the period of lost political liberties and foreign domination has been softened by time, and during the late Fascist period the whole body of Renaissance drama was rediscovered, as it had been to a lesser degree in the eighteenth century, and acclaimed as one of the most original and influential developments in European theater—which indeed it was in many respects. It was Benedetto Croce whose intermittent but continued interest in Renaissance comedy served as a link between the philological preoccupations of the late nineteenth century and the more varied approaches of modern criticism. In *Croce e il teatro,* Federico Frascani devotes a chapter to Renaissance comedy, and shows that Croce was particularly interested in Bruno, Beolco, Machiavelli, Annibal Caro, and Della Porta. His admiration of Sforza Oddi's *Erofilomachia* led him to publish in 1946 the first modern edition of that play. But he found Ariosto's comedies disappointing, and considered that in general the comedies of the period were lacking in "poesia."

The steadily mounting Italian interest in the genre has manifested itself since 1960 in a variety of ways. Of fundamental importance are numerous new editions of the plays themselves. Fifteen years ago, except for the works of a few major dramatists, only the original texts were extant, and scholars had to visit specialized libraries or work from microfilms and xeroxed copies. Now the most important plays are accessible in modern editions, many of them in the very inexpensive Collezione di Teatro published by Einaudi, and in the BUR series of Rizzoli. Of four important anthologies, three fall outside our period but must be mentioned here as forerunners. Anton Giulio Bragaglia's *Commedie giocose del '500* (1946) contains twelve plays, and Silvio D'Amico's *Teatro italiano* (1955), ten. The former volume has an introduction and a glossary, the second is without notes. The third, Aldo Borlenghi's *Commedie del Cinquecento* (1959) contains eighteen plays, an introduction, notes, and an appendix on Angelo Beolco. The fourth, Nino Borsellini's two-volume anthology of the same title, came out in 1962 and

1967; it provides ten plays, with an important introduction to each volume, notes to the texts, and a bibliographical note. There is naturally some overlapping: Dovizi's *La Calandria,* for instance, occurs in three of the four collections, Caro's *Gli Straccioni* in all four.

Only a few critical editions in the true sense of the word have recently appeared. *La Mandragola* was edited by Roberto Ridolfi in 1965; this edition and his "Contributo a un'edizione critica della *Clizia*" have both profited from newly discovered manuscripts. He has brought together the fruits of his long research on the plays in a volume of *Studi sulle commedie del Machiavelli,* which contains the article on *La Clizia.* For all Machiavelli research, his contributions to *La Bibliofilia* must be consulted. Recent editions of Machiavelli's comedies are too numerous to be listed here, though one may be mentioned; it has been edited with a good introduction by Franco Gaeta in Feltrinelli's *Biblioteca di classici italiani* (1965). A critical edition by Michele Catalano of Ariosto's plays was published in 1933; in 1962 Rizzoli brought out an inexpensive edition of his comedies which presents both versions of *Il Negromante, La Cassaria,* and *I Suppositi.* Torquato Tasso's *Intrighi d'amore* was published in 1968 when the play was performed in Sicily. Giorgio Petrocchi in 1971 edited Aretino's *Teatro,* containing all five comedies, with two texts, 1525 and 1534, of *La Cortegiana.* A critical edition of Giordano Bruno's *Il Candelaio* by Giorgio Barberi Squarotti appeared in 1965.

A new development in scholarly research is the publication of Renaissance critical treatises and controversies, hitherto accessible only in the original editions. Marvin Herrick, a pioneer in this as in other fields, studied Renaissance critical doctrines for his *Comic Theory,* reprinted in 1964 and so eligible for mention here. An appendix contained the first English translation of Francesco Robortelli's *Explicatio eorum omnium quae ad comoediae arteficium pertinent.* Bernard Weinberg in his *History of Literary Criticism in the Italian Renaissance* (1961) not only surveyed theories of comedy as well as of other genres, but provided scholars with many useful quotations in translation. In 1970 he published two volumes of some of the original *Trattati* on which he had based his history. Several of these, listed in the appended bibliography, are concerned with comedy.

They may be supplemented by a section edited by Ferdinando Taviani,

"Il Problema della moralità del teatro dopo il Concilio di Trento," in *Documenti di storia del teatro* (1967). It contains brief extracts from polemics by authors ranging from St. Carlo Borromeo and Cardinal Paleotti to such distinguished professional actors as G. B. Andreini and Nicolò Barbieri. Barbieri's *La Supplica,* a lively defense of the actor's profession, was published by Taviani in 1971, with variants, notes, and a critical study, as the third volume of a new series, Archivio del Teatro Italiano. The first volume made available Leone de' Sommi's *Quattro dialoghi in materia di rappresentazione sceniche,* edited in 1968 by Ferruccio Marotti. The author was a Jew, a native of Ferrara, and in 1584 he staged at the court of Mantua Bernardino Pino's *Gli ingiusti sdegni.* A playwright himself, he also directed at Mantua, in 1588, a performance of his own comedy *Le Tre Sorelle.* His theories of production, stage design, and costuming are thus based on practical experience.

Just as no general history of comedy has replaced that of Ireneo Sanesi, so no bibliography has yet superseded that of Leone Allacci, published in facsimile in 1961 by the Bottega d'Erasmo in Turin. Catalogues of individual collections have served to correct some of its errors and omissions. In 1966 Achille Mango published *La Commedia in lingua nel Cinquecento,* with an important introduction by Vito Pandolfi. It is a descriptive bibliography of 26 manuscripts and 81 printed editions of comedies: each is accompanied by a plot summary. These and other related publications can be traced through a series of review articles by Antonio Staüble in *Bibliothèque d'Humanisme et Renaissance.* A catalogue of sixteenth- and seventeenth-century comedies in the Palatina collection of the Biblioteca Nazionale in Florence was compiled by Giovanni Favilli and Maria Frulli Maggini for *Studi Secenteschi.*

The powerful influence on contemporary taste exercised by the Marxist critic Antonio Gramsci probably accounts for the recent popularity of Caro's *Gli Straccioni* and for the rediscovery of the plays of Angelo Beolco (Il Ruzante or Ruzzante) which Giorgio Zampa, writing in *Il Dramma,* has called one of the greatest triumphs of Italian culture, linguistic and dramatic, during the postwar period. Beolco, both dramatist and actor, portrayed the peasants and wrote in the dialect of his own Paduan region. His early plays had classical models, and were performed at the court of Ferrara with Ariosto's assistance in at least some of the productions. They are interpreted by the present generation as protests against the aristocratic and military society of Beolco's own day, and are consequently prized as having a relevance lacking in the plays of most of his contemporaries. His importance is evident in the anthologies of Silvio D'Amico and Borlenghi. Lodovico Zorzi brought out a complete edition of his works in 1967, including dialogues, orations, *canzoni,* and three letters. Innumerable articles have been written about him, and several books; two major monographs are Emilio Lovarini's *Studi sul Ruzzante e la letteratura padovana* and Mario Prosperi's *Angelo Beolco nominato Ruzante.* His plays have frequently been performed in Italy and elsewhere, for the Beolco vogue has been international. Gianfranco De Bosio reviewed his own productions of Ruzante over a period of twenty years in *Il Dramma* in 1968.

The manuscript of another dialect comedy, *La Venexiana,* was discovered and edited in 1928 by Emilio Lovarini. It has been printed several times, and the play has been translated into Italian and English, performed, and widely discussed. An excellent account of its fortunes by Bodo Richter, *"La Venexiana* in the Light of Recent Criticism," was published in 1970 in the *Festschrift for Leicester Bradner.* Its success has led to an interest in other dialect and rustic plays, particularly those written by the Accademia dei Rozzi in Siena. Roberto Alonge's *Teatro dei Rozzi di Siena* contains biographical and bibliographical notes on the authors and their comedies. *La Venexiana* has been compared to Giovan Aurelio Schiaffi's *La Ramusia* by Raffaele Sirri Rubes in his *Schede per il teatro del Rinascimento.* He describes a performance of the latter play in Verona in 1530, and also discusses the theater of Della Porta in relation to popular comedy. This interest in rustic plays can also be paralleled in the eighteenth century when *Ascetta,* a comedy by Francesco Mariani, was published in Paris (1756) with an introduction on the history of rustic theater and a long bibliography of such works, many of them in private libraries of Paduan scholars.

The current admiration inspired by Gramsci for proletarian or anti-establishment comedies has led to a plethora of critical attention directed to some half-dozen or so playwrights who are consistent with the new orthodoxy, and to almost complete neglect of more sober figures. Giulio Ferroni does include Raffaello Borghini among the four writers

studied in his *"Mutazione" e "riscontro" nel teatro di Machiavelli,* but
as might be expected he condemns Borghini's plays as insipid confections
suited only to courtiers' palates.

La Venexiana, Gli Straccioni, Il Candelaio, and many other comedies
of the sixteenth century have been staged in recent years; in an article in
Research Opportunities I included a check list of performances reviewed
in *Il Dramma* up to 1968. This can be supplemented by reference to subsequent issues of that periodical, as well as to reviews in Sandro De Feo's
In cerca di teatro. The new interest in their suitability for acting probably
provided inspiration for a volume of essays by several authors, *Lingua e
strutture del teatro italiano del rinascimento,* published in 1970 and edited
by G. Folena. Indeed, Franco Fido, in his "Reflections on Comedy by
some Italian Renaissance Playwrights," maintains that the great originality
of the plays of the period is their free, exuberant, unacademic use of
language.

Vito Pandolfi's *Il Teatro del Rinascimento e la commedia dell'arte*
studies the connections between erudite comedy and the professional
forms of dramatic art on which he has written the definitive reference
work, *La Commedia dell'arte: Storia e testo,* in six volumes, published
between 1957 and 1962. The *commedia dell'arte* can be mentioned here
only briefly, for the literature on the subject would require a detailed
study of some length. Present developments in this field parallel in many
ways those relating to written comedy. Two important older works in
English have been reprinted, Kathleen M. Lea's *Italian Popular Comedy*
in 1962 and Winifred Smith's *The Commedia dell'Arte* in 1964. The
latter is enriched with illustrations from the private collection of Mr.
David Allen of Baltimore. Also reprinted has been a translation by
Randolph T. Weaver of Pierre Louis Duchartre's *The Italian Comedy:*
in its 1966 issue it, too, has a new pictorial supplement.

A modern general account with lists of companies, passages from
scenari, and illustrations is Giacomo Oreglia's *The Commedia dell'Arte,*
translated by Lovett F. Edwards in 1968. The original appeared in
Sweden in 1961. Allardyce Nicoll's *The World of Harlequin* is international in scope, and is also distinguished for its fine illustrations, some of
them reproduced from the McGill Feather Book, which was the subject
of an article in *Renaissance Drama* in 1969. Ferdinando Taviani's *La*

Commedia dell'arte e la società barocca provides additional documentation for the seventeenth century. An article by Charles Felver in *Research Opportunities* offers suggestions for Anglo-Italian comparative studies. But except pictorially the delights of the *commedia dell'arte* cannot be captured on paper, as the published *scenari* have shown, even when they are by as great a figure as Flaminio Scala. A translation of his *Il Teatro delle favole rappresentative* by Henry Salerno appeared in 1968. The bare plot outlines can give little idea of what a brilliant actor could do to give them life and color; only those who were fortunate enough to see the great modern reincarnation of Arlecchino, Marcello Moretti, can imagine what the enchantment was that made such entertainment the rage in Europe for nearly three centuries.

Bibliography

Anthologies

BORLENGHI, ALDO, ed. *Commedie del Cinquecento.* 2 vols. Milan: Rizzoli, 1959.
    Vol. I: B. DOVIZI, *La Calandria*
        ANON., *Gli Ingannati*
        A. PICCOLOMINI, *L'Amor costante*
        L. DE' MEDICI, *L'Aridosia*
        L. CONTILE, *La Trinunzia*
        G. B. GELLI, *La Sporta*
        A. F. GRAZZINI, *La Strega; La Pinzochera*
        G. M. CECCHI, *L'Assiuolo*
    Vol. II: F. D'AMBRA, *Il Furto*
        A. CARO, *Gli Straccioni*
        S. ODDI, *L'Erofilomachia*
        G. B. DELLA PORTA, *La Sorella*
        ANON., *La Venexiana*
        A. BEOLCO, *La Pastorale; Moscheta; Fiorina; Saltuzza*
BORSELLINI, NINO, ed. *Commedie del Cinquecento.* 2 vols. Milan: Feltrinelli, 1962, 1967.
    Vol. I: D. GIANNOTTI, *Il Vecchio amoroso*
        A. F. GRAZZINI, *Il Frate*
        G. M. CECCHI, *L'Assiuolo*

ANON., *Gl'Ingannati*
A. PICCOLOMINI, *L'Amor costante*
G. BARGAGLI, *La Pellegrina*
Vol. II: B. DOVIZI, *La Calandria*
F. BELO, *Il Pedante*
A. CARO, *Gli Straccioni*
G. BRUNO, *Il Candelaio*
G. B. DELLA PORTA, *La Fantesca*
BRAGAGLIA, ANTON GIULIO, ed. *Commedie giocose del '500.* 4 vols. Rome:
Colombo, 1946–1947.
Vol. I: L. ARIOSTO, *La Cassaria*
G. M. CECCHI, *L'Assiuolo*
L. DE' MEDICI, *L'Aridosia*
Vol. II: P. ARETINO, *La Cortegiana*
A. CARO, *Gli Straccioni*
F. BELO, *Il Pedante*
Vol. III: N. MACHIAVELLI, *La Mandragola*
A. PICCOLOMINI, *L'Amor costante*
G. B. DELLA PORTA, *La Fantesca*
Vol. IV: G. BRUNO, *Il Candelaio*
B. DOVIZI, *La Calandria*
A. F. GRAZZINI, *La Strega*
D'AMICO, SILVIO, ed. *Teatro italiano.* 2 vols. Milan: Nuova Accademia, 1955.
Vol. I: L. ARIOSTO, *La Lena*
N. MACHIAVELLI, *La Mandragola*
P. ARETINO, *Il Marescalco*
A. BEOLCO, *Il Reduce; Bilora*
ANON., *La Venexiana*
A. CARO, *Gli Straccioni*
G. M. CECCHI, *L'Assiuolo*
Vol. II: G. B. DELLA PORTA, *L'Astrologo*
M. BUONARROTI, THE YOUNGER, *La Tancia*

Critical Texts and Translations

ARETINO, PIETRO. *Teatro,* ed. GIORGIO PETROCCHI. Milan: Mondadori, 1971.

ARIOSTO, LUDOVICO. *Le Commedie,* ed. ALDO BORLENGHI. 2 vols. Milan:
RIZZOLI, 1962. Text edited by MICHELE CATALANO, Bologna, 1933.

BARGAGLI, GIROLAMO. *La Pellegrina.* With introduction and notes by FLORINDO
CERRETA. Florence: Olschki, 1971.

BENTLEY, ERIC, ed. *The Genius of the Italian Theater*. New York: Mentor, 1964.

BERNARDO DOVIZI DA BIBBIENA, *The Follies of Calandro (La Calandria)*, trans. OLIVER EVANS

ANON., *The Deceived (Gl'Ingannati)*, trans. THOMAS LOVE PEACOCK

GIORDANO BRUNO, *The Candle Bearer (Il Candelaio)*, trans. J. R. HALE

BALDASSARE CASTIGLIONE, "The First Production of *The Follies of Cassandro*," trans. J. CARTWRIGHT

[BEOLCO, ANGELO] RUZANTE. *Teatro*. First complete edition. Edited, with translation and notes by LUDOVICO ZORZI. Turin: Einaudi, 1967.

BRUNO, GIORDANO. *Il Candelaio*, ed. GIORGIO BARBERI SQUAROTTI. Milan: Einaudi, 1965.

Comedia elegantissima in prosa nuovamente composta per Messer Bernardo Dovizi da Bibbiena intitulata Calandria, ed. COMITATO in honor of Cardinal Bibbiena on the 500th anniversary of his birth. Bibbiena, 1970.

MACHIAVELLI, NICCOLÒ. *La Mandragola*, ed. ROBERTO RIDOLFI. Florence: Olschki, 1965.

———. *Mandragola*, trans. ANNE and HENRY PAOLUCCI. New York: Bobbs-Merrill, 1957.

———. *Clizia*, trans. OLIVER EVANS. New York: Barron's, 1962.

———. *The Literary Works of Machiavelli*, trans. J. R. HALE. London: Oxford University Press, 1961.

PICCOLOMINI, ALESSANDRO. *L'Alessandro*. Critical edition with introduction and notes by FLORINDO CERRETA. Siena: Accademia Senese degli Intronati, 1966. Issued in the United States as Vol. X of Humanistic Series of University of Iowa.

SALERNO, HENRY F., trans. and ed. *Scenarios of the Commedia dell'Arte: Flaminio Scala's "Il Teatro delle favole rappresentative."* New York: New York University Press, 1967.

TASSO, TORQUATO. *Intrighi d'amore*. Government Tourist Bureau of Palermo and Monreale, 1968.

Critical Studies and Bibliographies of Plays

ALLACCI, LEONE. *Drammaturgia: Accresciuta e continuata fino all'anno MDCCLV*. Venice: Giambattista Pasquali, 1755. Facsimile edition, Turin: Bottega d'Erasmo, 1961.

ALONGE, ROBERTO. *Il Teatro dei Rozzi di Siena*. Florence: Olschki, 1967.

Annali di storia del teatro e dello spettacolo. Milan: Lerici, 1966. Contains essays on "Vincenzo Bracca e la Farsa cavaiola," by A. MANGO; "La Congrega dei Rozzi," by V. PANDOLFI; and texts of six *commedie rusticali.*

BARATTO, MARIO. *Tre studi sul teatro (Ruzzante, Aretino, Goldoni).* Venice: Neri Pozza, 1964.

BARBIERI, NICOLÒ. *La Supplica.* With critical study, notes, and variants by FERDINANDO TAVIANI. Milan: Il Polifilo, 1971.

BARR, ALAN P. "Passion, Extension, and Excision: Imagistic and Structural Patterns in Giordano Bruno's *Il Candelaio.*" *TSLL,* XIII (1971), 351–363.

BERTELLI, SERGIO. "When Did Machiavelli Write *Mandragola?*" *Renaissance Quarterly,* XXIV (1971), 317–326.

BOUGHNER, DANIEL C. *The Braggart in Renaissance Comedy: A Study in Comparative Drama from Aristophanes to Shakespeare.* New York, 1971. Originally published Minneapolis, 1954.

CERRETA, FLORINDO. "Una Canzone del Firenzuola e una vecchia teoria sulla paternità della commedia degl'*Ingannati.*" *Bibliofilia,* LXXIII (1971), 151–163.

———. "Le Edizioni cinquecentine della commedia de *Gl'Ingannati.*" *Bibliofilia,* LXXIV (1972), 215–224.

———. "*Gl'Ingannati:* The Problem of Overlapping Dates Reexamined." *BHR,* XXXIII (1971), 605–614.

———. "Italian Plays of the Renaissance." *Books at Iowa,* II (1965), 26–30.

———. "A Note on the First Performance of Bulgarini's *Scambi.*" *Italica,* XLV (1968), 83–86.

———. "The Sienese Manuscript of Bargagli's *Pellegrina.*" *BHR,* XXX (1968), 601–616.

CLUBB, LOUISE GEORGE. *Giambattista Della Porta: Dramatist.* Princeton, N.J.: Princeton University Press, 1965.

———. "Italian Comedy and the *Comedy of Errors.*" *Comparative Literature,* XIX (1968), 240–251.

———. *Italian Plays (1500–1700) in the Folger Library.* Florence: Olschki, 1968.

———. "Pictures for the Reader: A Series of Illustrations to Comedy, 1591–1592." *RenD,* IX (1966), 265–277.

———. "The Tragicomic Bear." *CLS,* IX (1972), 17–30.

CORRIGAN, BEATRICE. *Catalogue of Italian Plays, 1500–1700, in the Library of the University of Toronto.* Toronto: University of Toronto Press, 1961.

————. Supplements in *Renaissance News,* XVI (1963), 298–307; XIX (1966), 219–228.

————. "Commedia dell'Arte Portraits in the McGill Feather Book." *RenD,* N.S. II (1969), 167–188.

CRUCIANI, FABRIZIO. *Il Teatro del Campidoglio e le feste romane del 1513, con la ricostruzione architettonica del teatro di Arnaldo Bruschi.* Milan: Il Polifilo, 1968.

DE BOSIO, GIANFRANCO. "Per Ruzante 20 anni di fedeltà." *Il Dramma,* XLIV (October, 1968), 103.

DE FEO, SANDRO. *In cerca di teatro.* Milan: Longanesi, 1972. I, 119–154.

DERSOFI, N. D. "Ruzante: The Paradox of *Snaturalitè* in a *Mondo Roesso.*" *Yearbook of Italian Studies,* I (1971), 142–155.

DUCHARTRE, PIERRE LOUIS. *The Italian Comedy,* trans. RANDOLPH T. WEAVER, with a new pictorial supplement reproduced from the "Recueil Fossard" and "Compositions de rhétorique." New York: Dover, 1966. Originally published London, 1929.

FAVILLI, GIOVANNI. "Bibliografia della Collana Palatina di commedie." *Studi Secenteschi,* III (1962), 185–225; IV (1963), 193–223. Continued by MARIA FRULLI MAGGINI, IX (1968), 299–361.

FERRONI, GIULIO. *"Mutazione" e "riscontro" nel teatro di Machiavelli e altri saggi sulla commedia del '500.* With a preface by RICCARDO SCRIVANO. Rome: Bulzoni, 1972. Essays include: "Machiavelli"; "Le Commedie di Francesco Belo e il realismo dell'Irragionevole"; "Gli *Straccioni* del Caro e la fissazione maneristica della realtà"; "Edonismo e moralismo cortigiano nelle commedie di Raffaello Borghini." The last was originally published as an article in *La Rassegna,* LXXIII (1969), 37–63.

FIDO, FRANCO. "Machiavelli 1469–1969: Politica e teatro nel badalucco di Messer Nicia." *Italica,* XLVI (1969), 359–375.

————. "Reflections on Comedy by Some Italian Renaissance Playwrights." In *Medieval Epic to the "Epic Theater" of Brecht,* ed. ROSARIO P. ARMATO and JOHN M. SPALEK. *University of Southern California Studies in Comparative Literature,* I (1968), 85–95.

FOLENA, G., ed. *Lingua e strutture del teatro italiano del rinascimento.* Padua: Liviana, 1970.

FRASCANI, FEDERICO. *Croce e il teatro.* Milan and Naples: Ricciardi, 1966. Chapter 4, "La Commedia del Rinascimento."

GISOLFI, ANTHONY. "Ariosto's Delightful Prologue to *La Cassaria.*" *TA,* XXII (1965/66), 41–47.

HERRICK, MARVIN T. *Comic Theory in the Sixteenth Century.* New York, 1964. Originally published Urbana, 1950. University of Illinois Studies in Language and Literature, no. 34.

————. *Italian Comedy in the Renaissance.* New York, 1970. Originally published Urbana: University of Illinois Press, 1960.

————. *Italian Plays, 1500–1700, in the University of Illinois Library.* Urbana: University of Illinois Press, 1966.

LEA, KATHLEEN M. *Italian Popular Comedy: A Study in the Commedia del l'Arte, 1560–1620, with Special Reference to the English Stage.* New York: Russell, 1962. Originally published Oxford, 1934.

LIEVSAY, JOHN. *The Englishman's Italian Books, 1550–1700.* Philadelphia: University of Pennsylvania Press, 1969.

LOVARINI, EMILIO. *Studi sul Ruzzante e la letteratura padovana.* Padua: Antenore, 1965.

MANGO, ACHILLE. *La Commedia in lingua nel Cinquecento. Bibliografia critica.* Florence: Lerici, 1966.

MASTROPASQUA, FERNANDO, and MOLINARI, CESARE. *Ruzante e Arlecchino: Tre Saggi sul teatro popolare del Cinquecento.* Parma: Studium Parmense, 1970.

MELZI, ROBERT C. "From Lelia to Viola." *RenD,* IX (1966), 67–81.

MINOR, ANDREW C., and MITCHELL, BONNER. *A Renaissance Entertainment: Festivities for the Marriage of Cosimo I, Duke of Florence, in 1539.* Columbia: University of Missouri Press, 1968.

MITCHELL, BONNER. "Circumstance and Setting in the Earliest Italian Productions of Comedy." *RenD,* N.S. IV (1971), 185–197.

NAGLER, A. M. *Theatre Festivals of the Medici, 1539–1637.* New Haven: Conn.: Yale University Press, 1964.

NICOLL, ALLARDYCE. *The World of Harlequin: A Critical Study of the Commedia dell'Arte.* Cambridge: At the University Press, 1963.

OREGLIA, GIACOMO. *The Commedia dell'Arte,* trans. LOVETT F. EDWARDS, introd. EVERT SPRINGHORN. New York: Hill & Wang, 1968. Originally published in Stockholm, 1961.

ORR, DAVID. *Italian Renaissance Drama in England before 1625.* University of North Carolina Studies in Comparative Literature, Vol. XL. Chapel Hill: University of North Carolina Press, 1970.

PANDOLFI, VITO. *La Commedia dell'arte: Storia e testo.* 6 vols. Florence: Sansoni, 1957–1961.

————. *Il Teatro del Rinascimento e la commedia dell'arte*. Rome: Lerici, 1969.

————. *Teatro goliardico dell'Umanesimo*, ed. VITO PANDOLFI and ERMINIA ARTESE. Milan: Lerici, 1965.

PARRONCHI, ALESSANDRO. "La Prima Rappresentazione della *Mandragola*." *La Bibliofilia*, LXIV (1962), I, 37–86.

PERRUCCI, ANDREA. *Dell'arte rappresentativa premeditata ed all'improviso*. Ed., with bibliography, by ANTON GIULIO BRAGAGLIA. Florence: Sansoni, 1961.

PROSPERI, MARIO. *Angelo Beolco nominato Ruzante*. Padua: Liviana, 1970.

RADCLIFF-UMSTEAD, DOUGLAS. *The Birth of Modern Comedy in Renaissance Italy*. Chicago: University of Chicago Press, 1969.

RAIMONDI, EZIO. *Politica e commedia: Dal Beroaldo al Machiavelli*. Bologna: Il Mulino, 1972.

Research Opportunities in Renaissance Drama:

VI (1963): LOUIS A. SCHUSTER, "Pioneering in Neo-Latin Drama," pp. 14–17.
LEICESTER BRADNER, "Desiderata for the Study of Neo-Latin Drama," pp. 17–20.
MARVIN HERRICK, "Italian Drama of the Renaissance," pp. 21–23.
CHARLES S. FELVER, "The Commedia dell'Arte and English Drama in the Sixteenth and Early Seventeenth Centuries," pp. 24–34.
VII (1964): DANIEL C. BOUGHNER, "Italian and English Comedy," pp. 6–7.
JOHN LEON LIEVSAY, "Anglo-Italian Renaissance Drama," pp. 10–12.
IX (1966): MARVIN T. HERRICK, "Opportunities for Research in Italian Comedy of the Renaissance," pp. 13–16.
XI (1968): BEATRICE CORRIGAN, "Opportunities for Research in Italian Renaissance Drama, 1967," pp. 9–20.
XII (1969): BEATRICE CORRIGAN, "Problems in Staging Italian Renaissance Drama," pp. 7–11.

RHODES, DENNIS E. "The Printer of Ariosto's Early Plays." *IS*, XVIII (1963), 13–18.

RICHTER, BODO L. O. *"La Venexiana* in the Light of Recent Criticism." In

The Drama of the Renaissance: Essays for Leicester Bradner, ed. ELMER M. BLISTEIN. Providence, R.I.: Brown University Press, 1970.

RIDOLFI, ROBERTO. *Studi sulle commedie del Machiavelli.* Pisa: Nistri-Lischi, 1968.

RODINI, ROBERT J. *Antonfrancesco Grazzini: Poet, Dramatist, and Novelliere, 1503–1584.* Madison: University of Wisconsin Press, 1970.

SIRRI RUBES, RAFFAELE. *L'Attività teatrale di G. B. Della Porta.* Naples: De Simone, 1968.

——. *Schede per il teatro del Rinascimento.* Naples: Il Tripode, 1965.

SMITH, WINIFRED. *The Commedia dell'Arte.* With illustrations gathered by David Allen and Benjamin Blom. New York: Blom, 1964. Originally published (with no illustrations) New York: Columbia University Press, 1912.

SOMMI, LEONE DE'. *Quattro dialoghi in materia di rappresentazioni sceniche,* ed. FERRUCCIO MAROTTI. Milan: Il Polifilo, 1968.

STAÜBLE, ANTONIO. *La Commedia umanistica del Quattrocento.* Florence: Sede dell'Istituto Palazzo Strozzi, 1968.

——. "Nuove edizioni di commedie rinascimentali." *Bibliothèque d'Humanisme et Renaissance,* XXX (1968), 203–208.

——. "Nuove pubblicazioni sul teatro del Rinascimento." *BHR,* XXXII (1970), 649–675.

——. "Quelques considérations sur les comédies des humanistes: À propos de deux publications récentes." *BHR,* XXVIII (1966), 458–475.

——. "Rassegna di testi e studi sul teatro del Rinascimento." *BHR,* XXIX (1967), 227–245.

SUMBERG, THEODORE A. "*La Mandragola:* An Interpretation." *Journal of Politics,* XXIII (1961), 320–340.

TAVIANI, FERDINANDO, ed. *La Commedia dell'arte e la società barocca: La Fascinazione del teatro.* Rome: Bulzoni, 1971.

——, ed. of section. "Il Problema della moralità del teatro dopo il Concilio di Trento," in *Documenti di storia del teatro.* Rome: Bulzoni, 1967.

WEINBERG, BERNARD. *A History of Literary Criticism in the Italian Renaissance.* 2 vols. Chicago: University of Chicago Press, 1961.

——. *Trattati di poetica e retorica del Cinquecento.* 2 vols. Bari: Laterza, 1970. Treatises on comedy.

Vol. I: VITTORE FAUSTO, *De comoedia libellus*

ALESSANDRO VELLUTELLO, Preface to AGOSTINO RICCHI's *Tre tiranni*

Francesco Robortello, *Explications de satyra . . . de comoedia . . .*
Vol. II: G. G. Trissino, *La Poetica,* Vols. V–VI.

Vincenzo Maggi, *De ridicules*

Bernardino Pino, *Breve considerazione intorno al componimento de la commedia* (preface to Sforza Oddi's *Erofilomachia*).

Williams, Robert I. "Machiavelli's *Mandragola,* Touchwood Senior, and the Comedy of Middleton's *A Chaste Maid in Cheapside.*" *SEL,* X (1970), 385–396.

Zampa, Giorgio. "Bilancio d'una stagione," *Il Dramma,* XLVII (October, 1971), 48–51.

Shakespearean Pastoral

Review Article

DOUGLAS COLE

McFARLAND, THOMAS. *Shakespeare's Pastoral Comedy.* Chapel Hill: The University of North Carolina Press, 1972. Pp. x + 218. $8.95.
YOUNG, DAVID. *The Heart's Forest: A Study of Shakespeare's Pastoral Plays.* New Haven and London: Yale University Press, 1972. Pp. xi + 209. $7.95.

SHAKESPEARE'S "GREEN WORLD," already a cliché in undergraduate blue-book criticism, has also become a territory for more ambitious explorers, mappers, and surveyors. Critical interest in Renaissance pastoral generally has never been wanting, and in recent years it seems to have reached new intensity; hence, one is hardly surprised to find these latest studies in Shakespearean versions of pastoral. Nor should it be surprising to find that the maps of the territory differ markedly in many ways: almost every study of "pastoral" defines its subject (genre, mode, concept, or what you will) differently, and in so doing establishes boundaries and limits of various range. McFarland's book devotes separate chapters to five plays; Young's, to four; and they share only three in common: *As You Like It, The Winter's Tale,* and *The Tempest.* McFarland adds *A Midsummer Night's Dream* and *Love's Labour's Lost* to his set, and includes an appendix on Falstaff as "exile" from a pastoral world.

213

Young's more paradoxical addition is *King Lear*—taken, according to an earlier suggestion by Maynard Mack, as a kind of "anti-pastoral" drama.

The phenomenon of the variable set is not an unfamiliar one: in the several studies of Shakespeare's "problem plays," for example, differing sets of plays have been suggested as "belonging" in the category, and the category itself has been variously defined. Nor has there been much argument about whether or not a given play should be included or excluded, for, as in most studies of this sort, the category itself seems less important than either the challenge involved in describing it (Young points tellingly to Polonius' "tragical-comical-historical-pastoral") or the special attention it permits to particular aspects of individual plays. Ever since Empson, "pastoral" itself has covered a multitude of literary applications. In some cases the concept seems to have been stretched beyond all practical utility. But it is nonetheless informative to watch the categorizing process in action: to see how a special way of mapping the pastoral territory predetermines the range of discoveries made possible within it.

Young's approach is by way of the context provided by Renaissance pastoral poetry, drama, and prose romance. Though not presented in detail, his survey of the tradition sketches in a familiar complex of recurrent themes, plot patterns, and qualities of setting: contrasts or antitheses involving court and country, rich and poor, worldliness and innocence, nature and nurture, nature and art, nature and fortune; a loose structure involving initial disruption or separation, a sojourn in or retreat to a pastoral environment, followed by reunion or reestablishment of social harmony; an emphasis on the way landscape mirrors spirit, the idyllic or idealized setting (even with its characteristic antitheses and intrusions) as image of human dream and desire, the "green world" seen as a special variant of what Sidney called the "golden world" of poesy. McFarland, less concerned with the historical tradition of pastoral in Shakespeare's time, fastens more eagerly on the aspect of dream or wish fulfillment, developing it in terms supplied by psychological and myth criticism. Thus, pastoral's "semiological basis" (p. 20) is what intrigues McFarland—it turns out to be "the structure of hope" (p. 38) in human experience as analyzed by psychiatry, theology, and phenomenology. Theology embodies that structure in the idea of paradise, and the "fictional co-ordinate" of that idea turns out to be pastoral comedy: "the pastoral vision is, in its potentiality and inner logic, a vision of paradise in which death is repudiated" (p. 36), and comedy's way of presenting that vision is to combine "happy society and blessed place" (p. 37). Young's paradigms are provided by Spenser, Sidney, Lyly, Greene, and Fletcher; McFarland's by Freud, Eriksen, Huizinga, Jaspers, Moltmann, and Bloch. The modernity of the latter set may provide an illusion of greater profundity and resonance, but in the end we discover we are in the same territory: the green world is the golden world, the perfectibility we hope for but never possess, an image of hope, joy, and community.

McFarland's focus on pastoral as an aesthetic image of the paradise we hope for proves far too narrow in the long run. The perspective it provides for our view of individual plays is foreshortened or confining; the whole picture of complex relationships in a given play is sacrificed to the highlighting of certain colors, tones, and themes. We are but dimly aware of the real toads in these imaginary gardens, the strangers in paradise, the comic and the more serious threats to whatever harmony exists there, the notes (or must we say touchstones?) of irony, parody, and skepticism that test the resilience of the idealized environment. McFarland is certainly conscious of such aspects, as his discussion of *As You Like It* and *The Winter's Tale* demonstrates, but he is uneasy about them, and tends to interpret them as deviant elements which Shakespeare was finally able to exorcise by the time he wrote *The Tempest*. The uneasiness reflects an assumption and a norm that is, in fact, unwarranted: namely, that the ideal pastoral ought to reflect or embody an ideal state; that there should be neither serpents nor insects in paradise. Hence it is that McFarland traces through the course of Shakespeare's dramatic progress an initial vision of innocence and artful play (in *Love's Labour's Lost* and *Midsummer Night's Dream*), followed by an intrusive quality of ambiguity (in *As You Like It*) which expands to tragic dimensions before it is purged and Shakespeare returns to a restored hope:

In *The Winter's Tale*, great cracks run through the artifice of happiness, and are caulked only with difficulty. Not until *The Tempest* does Shakespeare's art, having traversed the bitter complications of the middle and late comedies, find quiet harbor in a renewed paradisal hope. There at last, in the enchanted island's golden world, the storm of cynicism and tragic disharmony, with a final rage, blows itself out.

(p. 121)

This passage, which may recall to some Dowden's older view of the late Shakespeare, "On the Heights," discloses a bias which may in fact be very unfair to the more distinguished examples of pastoral art, including Shakespeare's own, which characteristically (and not atypically) play upon the tensions between the ideal and the real, the sentimental and the grotesque, that which can be hoped for and that which ought to be hoped for. Fools, knaves, and satyrs abound in pastoral; to exile them as deviants is to alter the nature of the art, if not to alter the nature of Nature. For all its idyllic possibilities, pastoral is still this side of paradise.

Although McFarland's discussions of individual plays are not Procrustean in any extreme sense, they show some tendency to overemphasize the idealistic side of pastoral as defined or described in the book's initial chapter. Thus, the King of Navarre's park in *Love's Labour's Lost* becomes a pastoral paradise by an etymological sleight-of-logic: *"Paradeisos . . .* originally meant 'a royal park,' and the setting of *Love's Labour's Lost* in the King of Navarre's park can be seen as bypassing the Arcadian mediation in favor of a direct attainment of paradise at the outset" (p. 50). This paradise, McFarland goes on to argue, rules out any "real trouble" and rules in only playful games that determine mood, theme, and action. The quality stressed, above all, is playfulness, a playfulness worked out in symmetries of situation and language that approach the formalities of dance. Parody, mockery, and folly abound, but are to be gauged as defenses against various threats to comic blissfulness. In his eagerness to prove this paradise a threatless environment, McFarland tends to make more of the presumed hostile themes than seems reasonable: we are asked to interpret the mocking of romantic love as a communal defense against any claims of individual love for transcendent dignity, to interpret the business of the Nine Worthies as a similar defense through ridicule against "heroism" (the presumption being that both individual romantic love and heroism are threats to social norms), and to see in Armado a defense against whatever threatening feelings his name was supposed to call up to the Elizabethans by association with the Spanish Armada. When metaphors of warfare are used by the courtiers to describe their wit-combats in the service of love,

McFarland claims still another defusing of the threat of warfare. When the news of the death of the Princess' father is announced, and becomes the basis of a new rule of the game being played between the men and the women (the year's postponement of love-matches), the conclusion McFarland draws is that the paradisal park is "proof against death" (p. 63). Obviously, comedy will treat themes of love, death, heroism, and warfare in ways different from those in tragedy and epic; but to see the function of pastoral comedy (if, indeed, *Love's Labour's Lost* deserves its pastoral label) as one of systematically defeating these "threatening" themes is to displace its center of levity, to stress what may be a therapeutic fringe benefit at the expense of the conscious artistry. Braggart warriors and braggart lovers are conceived not so much to put down war and love as to demonstrate the delightful vulnerability of pretenders; one may go on to ask whether pastoral in the hands of its better artists is less an invitation to recreational living in a land of let's pretend and more a delightful exploration of the vulnerable limits of the ideals which define our notions of earthly paradise. Shakespeare, clearly, seems less interested in banning the real toads from his imaginary gardens than in deliberately introducing them in order to see what we can learn about both toads and gardens.

When McFarland moves from the playful park of the King of Navarre to the enchanted forest of *Midsummer Night's Dream,* he continues to stress the paradisal motif. One cannot argue with his keen appreciation of the gorgeous language which conveys its landscape, of the hilarity of action both in the wood and in the court at its celebrations. Nor is it likely that many—apart from Jan Kott, whose reading of the play converts it into something like a sexual nightmare—will disagree with McFarland's keynote of "happiness" as the play's dominant tone. What disappoints is the simplicity of the discussion, the assertions of happy mood and decorative language, without much special notice of the ambiguities of the forest happenings and their relation to the wedded themes of love and imagination set against reason and folly. With magic in charge, the dissensions, rivalries, and infidelities of the forest events cannot trouble us overmuch; and yet their presence is both notable and nonidyllic. What is more, it takes more doing (and more authority) than the green world can provide in order to unravel the whole complicated tangle of mismatched lovers. Happiness and blessings abound, but we are not pressed by McFarland's analysis to understand why. It is significant (and important in terms of his thesis about pastoral as defying death) that he sees the chief threat to the enchanted world's happiness as the tragic love story of *Pyramus and Thisbe,* a threat defused by a manner of presentation that renders it comical. The thematic implications of whatever threats to harmony exist in Oberon's forest itself are never taken up directly.

McFarland faces such themes and dimensions more squarely in his treatment of the forest of Arden, a paradise he must admit is more equivocal than the others. Its notes of discomfort and danger, and the initial plot problems concerning brotherly usurpation, lead him to assert, rather extremely, that the play represents "the first massive assault of the forces of bitterness and alienation upon the pastoral vision of Shakespeare" (p. 101). Jaques embodies those forces most clearly for McFarland, who then suggests that Touchstone is provided as a kind of antidote to the former's melancholic poison. Following Jenkins, he traces the major encounters and confrontations in the play, develops rather briefly the idea that romantic love is seen as a "social sickness" (p. 112) finally controlled by Rosalind (who operates as a kind of love doctor) and ends with an uneasy consideration of the ragged (less than totally harmonious and blissful) ending. The over-all impression is that McFarland finds here a disturbing doubt of pastoral ideals, rather than a testing of them. Unlike Young, who comes to the play with a perspective that highlights Shakespeare's conscious gaming with pastoral conventions, he uses terms that are too limited to handle the dimensions of artifice and parody other than as signs of a growing bitter skepticism.

Young's approach here is more flexible and far richer, informed as it is by a more direct appreciation of the self-conscious quality of Renaissance pastoral (rather than its unconscious and mythic thirst for paradise). He can point out how the enhancement of artifice in pastoral becomes a way to make the idea of pastoral itself an important part of the play's subject matter. Thus, the green world becomes not a place for magic cures to be enacted, but a mirror for the wide range of attitudes and sensibilities that respond to its qualities and judge them to be ideal or otherwise. The encounters and juxtapositions that define the structure of the play finally work not toward a concluding feeling of threats imperfectly resolved, but rather toward a paradoxical and ultimately balanced judgment that sees how both the artificial world and the real world disclose truths about each other. The comic victory is not a matter of the golden world winning out over the dross, but more a triumph of wit and wisdom over both sentimentalism and cynicism. Rosalind, rather than Jaques, stands finally as the more central figure, "liberating love from folly and pastoral from artifice" (p. 68). She herself tests the ideals that move her, just as the play tests the conventions that generate it. Young's conclusion is important, for, among other things, it serves as a basic foundation for his treatment of the other plays as well:

Shakespeare had the wisdom to recognize that the pretense [of pastoral's not "seeing" the sophistication with which it expresses its recurrent themes of simplicity and innocence] could be abandoned and allowed to grow comic without destroying the value and meaning of pastoral, just as Rosalind could be allowed to mock love without losing her status as an ideal lover. The result, in both cases, is rather an enhancing and strengthening of what can survive the tests of criticism and laughter. In *As You Like It* we are invited to view the pastoral convention simultaneously from the inside, as in Lodge, and from the outside, as a frankly artificial and illusory construction. The effect is to make the play a consideration, not only of the typical pastoral themes, but of the pastoral itself.

(p. 70)

Seen this way, the play becomes not a sign of a crack in the golden world but an artful exercise in distinguishing fool's gold from true.

Cracks and doubts are more clearly the subject of *King Lear*, Young's nomination for pastoral tragedy. Young judiciously admits that *Lear's* "use of pastoral is submerged, eccentric, and in no way bound by conventions" (p. 75), and wishes only to explore aspects of the tragedy which bear close relation to two major features of the pastoral tradition: the sojourn (after a break with society) in a natural setting, which in many ways can mirror the mind and allow some measure of self-knowledge and self-discovery; and the exploration of the theme of human harmony with nature. The variant of the sojourn, with its reduction of courtly comforts to more primitive contact with nature, is obvious enough; so, too, the amplification of the main plot by the Gloucester story taken from the *Arcadia*. The consequences of Shakespeare's treatment of such patterns lead Young to the following conclusion:

When we have recognized that *King Lear* employs the pastoral pattern in order to negate it, that it denies its characters and audience the consolations supposed to accompany poverty, isolation, and humiliation, that it suggests that renunciation is no insurance against suffering, we are a long way toward identifying its central vision. Having disrupted and challenged the conventions of pastoral, *Lear* drives on to challenge its basic assumption about the essential harmony of man and nature.

(p. 93)

Man's kinship with the elements is finally called into radical question, not merely tested, and neither man nor nature is left "idealized." Young then falls back on a familiar response to such a vision: what we have left to sustain ourselves is the art that reveals that vision: "the play, as a work of art, offers the miracle of recurrent experience . . . stripped of its destructive character" (p. 103).

Because of *Lear's* transforming use of some conventional pastoral themes and structures, Young's discussion of this "anti-pastoral" is far more convincing than McFarland's argument (in an appendix) that the "Henriad" is a kind of anti-pastoral. McFarland wants to demonstrate that Falstaff, whose vivacity and childlike enthusiasm for life's comforts make him a representative of the playful pastoral world, becomes a scapegoat to the harsh policy of the Machiavellian world that Hal learns so well to manage. McFarland, reminding us that Falstaff on his death-bed may have "babbl'd of green fields," revives the somewhat sentimentalized arguments in behalf of Sir John made by Maurice Morgann in 1777, and tries to convince us that Falstaff, a frustrated idealist, would be most at home in "the pastoral world of ideal social harmony" (pp. 191-192). I find this notion very difficult to understand, unless Falstaff in such a world would be able to do with it what Autolycus does in *The Winter's Tale;* it is far easier to "place" a character like Falstaff in Ben Jonson's comedic universe of delightfully energetic frauds. McFarland's arguments are nowhere more strained than in this essay, which establishes Falstaff's role as a tragic scapegoat by paralleling him with Socrates (they were both charged with leading youth astray, they were both physically grotesque, they were both gadflies to the state, they both met censure which led to their death, etc.), and which claims that Falstaff's association with a paradisal and religious world is suggested by such things as the Hostess' report of his death—"he's in Arthur's bosom" (p. 179)—or his statement to the Chief Justice that he has lost his voice by too much "singing of anthems" (McFarland sees "sacramental commitment" [p. 196] in this!). Few great comic figures deserve or need such sanctification.

Perhaps inevitably, both McFarland and Young, in treating *The Winter's Tale* and *The Tempest,* devote more attention to problems that arise from Shakespeare's use of the stylized and archaic conventions of narrative romance than to strictly pastoral motifs. Even so, the defining perspectives are still visible. McFarland sees the ugliness of Leontes' emotions and judgments as attacking "pastoral bliss at its very heart" (p. 123); the disruption will be healed by "the balm of pastoral" (p. 131) in the later acts. He writes glowingly about the sheep-shearing scene, concentrating on the lyrical language that accompanies the giving of flowers. But the glow does not illuminate very much, for there is no serious attention paid to the way in which the pastoral celebration is itself disrupted by the harsh fury of Polixenes. McFarland is not alone in wishing to dissolve that interruption away; he must admit it is there, but even in doing so asserts that "Polixenes's wrath is filtered through the magic fact of pastoral, as is shown by his acknowledgments of Perdita's charm ['And thou, fresh piece / Of excellent witchcraft . . .'] and even by his threats to have her beauty 'scratch'd with briers' " (p. 137). It is as if tone were more instrumental than actual event or turn of plot, or, indeed, as if the tone of the start of this scene were *not* shattered by the new disharmony of authority's challenge. The critic's belief in the magic charm of pastoral setting or pattern will not permit him to see how effectively Shakespeare has broken that charm at this moment in the play. The balm that actually begins to restore things at the literal level of decision and event is Camillo's counsel; without it (and, by the way, without its counterpart in Paulina's actions in Sicilia) the green world would have been helpless.

Young, too, does not meet honestly the shattering of the carefully and winningly constructed pastoral mood. His concern is not with the charm of the shepherd's world, but rather with the larger aesthetic issues suggested by what he sees as Shakespeare's experimentation with an old-fashioned and highly artificial mode of dramatic narrative. He comments lengthily on the familiar themes of Time and of Nature vs. Art in the play, integrating this part of his discussion with his main purpose: to stress the self-conscious quality of Shakespeare's art, which here seems to be calling attention to itself in order to make its audience question their own delight in and need for the patently fictive. The efficacy of the green world in criticizing reality is still intact; and its relative helplessness as a cause of restoring order is subsumed under a more pervasive concern with romance's artificial ways of setting things straight. The central question that emerges comes without an obvious answer: why do we need the golden worlds of the poet, of which the green world is but one special reflection?

McFarland's essay on *The Tempest* answers that question with a repetition of his original connection between pastoral and paradise:

> . . . the pastoral ideal reveals itself as something far more necessary than a merely historical tradition in literature. As an analogue of the Christian heaven that exists as the goal of struggling mortals, of Jaspers's "transcendence" that flickers unattainably before all existence, it represents the deepest authentication of the meaning of human hope.
>
> (p. 159)

The repetition involves a modification: paradise has become, more specifically, the Christian heaven. It is largely in terms of that modification that *The Tempest* itself is analyzed: McFarland stresses the qualities of religious parable in the play, as so many have done before him. The storm becomes the metaphor for existence, Prospero a godlike figure who turns adversity to harmony, blending justice with forgiveness, and constraining the power of evil with a greater power of goodness. There is a greater wealth of supporting detail provided in this essay than in most of McFarland's others (in several, there are nearly as many lines of quoted material as there are of the author's), but a nagging quality of oversimplification still persists. The ambiguous and the paradoxical are brushed aside in the effort to underline the religious themes and tones.

Young's approach is along the continuum that links his discussion of the four plays, the self-consciousness of Shakespeare's experiments with pastoral forms and themes. Hence, Prospero as artist becomes more important than Prospero as god, and the island setting becomes not only a locale for providential harmonizing but still another multiple mirror for the contrasting spirits and men that inhabit or visit it: the ambiguous borders of illusion and reality, nature and art are probed more subtly in a process that leads not to an ideal happiness but to a more comprehensive vision of possibilities:

. . . realities are not merely juxtaposed, but tend to give way to one another, creating a world in which we are pulled further and further into an over-whelming sense of the basically illusory character of experience and of firm categories, a reality so shifting and impermanent that only a man who has penetrated and accepted its protean nature, like Prospero, can have any mastery of it.

(p. 178)

The strengths and limitations of nature, of art, and of man are all within the compass of this play, which Young sees finally as working upon the audience in ways analogous to those employed by Prospero's theatrical magic working upon the characters cast ashore: "In both cases the experience will be illusory—the result of art, shadowy, an insubstantial pageant—but that will not make it any less valuable. On the contrary, it will make possible events and recognitions not otherwise attainable" (p. 190). The range and quality of recognition will probably vary as much as the spectrum defined by the reactions of the various characters to Prospero's art, including Prospero himself; and is there not an important recognition implicit in that very variety? If the enchanted island is some figure for paradise, it is finally one, like Dante's perhaps, that admits of varying modes and levels of appreciation. To honor that aspect is to respect the complexity of Shakespeare's vision, and finally to understand that his golden world has answered, and will continue to answer, varying needs for varying spectators.

It is not likely that these two books will be the last to address themselves specifically to Shakespeare's use of pastoral. In the final analysis, McFarland's study is grounded on too simple a conception of pastoral, a limitation that imparts a kind of tunnel vision to his discussions and discoveries. Young's is the more flexible, open-ranging, and better informed with respect not only to other Renaissance practices with pastoral, but also to the considerable body of recent criticism on the Shakespearean plays he treats. For that reason it is a better general introduction to the subject and its problems. Nonetheless, its own achievements somehow seem less than satisfactory, given the ambition of the enterprise. "When I began this project," he notes in his epilogue, "I thought to write a book that divided its interest fairly evenly between Shakespeare and the pastoral convention as his age defined and practiced it. I ended, obviously, by writing a book about Shakespeare" (p. 193).

The first "book" is still needed, and indeed might have been one that would have led to more discoveries about Shakespeare's own art in the long run. As it is, Young's movement through the plays traces many paths that are well-blazed and well-trodden. The map is a convenience, in that it is compact and clear, bringing together many useful details from the work of others. But its scale does not quite permit a full appreciation of the territory. More exciting discoveries may still await those who travel deeper into the forest and the heart.

The Medieval Origins of Elizabethan Comedy

Review Article

JOEL H. KAPLAN

FARNHAM, WILLARD. *The Shakespearean Grotesque: Its Genesis and Transformations*. Oxford: Clarendon Press, 1971. 3 pls. Pp. x + 175. $7.00.

FELDMAN, SYLVIA D. *The Morality-Patterned Comedy of the Renaissance*. The Hague and Paris: Mouton & Co., 1970. Pp. 165. 18 glds.

DESSEN, ALAN C. *Jonson's Moral Comedy*. Evanston, Illinois: Northwestern University Press, 1971. Pp. ix + 256. $7.95.

THREE VERY DIFFERENT BOOKS published in 1970–1971 find common ground in their attention to the medieval origins of Elizabethan and Jacobean comedy. Willard Farnham takes the broadest path, conducting us on a wide sweep of classical and Gothic sensibilities in an attempt to explain a perplexing side of Shakespeare's comic art. And in so doing, *The Shakespearean Grotesque* is able to extend its discussion to the tragedies and histories as well. Farnham's starting point is St. Bernard's irritation at the fantastical shapes and monsters that decorated Cluniac cloisters, threatening to draw monks away from their devotions toward the dangers of aesthetic speculation. Adopting St. Bernard's description of such art as "deformed beauty and beautiful deformity," Farnham defines the medieval grotesque as a tension of opposites, "a breaking down of normal creatures and a recombination of parts of them in a form where the parts must be at war with each other in their incongruity" (p. 4). This incongruity is, Farnham argues, completely foreign to the grotesquerie of the classical world. It becomes, in the centuries preceding Shakespeare, the route by which comedy first joins itself to serious matter to produce an image of low jostling high in a world turned upside-down—an image that Farnham goes on to explore in the figures of Falstaff and Hamlet, as well as in the vision of "diabolic grotesqueness" that he finds in *Troilus and Cressida, Othello,* and *The Tempest.*

In his opening chapter Farnham is concerned with how and where this image parts company with classical notions of the grotesque; and in the process he moves with breath-taking agility from Roman grottos to Gothic illuminations, from the English mystery cycles and moral interludes to the decorative borders used by Elizabethan printers. There is much to be learned here, both from the author's easy and wide acquaintance with things ancient and medieval, and from his analysis of the individual works singled out for special attention. Of particular value are his remarks on the drolleries of the Luttrell Psalter and B. M. Lansdowne MS. 420 (pp. 24–26), and a detailed reading of the Wakefield *Second Shepherds' Play* (pp. 42–46), vastly different but apt examples of Farnham's point about low echoing high in a manner that ultimately affirms both. One might quibble about the occasional interpretation, as in the discussion of a twelfth-century Book of Job in which much rests upon our seeing an "explorer of evil" in the rather expressionless features of a figure trapped in a maze of interlaces (pp. 22–23). But on the whole the performance is impressive. If there is room for uneasiness, it lies rather in Farnham's failure to define the classical grotesque that he tells us was transformed by the spirit of medieval Christianity. He talks, for example, of "a low-keyed spirit of gaiety" and "mild deformation" in the Mausoleum of Constantia and a third-century sarcophagus now in the Museo Lateranese (pp. 6–8). But we are never told of what this gaiety or deformation consists. In neither piece is monstrosity a theme, and one is left wondering whether "formalization" alone is enough to qualify a work as "classically grotesque." It may seem ungrateful to raise the point, as Farnham is primarily concerned with a later form of grotesquerie and the changes that Shakespeare is able to ring upon it.

Yet without such controls the medieval grotesque runs the risk of becoming a distorting mirror for Renaissance drama. The oversimplifications that result have some unfortunate consequences in the Shakespeare chapters that follow.

A case in point is Farnham's extended discussion of the *Henry IV* plays (Chapters 2 and 3), in which Falstaff is presented as an animal body of "savouriness and unsavouriness strangely joined to help make him complexly monstrous" (p. 51). Farnham explores with great sensitivity the double function of the food and animal imagery associated with Falstaff, and includes an important section on the pun as grotesque language arising from "a monstrous union of incompatible things" (p. 61). He also makes good use of the morality vices as well as the marginal figures of the Gothic Psalters described in the previous chapter in a discussion of Falstaff's lineage. Yet valuable as such analysis may be, it skirts the larger problem of Falstaff as a peculiarly Shakespearean grotesque. The critical phrase in Farnham's initial description of Falstaff is not that he contains both "savouriness and unsavouriness," but that in him these qualities are "strangely joined." It is, however, just this matter of joining that is most taken for granted, and least commented upon. As a result, although Farnham quite rightly warns us of the dangers of rejecting either side of Falstaff's dual nature, we are left with the impression of the fat knight as a thing of shreds and patches, more interesting in his component parts than in their assembly.

In such a context Farnham's use of the medieval grotesque often seems reductive. We are told, for instance, that Falstaff's verbal dexterity is a *sine qua non* for his role as man-animal, binding him to the whole notion of the grotesque set forth in Chapter 1. As such, Farnham seems to feel that Falstaff's wit must be defended in all instances, and so we find the rather feeble dialogue with the Lord Chief Justice at the opening of *2 Henry IV* elevated to the level of the Gadshill explanations. The logic is plain enough. But do we actually feel that Falstaff is "at his masterful best" in both episodes? Farnham's account of Falstaff on the battlefield lays itself open to similar objections. It is true, of course, that the vices of Tudor interludes often become soldiers to foment strife more effectively; it is also true that Falstaff, who shares some unmistakable traits with these figures, goes to war. But are we then justified in attributing to Falstaff, as Farnham does, the motives of an Ambidexter or Courage-

Revenge? Does Falstaff, or even a part of him, really display "a fascination with combat and an urge to enter into it, even with some daring" (p. 92)? Again, Farnham is not so much wrong as off-center, constructing from *disjecta membra* a Falstaff whose "doubleness" is far too regular and predictable to square with our experience of him in the theater, study, or classroom.

Such reservations are only partially dispelled by Farnham's concluding chapters. "Hamlet among Fools" begins with a promising section on monstrosity and idealism, but soon entangles itself in the same kind of circular explanations and special pleadings that mar the Falstaff discussion. Thus Hamlet, as a figure "so deeply invaded by the grotesque he has a double nature," is permitted to wield puns like so many two-handed engines. But when Laertes on one occasion seems to do the same, Farnham can only find "Shakespeare alone, standing out from behind his Laertes to plead joy of contrivance" (p. 106). More successful is Farnham's final chapter on "Diabolic Grotesqueness," which seeks to demonstrate the "capacity of the Shakespearean grotesque to develop enmity toward the non-grotesque" (pp. 151–152). Of particular interest is an all-too-brief account of *The Tempest* (pp. 152–169), in which the play's grouping of Caliban, Trinculo, and Stephano is put to excellent use. Both Trinculo and Stephano, it is argued, are holdovers from an earlier and simpler concept of monstrosity, happy (like Falstaff) to find niches for themselves in a world controlled by the nongrotesque. Caliban, however, represents something new for Shakespeare: a grotesque revolutionary whose designs against the established order are charged with a sense of sacred purpose denied to his companions. The drollery, in effect, has crept out of the margin and now makes a direct assault on the world that has tried to contain it. Yet in making Caliban a literal man-animal, Shakespeare has at the same time given us an "objective correlative" for "that strange union of the more-than-animal and the merely-human which is a finding within man in general" (p. 166). And this, Farnham goes on to suggest, may help to explain the complex attitude we are asked to take toward both Caliban and his rebellion.

If Farnham is not always this helpful, it would be well to keep in mind the Herculean task he has set out to accomplish in one hundred and sixty-nine pages. One wonders, in fact, how much limitations of space have to do with Farnham's failure to make an adequate case for the classical grotesque, or the reductive method of the Falstaff and Hamlet chapters. An admirable but perhaps overzealous desire to compress may also account for Farnham's reluctance to consider the Shakespearean grotesque within its Elizabethan and Jacobean context. It may be instructive to trace Shakespeare's grotesquerie back to its medieval and Tudor roots. But one would also like to know just how "Shakespearean" this Shakespearean grotesque is. Is Falstaff's "animal doubleness" shared, say, by Jonson's Ursula or some of Middleton's more energetic overreachers? Or might we find in *The Revenger's Tragedy* or *The Duchess of Malfi* the same type of complex monstrosity that Farnham encourages us to see in *Hamlet?* In the absence of such considerations we do not know if Farnham's category describes what we might loosely call a "Jacobean grotesque," in which Shakespeare differs in quality but not in kind from his contemporaries, or if it means to imply a uniquely Shakespearean use of medieval conventions and sensibilities. This confusion is all the more regrettable when one considers what an admirable guide Farnham would have made for the task. It would, however, be churlish to close with an attack on Farnham's book for what it does not attempt. In spite of these shortcomings *The Shakespearean Grotesque* remains rich in suggestion and detail, and if at times it resembles a jigsaw puzzle imperfectly fitted together, Farnham has at least given us enough pieces to keep us busy for some time to come.

Unfortunately, the same cannot be said for Sylvia D. Feldman's *The Morality-Patterned Comedy of the Renaissance*. Miss Feldman begins by suggesting a quite different relationship between medieval convention and Renaissance drama. Noting the optimism that the early moral plays share with English comedy in general, she concludes that "the morality structure" must be inherently comic, and that "any fully developed morality play or moral interlude is associated with the comic genre." On the basis of this observation a new category of Elizabethan and Jacobean drama is called into being, the "morality-patterned comedy." This subgenre, we are told, consists of a "central core" of five plays (*How a Man May Choose a Good Wife From a Bad, The Fair Maid of Bristow, The Dutch Courtesan, 1 The Honest Whore*, and *Eastward Ho!*), each "a Renaissance work employing the didactic intentions, character groupings, action, and structure of the morality play" (p. 14).

To the list Miss Feldman would add another dozen or so plays that follow the pattern, but with some variation. Since the value of such a category would seem to lie in its ability to tell us something new about those works that comprise it, the most baffling feature of this book is Miss Feldman's refusal to talk in any detail about the handful of plays that form her "central core." In her opening chapter we find an eight-page plot summary of *How a Man May Choose a Good Wife From a Bad,* intended to demonstrate that this work, like the early moralities, "begins in trouble and ends in peace" (pp. 17–23). The bulk of the chapter, however, consists of laboriously spun-out plot rehearsals of five additional Renaissance plays, designed to show us what a "morality-patterned comedy" is not. The remaining "core" plays are huddled together in the space of nine pages at the beginning of Chapter 4 (pp. 93–101). Here, too, discussion is limited to plot summary, much of which either misunderstands or misrepresents the plays described. (To call Malheureux a "mankind figure [who is] in a state of virtue" at the opening of *The Dutch Courtesan* makes nonsense of the action that follows.)

Largely because Miss Feldman has so little to say about "morality-patterned comedy," her central thesis that such a category exists or is at all useful must rest unproven. What remains (and what the book must ultimately be judged by) is a hair-raising account of allegorical drama in medieval and Tudor England that does little to inspire confidence in its author as either a critic or literary historian. To begin with, Miss Feldman takes a strangely blinkered view of "the morality play" and "morality structure," maintaining that there is *only one action* in the moralities: the conflict between the Vices and Virtues for the possession of mankind's soul," and that this struggle can have *"only one outcome . . .* mankind *always* repents and, consequently, *always* saves his soul" (pp. 46, 48; italics mine). These propositions are maintained by a tautological argument that simply removes from consideration those plays that do not conform to the pattern. The first to go is *The Pride of Life,* excluded, we are told, because it is a fragment and therefore "useless for the purposes of analyzing the basic morality elements" (p. 40). Such a statement conveniently overlooks the speech of the Prolocutor that opens the piece, giving us a full account of the play's action—enough at any rate to tell us that this earliest of English moral plays is patently not about "the conflict between the Vices and Virtues." (On page 76 Miss Feldman is willing to admit as evidence Rastell's *Four Elements,* also a "fragment" but one that supports her argument.) This kind of special pleading reaches a ludicrous climax in Chapter 3 ("Evolution, as Reflected in Some Tudor Moral Interludes"), in which a single footnote is used to dispatch some eighteen plays, among them the works of John Bale, *Godly Queen Hester, The Trial of Treasure, Like Will to Like, All for Money, The Tide Tarieth No Man, Nice Wanton, The Disobedient Child, Horestes, The Three Ladies of London,* and the moral tragedies of W. Wager (p. 65). At the end of the chapter Miss Feldman asks incredulously why all of the plays she has been examining have "comic structures." One is tempted to answer that it is because everything else has been thrust out of doors.

One might suspect such arguments to grow out of an insufficient understanding of particulars; this proves to be the case. A few examples will have to suffice. Miss Feldman is incorrect in claiming that topical references or the noting of social abuses are indications of a late date (p. 72). We have only to think of *Mankind,* or the Wakefield *Second Shepherds' Play* for that matter. Nor is the appearance of *Humanum Genus* as king a sign of dramatic evolution (p. 66); again the excluded *Pride of Life* comes to mind. On pages 84–85 Miss Feldman implies that she is citing the 1540 version of Lindsay's *An Satire of the Three Estates,* a version that exists only as a brief description of the Linlithgow performance. And an appendix on "Education Drama" (pp. 138–150) draws heavily upon Palsgrave's translation of *Acolastus,* apparently unaware that this school exercise was never meant to be acted. The frequency of misprints and misquotes also runs high (p. 68, for "syght" read "wyght," for "pelly can" read "pellycan"; p. 81 for "Related" read "Belated"; p. 108, for "struck" read "stuck"; p. 79, n. 11, for *"Renaissance Drama,* Vol. XIII" read *"Renaissance Drama,* Vol. VIII"), and one is puzzled by Miss Feldman's choice of edited texts. Manly is not a reliable guide for the late moralities, nor does a contemporary critic need to go to Glover for a text of *A King and No King,* or the Pearson reprint of 1873 for Chapman's *All Fools.* (One has visions of the Illinois Chapman editors weeping over their collators.) In themselves these may be minor irritations. But in context they are symptomatic of the larger problems that plague Miss Feldman's book: a doctrinaire view of what morality plays and moral interludes ought to be, and an insistence on applying this view dogmatically in the face of an inadequate knowledge of either the period or its drama. Perhaps, though, the responsibility for such a performance should not fall on the author alone. This is not the first time that Mouton Press has used its *de Proprietatibus Litterarum* series to present us with premature work that might have benefited from a longer period of incubation. Such a practice not only does an obvious disservice to scholarship, but may have the unfortunate effect of prejudicing once-burned readers against some of the worthwhile titles that have appeared in the same series.

These faults are all the more glaring when Miss Feldman's book is set alongside of Alan C. Dessen's *Jonson's Moral Comedy*. Dessen is also interested in the impact of the moral play and morality techniques upon a number of Elizabethan and Jacobean comedies. But he is fully aware of the complexities of the tradition he seeks to define and advances his arguments with appropriate caution. Dessen begins with a reassessment of the dramatic legacy bequeathed to Renaissance drama by the morality play and moral interlude. His initial point is that in attempting to establish a link between these plays and their Elizabethan descendants we have often looked in the wrong places, fixing our gaze upon *The Castle of Perseverance, Mankind,* or *Everyman,* while dismissing as formless and crude the output of the mid- to late sixteenth-century. Dessen acknowledges the importance of the *Humanum Genus* structure both for the early moralities and for a handful of Renaissance works (*Doctor Faustus, Macbeth,* and *Othello* among them), yet finds a broader and more immediate influence in those plays of the 1560s–1590s that take as their central concern not the soul of mankind but the health and well-being of the kingdom. Such pieces, Dessen claims, are more representative of the moral play as Jonson and his fellows found it, and may be able to tell us more about Jonson's own handling of morality themes and conventions. The point is well taken, and after a brief discussion of Jonson's early comedies, Dessen devotes the greater part of his book to substantial readings of *Volpone, The Alchemist,* and *Bartholomew Fair* that trace this influence in considerable detail. A penultimate chapter on "The Decline of Moral Comedy" looks at Jonson's more explicit use of morality devices in *The Devil is an Ass* and *The Staple of News,* attempting in the process to account for the comparative failure of these late plays.

Dessen's opening section on the "estates" morality should be of particular interest to students of Renaissance drama. The fate of the morality play in the sixteenth century has often been viewed as a simple degeneration: mankind shatters into a collection of social types, the argument of the *psychomachia* collapses, and the figure of the Vice is left to range at will through a chaotic world that has lost both coherence and purpose. Dessen does not deny this abandonment of mankind or the increased scope given to the Vice. But he sees both as part of a larger movement by which the moral play acquires a new *raison d'être,* shifting its focus from the spiritual plight of a central hero to the social and economic problems of society at large. What previous critics have tended to see as a degeneration is for Dessen a form of development. If the Vice forsakes his former role of personal or psychological process, he does so to become "a dramatic symbol for that attitude or force within the kingdom which the dramatist wishes to single out as a basic cause of contemporary evils" (p. 16). And in juxtaposing this new function with the misdeeds of a cross-section of the commonweal, plays like *All for Money* (1577), *Like Will to Like* (1568), and *The Tide Tarieth No Man* (1576) present us with a "thesis-and-demonstration" structure that illustrates "the effects of such corruption upon the various 'estates' or segments of London society" (p. 24). The chapter concludes with an examination of a number of pieces from the 1590s that show us the full potential of this movement from Mankind to Respublica. The "estates" structures of Wilson's *The Cobbler's Prophecy* (1590) and the anonymous *A Knack to Know a Knave* (1592) are admirably sketched out, and in his analyses of Greene and Lodge's *A Looking Glass for London and England* (1590) and Marston's *Histriomastix* (1599) Dessen brings us across the illusory line that too often separates these neglected plays from the work of the major Elizabethan and Jacobean dramatists.

In the chapters that follow, Dessen applies his findings to Jonson's mature work, showing us how the stuff of the late moralities is turned into comedy of the very highest order. The comical satires are seen as interesting experiments in this general direction, but it is in *Volpone* that Jonson first succeeds in rendering into literal drama the themes and structure of the "estates" play. In this piece Jonson (like the writers of

the late moralities) constructs a fable that will demonstrate "how Lucre
has gained control over the minds and hearts of men" (p. 75). Volpone
and Mosca are "pseudo-Vices" in Jacobean cloaks, the play's opening
hymn to gold an initial postulate to be tested in "thesis-and-demonstration" fashion, and Corvino (merchant), Corbaccio (miser), and Voltore
(lawyer) the representative "estates" whose actions point up the perilous
condition of society. Even Celia and Bonario are shown to have morality
precedents in figures like Heavenly Man and Faithful Few, who provide
us with a perspective from which we may view and condemn the
venality of Respublica. Yet Dessen is careful to distinguish morality
conventions from Jonson's "comic or satiric equivalents" for such devices, and in his analysis of the play's stage imagery shows us how
Jonson transforms the simple didacticism of the morality play proper
into a series of complex and disturbing theatrical emblems; his discussions of the attempted rape of Celia (pp. 84–90), Volpone's sickbed appearance before the Scrutineo (pp. 93–95), and the "sham dispossession"
of Voltore (pp. 97–101) are of particular value. One wishes that Dessen
had more to say about the play's subplot (does it blur the play's focus, as
he claims, or only its indebtedness to the "estates" tradition?), and a
section on the final meting out of punishments seems regrettably abrupt
(are our moral sensibilities this easily satisfied? or is Jonson's own concern about his comedy's rigorous conclusion worth a fuller consideration?). But these are minor reservations about a chapter that as a whole
vindicates Dessen's approach and gives us some of the best writing yet on
a very difficult play.

   If one has more substantial reservations about Dessen's readings of
The Alchemist and Bartholomew Fair, it is not that these plays prove
less amenable to his over-all argument. The Alchemist especially, he
persuades us, is an "estates" comedy to the hilt. Face, Doll, and Subtle
burst upon us as another band of Vice-intriguers, while the paler gulls of
Volpone scatter before a fantastical jumble of "estates" types, as city and
country, knight, merchant, and divine stumble over one another in
pursuit of ill-gotten gain. Once more the true victim is shown to be
society itself. Dessen draws some suggestive distinctions between the
play's various dupes, sorting them out along morality lines into those
who embody forces that are a real threat to the commonweal (Mammon,
Ananias, Tribulation Wholesome) and those whose victimization il-

lustrates the breakdown of social responsibility (Dapper, Drugger, Kastril). And again Dessen is good at picking out the stage images that show us this process; Dapper's casting away of worldly goods (p. 112) and the expulsion of Surly (pp. 128–129) are especially apt examples of Jonson's increasing ability to find ironic emblems for moral propositions. What one is uneasy about is the solemnity that often creeps into Dessen's tone. He tells us at the outset that *The Alchemist* is "not as dark" a play as *Volpone* (p. 113). But is it dark at all? Ananias may be less of a rogue than Tribulation Wholesome, but do we really find his discomfiture "disturbing in its disclosure that such scruples in this world are only worthy of our laughter" (p. 121)? And is it quite fair to say that Face is playing upon Lovewit's "fear of age" in promising his master a widow who "will make [him] seuen yeeres yonger" (pp. 131–132)? (William Blissett has also written on the morality roots of this play, coming to some very different conclusions about its comic mood; a consideration of his essay might have been useful here.) But perhaps such misgivings amount to no more than a confirmation of Dessen's verdict that *The Alchemist* is a more complex and sophisticated piece of work than *Volpone*. What is impressive is that in spite of these disagreements his general thesis works so remarkably well.

Dessen's eighty-two page chapter on *Bartholomew Fair* is something of a tour de force and the high point of his book. Given the "pessimistic appraisal of society and its diseases" that he finds in *Volpone* and *The Alchemist* (and in nondramatic pieces like "A Speech according to Horace"), Dessen expresses dismay at recent interpretations of this play that see it as little more than an amoral romp. Drawing our attention to Jonson's praise of Pembroke, Overbury, and Lady Aubigny (as well as their stage counterparts in figures like Cicero and Augustus Caesar), Dessen underscores Jonson's belief that virtuous men in positions of responsibility are society's only defense against the forces of vice and ignorance. It is against this backdrop that he challenges the "kill-joy" thesis of *Bartholomew Fair* that sees opposition to the world of Smithfield as the principal target of Jonson's satiric wrath. Wasp, Zeal-of-the-Land Busy, and Justice Overdo may be laughable in their hyperbolic attacks upon the fair, yet Dessen finds another and more serious purpose behind them. Each is a "man in authority" who abuses his "estates" position, abdicating "a role necessary for the health of society" and betraying both himself and those individuals entrusted to his care. When Good Counsel becomes Wrath (Wasp), Religion Hypocrisy (Busy), and Law Self-Delusion (Overdo), the commonweal falls prey to the amoral and anarchic energies fleshed out in the sharpers, thieves, bawds, and whores who inhabit Jonson's Smithfield. The effects of this failure are illustrated in the progress of a figure like Cokes, who retraces the steps of a Youth, Moros, or Lusty Juventus in his idiotic acceptance of the fair's folly (pp. 166–176). The process as a whole finds a fitting emblem in the stocking of the play's three authority figures, another bit of stage business specifically borrowed from the late moralities (pp. 187–190). As with *The Alchemist,* there are moments when one feels that Dessen is taking it all a bit solemnly. It is hard to see Quarlous' final advice to Justice Overdo ("you haue your frailty") as "ominous [in its] implications for the future health of society" (p. 216). If, as Dessen himself claims, Overdo's pretentious posturing has infected his dispensing of justice all along, what could be more fitting than a reminder that he too is *"Adam,* Flesh, and blood"? And it requires some stretching to see the play's exit to a feast as a "violation of quality" that threatens to "project into the future the abuses found in both the fair and the puppet show" (p. 218). But once again, one is struck by the persuasiveness of Dessen's larger arguments and comes away, from this chapter especially, convinced of the real importance of his book. There may be room for disagreement with a number of his conclusions, but in *Jonson's Moral Comedy* Dessen has given us a valuable methodology and demonstrated some of the new insights it is capable of yielding. For both its scholarship and ingenuity this is a work that one feels Jonson himself would have appreciated.

Review

LEVIN, RICHARD. *The Multiple Plot in English Renaissance Drama.* Chicago and London: The University of Chicago Press, 1971. Pp. xiv + 277. $9.50.

THE PRESENCE of double or multiple plots in Elizabethan plays has served as both irritant and stimulant. After several shifts in the winds of critical taste, the situation seems to have stabilized, for, as Richard Levin observes in his opening sentence, "it takes no great courage today to rise to the defense of the multiple plot." Heretofore, arguments for the virtues of that multiple plot have usually been limited to studies of individual plays (e.g., *King Lear, Volpone, Doctor Faustus*), but Levin now offers us a full-scale exploration of this phenomenon in English Renaissance drama with attention to both theory and practice. This ambitious study deserves our careful attention.

Levin's first chapter establishes his assumptions and theoretical framework—in particular, his use of Aristotle's four causes to characterize the four possible kinds of interplot connection. Thus, for Levin, Aristotle's material cause would correspond to static relationships included in the original matter with which the playwright began (as when characters in different plots are blood relatives or neighbors). Similarly, the efficient

237

cause would characterize causal links resulting from mutual interaction between plots, whereby one line of action affects the other (as with the Lear and Gloucester plots). As Levin notes (p. 9), much of the hostility of older critics to the multiple plot can be traced to the often unstated assumption that the material and efficient modes were the only means of integrating multiple plots; two plots would thereby be properly "unified" only when one line of action significantly affected the other.

Of greater interest for critics today is the third or formal cause, which characterizes the logical or analogical relationships between the plots. As Levin argues:

> Unlike the material mode, it must be rendered through the action itself; but unlike the efficient mode, it is a dramatic constant, no more subject to time or change than a mathematical equation. Not only does the formal relation exist outside of time, but it is also ultimately perceived in this way, for although we infer it from the single sequence of alternating scenes which enact the separate plots, we do not fully comprehend it until we have abstracted these plots from the sequence and compared them as complete wholes placed, as it were, side by side. It is, to continue the figure, a spatial integration of plots, whereas that produced by the efficient mode is temporal.
>
> (p. 10)

Since this mode was given little attention by earlier commentators, it is here, according to Levin, that we are likely to find the unity formerly denied such plays.

But to stop here, seeing the formal cause as an end in itself, is a mistake, continues Levin; rather we must recognize a higher level of integration, corresponding to Aristotle's final cause, in which the analogies "relate the separate plots, intellectually and emotionally, in such a way that our reaction to one conditions and is conditioned by our reaction to the other, in order that both sets of responses can be synthesized, if the dramatist is successful, into a coherent overall effect which constitutes the real unity of the play" (p. 16). For Levin, this final cause is the most complex and the most important, "a composite response" produced by both similarities and differences between plots, a response that transcends the play "as a mere aggregation of homogeneous parts" but sees the components as "heterogeneous and complementary, each contributing in its own way to the total living process" (p. 17).

In the chapters that follow, Levin sets up categories derived from his third or formal mode, "the one that most directly determines the specific structure and effect of the plays" (p. 20). Thus in Chapter 2, "Direct Contrast Plots," he deals with the simplest way to integrate separate actions—the use of "a negative analogy built on direct moral contrast" (p. 38); included here are detailed, deft analyses of *The Changeling* and *The Second Maiden's Tragedy*. In Chapter 3, "Three-Level Hierarchies," Levin covers a wide range of "two-and-one-half-plot plays" with particular emphasis upon *The Family of Love, A Fair Quarrel,* and *The Atheist's Tragedy* and a final section devoted to *As You Like It* and *1 Henry IV*. In such plays he finds "a hierarchy of descending magnitude and seriousness," often expressed through "a main plot consisting of characters deliberately elevated above the others, usually in heroic or romantic terms; a subplot of more ordinary people viewed from a more realistic and often ironic or satiric perspective; and a third group debased to the level of low comedy" (pp. 55–56).

For me, Chapter 4, "Clown Subplots: Foil, Parody, Magic," was the most provocative in the book. At the outset Levin distinguishes carefully between foils and parodies. Thus a clown can serve as a foil when the dramatist stresses the negative aspect of the analogy, so that "a devalued background" brings out "the superior qualities of 'centerpiece' characters belonging to a very different order of being." On the other hand, "if there is a positive emphasis on the similarity between the two actions, the result is not just parallelism but 'parody,' because the clown matter will assimilate the main plot and draw it down to its own level" (pp. 111–112). Earlier critics, Levin observes, discovered foils everywhere, whereas critics of the present generation, when discussing analogies between low and noble characters, usually find parodies at work. As Levin points out, "we are led to find in these subplots what we want to find, what we feel is needed to rescue the play from sentimentality, naïveté, directness, univocality, and the other moral and esthetic sins of our day" (p. 112). To defend the almost forsaken foil, Levin draws upon a wide range of materials (including Hollywood westerns and Broadway musicals) to build a persuasive argument against the current overemphasis upon parody and backs up his claims with careful analyses of the comic materials in *Henry V* (foil) and *Doctor Faustus* (parody). Elsewhere in this chapter Levin describes the "lightning rod" function of such clown plots, by which they can "drain off a potentially undesirable response to the main action" (p. 134); in another interesting passage he argues for "comic release" rather than "comic relief" (p. 139). All in all, this chapter provides challenging reading for anyone interested in the clown subplot.

Thus far, the analogies considered have drawn upon common subject matter (e.g., two fathers misjudging their children or two wives threatened with sexual blackmail). But in Chapter 5, "Equivalence Plots," Levin treats multiple-plot plays which contain actions that draw upon quite different aspects of life but still in some sense can be equated on the formal level. As he notes, there is an obvious danger here, because, no matter how disparate two plots may be, an ingenious reader can always find some common denominator that can subsume them both. But he proposes to discuss "the more extreme examples in which we are clearly meant to understand that two distinctly different subject matters have been made equivalent by the inter-plot parallel" (pp. 148–149). For example, he discusses the love-honor equation in *A Fair Quarrel, A Challenge for Beauty,* and *Troilus and Cressida;* the money-sex equation in *A Mad World, My Masters* and *Michaelmas Term;* and the abuses of money and language in *The Staple of News.* The larger process at work, Levin argues, is an outgrowth of "the impulse to construct or discover satisfying connections among the disparate aspects of our experience by the sort of analogical reasoning that underlies so much primitive myth and ritual" (p. 149). This kind of reasoning is taken even farther in the next chapter, "The Limits of Multiplicity," which is devoted to two exceptionally rich multiple-plot plays, *A Chaste Maid in Cheapside* and *Bartholomew Fair.*

In his final chapter, "Beyond the Categories," Levin forestalls some of the slings and arrows of outrageous reviewers by briefly considering alternative ways of approaching the Elizabethan multiple plot. First, he discusses the assets and difficulties in a historical or chronological approach to this material; he argues, for example, that "the conceptions underlying the categories of multiple-plot integration" can "be found in the universal processes of the mind, quite apart from their literary manifestations," so that in reality "the multiple plot required no prior literary 'cause,' since it was always there" (p. 216). Considering next the genre approach, he offers some interesting generalizations about the efficacy of multiple plots in comedy, tragedy, and history. In his final paragraphs Levin discusses multiplicity and dramatic inclusiveness, arguing that the multiple plot became a means for both "generating and controlling the variegated panoramic richness which is one of the most characteristic and most glorious attributes of this great theater" (p. 224).

Here, then, is an ambitious book which tackles a formidable problem by setting up a series of categories and then treating representative plays. How are we to assess Levin's achievement? Our yardstick, it seems to me, should be something more than agreement or disagreement with interpretations of individual plays. Although readers at times will certainly find themselves disagreeing with the analyses, Levin's claims are inevitably backed up by citations and careful argument. To evaluate this book fairly, some larger questions must be raised.

First, we should consider Levin's methods and tools. At the outset he acknowledges the dangers besetting such a study, especially in what he terms the "atomic" approach, whereby the critic piles up "miscellaneous isolated details of character or incident or diction shared by both plots" (p. 13). But there are other traps awaiting the critic who pursues inter-plot parallels and analogies, traps that can produce subtle distortions of the plays. Thus, from Levin's analysis of *Much Ado About Nothing* (p. 90) a reader would conclude that the audience witnessed a scene in which Claudio and Don Pedro saw the false Hero on the balcony. Or earlier (p. 47) we find Levin suggesting a lost scene in *The Changeling* which would have included the masque, a fight between Antonio and Franciscus over Isabella, and their subsequent arrest for the murder of Alonzo—a scene, in short, that would cinch his analysis. Neither point is a flaw in the book, but both suggest a larger problem whereby the concern with spatial relationships overshadows the actual experience of the viewer in the theater or the reader. Those sensitive to this problem will also be troubled by the diagrams of plot relationships (e.g., p. 82). If such relationships as diagrammed are there to be perceived, who is perceiving them and at what point?

Levin is by no means insensitive to such questions. For example, he argues forcefully that the critic must take into account the temporal organization of the play, because atemporal or spatial relationships "must be enacted in and inferred from the single sequence of alternating scenes which we actually experience and which inevitably colors our perception of them" (p. 15). Some of his analyses (e.g., of *The Second Maiden's*

Tragedy) then make adept use of such alternating scenes. Nonetheless, for me the most disappointing feature of Levin's presentation was his general failure to use the visual / theatrical effects built into the plays that often buttress the analogies or relationships being discussed. An audience watching *The Tempest,* for example, does not need critical guidance to compare and / or contrast Caliban and Ferdinand, because in consecutive scenes (II.ii, III.i) Shakespeare brings these two figures on stage *"with a burden of wood"* and *"bearing a log."* Such a clear visual analogue can underscore a spatial relationship. Or consider *1 Henry IV*. Most critics agree that the Gadshill robbery in some way corresponds to the rebellion of the main plot, but again the relationship could be quite clear to the viewer. Thus, after the merchants have been robbed by Falstaff, Gadshill, Bardolph, and Peto, the stage direction announces: *"As they are sharing, the Prince and Poins set upon them"* (II.ii.97); clearly, when interrupted by Hal and Poins, the four figures are somehow dividing up the spoils. A few scenes later in Act III, scene i, Shakespeare sets up a clear theatrical parallel for the eye when again he places on stage four figures (Hotspur, Glendower, Worcester, and Mortimer) who are standing around a map and dividing up the spoils (this time the kingdom itself). Once more an atemporal relationship is called to the attention of an audience in the theater by a device peculiar to the medium of drama. Without disputing Levin's explications, one can still ask for more theatrical evidence to bolster his argument.

Even more important to an assessment of Levin's achievement is the question: how valid or helpful are his categories and terms? All in all, they stand up rather well. At the least, future critics and readers will have a vocabulary to draw upon (and perhaps refine); so, building upon Levin, we can now think in terms of direct-contrast plots, foils, parodies, and three-level hierarchies. The term "equivalence plot" struck me as the vaguest of the major categories, so I felt Chapter 5 to be the least cohesive in the book. But the weight of the entire study gives an authenticity and added respectability to multiple plots and multiplicity, which *do* emerge as distinctive features of this great age of drama.

But Levin's categories and his main thrust can at times be overly exclusive. Thus, many of the questions raised about the multiple *plot* relate somehow to the larger category of multiple *action,* whether in two or more plots or even within the same story line. For example, *Othello* would not be considered a multiple-plot play, yet, within the terms of Levin's formal mode, figures in Acts I and II are clearly analogous to the tragic hero in the second half of the play. Thus Brabantio's susceptibility to Iago's statements about Desdemona prepares us for Act III, scene iii; the Duke and Senate of Venice provide a direct contrast to Othello's later credulity; and Cassio's degradation in Act II, scene iii, owing to his own particular weakness (for wine), is equivalent to the Moor's similar degeneration. Or again, Lady Macbeth's handling of her husband in Act I, scene vii, is analogous to Macbeth's handling of the two murderers in Act III, scene i (with the stress upon similar definitions of manhood). Admittedly, to take on multiple action rather than multiple plot would have greatly expanded (and perhaps distorted) Levin's project, but not to consider such a related phenomenon strikes me as arbitrary and potentially misleading.

In his conclusion Levin does raise some challenging questions about multiplicity and the experience offered by Elizabethan plays. But, in eschewing any historical approach, he relies largely upon general impulses present in all ages ("universal processes of the mind") to explain the presence of this phenomenon in this period. But is there not something distinctly Elizabethan in such multiple plots or such use of analogy? Heinrich Wölfflin and Madeleine Doran (to name only two) have discussed "multiple unity" as a distinctive way of perceiving the world and conveying that perception in Renaissance art and literature. Although it may be impossible to chart the clear chronological development of the multiple plot, we may nonetheless lose a great deal of perspective if we divorce this technique from contemporary practice in the visual and literary arts and indeed from the so-called Elizabethan world picture. In short, readers with a historical or contextual bent will not be fully satisfied with Levin's framework or conclusions.

My purpose, however, is not to carp at those conclusions, which are usually sound, or at Levin's achievement, which is substantial. But since this book will stand as a point of departure for future discussion of the multiple plot (a lightning rod effect), it is particularly important to call attention to territory yet to be explored. We should be grateful to Professor Levin for taking us this far.

ALAN C. DESSEN

Notes on Contributors

Jonas A. Barish, Professor of English at the University of California, Berkeley, is well known for his many studies of Renaissance literature, especially *Ben Jonson and the Language of Prose Comedy* (1960). He is currently at work on a study of antitheatrical prejudice.

Douglas Cole is Professor of English at Northwestern University and the author of *Suffering and Evil in the Plays of Christopher Marlowe* (1962). His current project is a book on the drama of ideas.

Beatrice Corrigan, Professor Emeritus of Italian at the University of Toronto, has published *A Catalogue of Italian Plays, 1500–1700, in The Library of The University of Toronto* (1961). She is a member of the Editorial Committee of *Renaissance Drama* and has contributed to previous volumes.

Alan C. Dessen is Professor of English at the University of North Carolina and coeditor of this volume. He is the author of *Jonson's Moral Comedy* (1971) and will be guest editor of Volume VI of this series of *Renaissance Drama*.

Donna B. Hamilton, Assistant Professor of English at the University of Maryland, has contributed essays on Shakespeare to *Shakespeare Studies, Studies in Philology,* and *Shakespeare Quarterly.*

Joel H. Kaplan, who teaches English at the University of British Columbia, has published articles on early English drama and has directed and produced medieval and Renaissance plays. At present he is preparing an edition of Massinger's *The City Madam* for the Revels series.

LAWRENCE L. LEVIN, Assistant Professor of English at the University of California, Santa Barbara, has published articles on *Sejanus* and *Every Man in his Humour*.

JOHN REIBETANZ teaches at Victoria College in the University of Toronto and has recently completed a study of *King Lear* in the context of Elizabethan and Jacobean theatrical traditions.

BROWNELL SALOMON, Associate Professor of English at Bowling Green State University, has contributed essays to *Research Opportunities in Renaissance Drama* and *Studies in English Literature*.

SUSAN SNYDER is Associate Professor of English at Swarthmore College and has published articles on Shakespeare, Spenser, Marlowe, and Donne. She has recently completed a critical edition of Sylvester's Du Bartas and is now writing a book on the role of comic conventions in some of Shakespeare's tragedies.

EDWIN J. WEBBER is Professor of Spanish at Northwestern University and a member of the Editorial Committee of *Renaissance Drama*.